Interactive Conflict Resolution

Syracuse Studies on Peace and Conflict Resolution
Harriet Hyman Alonso, Charles Chatfield, and Louis Kriesberg,
Series Editors

Interactive
Conflict
Resolution

Ronald J. Fisher

WITHDRAWN

Syracuse University Press

First Edition 1997

97 98 99 00 01 02   6 5 4 3 2 1

Permission to reprint figures from the following sources is gratefully acknowledged:

World Game Institute from M. Gabel, and E. Frisch, *Doing the Right Things*, 1991.

Dartmouth Publishing Company from E. E. Azar, *The Management of Protracted Social Conflict*, 1990.

R. J. Fisher, "Third Party Consultation: A Skill for Professional Psychologists in Community Practice," *Professional Psychology* 7 (1976). Copyright 1976 by the American Psychological Association. Reprinted by permission of the author.

Reproduced from *The Consulting Process in Action*, 2d. ed., by G. Lippitt and R. Lippitt. Copyright © 1986 by Pfeiffer and Company, San Diego, Calif. Used with permission.

Human Sciences Press from R. J. Fisher, and J. H. White, "Reducing Tensions Between Neighborhood Housing Groups," *International Journal of Group Tensions* 6 (1976).

R. J. Fisher, "A Third Party Consultation Workshop on the India-Pakistan Conflict." *Journal of Social Psychology*, 112 (1980). Reprinted with permission of the Helen Dwight Reid Educational Foundation. Published by Heldref Publications, 1319 18th St. N.W., Washington, D.C., 20036-1802. Copyright © 1980.

Springer-Verlag from R. J. Fisher, *The Social Psychology of Intergroup and International Conflict Resolution*, 1990.

Blackwell Publishers from R. J. Fisher, "The Potential for Peacebuilding: Forging a Bridge from Peacekeeping to Peacemaking," *Peace and Change*, 18 (1993).

Yale University Press from L. Kriesberg, *International Conflict Resolution: The U.S.-USSR and Middle East Cases*, 1991.

The Society for the Psychological Study of Social Issues from R. J. Fisher, "Generic Principles for Resolving Intergroup Conflict," *Journal of Social Issues* 50 (1994).

The paper used in this publication meets the minimum requirements for American National Standard for Information Sciences—Permanence of Paper for Printed Library Materials, ANSI Z39.48–1984. ∞™

Library of Congress Cataloging-in-Publication Data

Fisher, Ronald J.
    Interactive conflict resolution / Ronald J. Fisher.
        p.   cm. — (Syracuse studies on peace and conflict resolution)
    Includes bibliographical references and index.
    ISBN 0-8156-2714-9 (cloth : alk. paper). — ISBN 0-8156-2715-7 (pbk. : alk. paper)
    1. Mediation, International.   2. Conflict management.   3. Pacific settlement of international disputes.   I. Title.   II. Series.
JX4475.F57   1996
327.1'7—dc20   96-19792

Manufactured in the United States of America

*To John W. Burton, the innovator,
and Herbert C. Kelman, the master,
of interactive conflict resolution*

Ronald J. Fisher is professor of psychology and founding coordinator of the Applied Social Psychology Graduate Program at the University of Saskatchewan. He is the author of *Social Psychology: An Applied Approach* and *The Social Psychology of Intergroup and International Conflict Resolution,* and his professional interests include studying protracted social conflict and developing the scholar-practitioner field of interactive conflict resolution.

Contents

Part Three
The Prospects for the Future

Illustrations

Preface

This book has been a long time in the making, from my efforts in the early 1970s to develop a generic model of third party consultation to my current activities in helping organize a network of scholar-practitioners interested in interactive conflict resolution. During this time, the social problem to which these and other efforts are directed, destructive and protracted conflict between identity groups, has grown in both complexity and ferocity. Thus, as in all advances of civilization, we require social institutions to control the potential destructiveness of human beings toward one another and to provide cooperative alternatives for the satisfaction of basic human needs.

Interactive conflict resolution is one such social innovation that is yet to receive widespread acceptance and support as an additional method directed toward improving the quality of life on this endangered planet. The past thirty years have seen the development and proliferation of small-group discussion methods for analyzing social conflict and creating alternative directions toward management and resolution. This book provides a description and evaluation of that history at the intercommunal and international levels in a supportive and yet candid manner. It also attempts to extend our thinking about how interactive methods can influence decision making, policy formation, and conflict resolution in ways that complement existing methods. If issues such as funding, training, institutionalization, and professionalization can be successfully addressed, I am confident that interactive conflict resolution can move forward to develop its potential as a unique and sometimes essential method of peacebuilding.

The completion of this work has been a wide-ranging effort drawing on the contributions of many persons and organizations, many of which are acknowledged in the text. The starting point was a research project supported by the unfortunately now-defunct Canadian Institute for International Peace and Security, which enabled me to interview most of the senior scholar-practitioners in the field. I would like to thank Geoffrey Pearson, the first executive director of CIIPS, for his willingness to generously support the development of a method that he held in some skepticism, and his successor, Bernard Wood, for being challenging but not dismissive of interactive conflict resolution methods. Also at the institute, my colleagues Roger Hill, Philip Lemieux, and Doina Cioiu provided many forms of advice and assistance that contributed to the successful completion of the project. The persons who were interviewed are also worthy of appreciation for their willingness to provide comprehensive and candid answers to my questions, often under the time pressure of other demands.

CIIPS also provided support for my first two workshops on the Cyprus conflict, which were extended to two further workshops with the assistance of the also now-defunct Cooperative Security Competition Program of Foreign Affairs and International Trade Canada. For their essential involvement and collaboration in the Cyprus work, I wish to thank my colleagues and friends Louise Diamond, A. J. R. (John) Groom, Loraleigh Keashly, Herbert Kelman, Brian Mandell, Chris Mitchell, and Jay Rothman, and my Cyprus associates and participants who continue to work toward peace under difficult and at times risky conditions.

The preparation of a lengthy manuscript is an arduous task to which many people contribute. I would like to thank the following colleagues, who provided very useful comments on one or more chapters: Kevin Avruch, David Bargal, Reena Bernards, John Burton, Cynthia Chataway, Stephen Cohen, A. V. S. (Tony) de Reuck, Leonard Doob, William Foltz, Alexander George, Ted Gurr, Paul Hare, Herbert Kelman, John McDonald, Chris Mitchell, Robert Ricigliano, Jay Rothman, Dennis Sandole, Pamela Steiner, Janis van der Westhuizen, Vamik Volkan, and Andrew Willard. In addition, Louis Kriesberg and John Paul Lederach read the entire manuscript and provided candid evaluations and useful suggestions for improving it. At Syracuse University Press, I especially wish to thank Cynthia Maude-Gembler for her attentive management of the acquisition process. Thanks also to Medard Gabel of the World Game Institute for providing a copy of their figure "What the World Wants" and to Martin Rempel for providing expeditious library research at a number of different points in manuscript preparation. Lastly, I want to express my appreciation to my wife, Carol, for her patient understanding and quiet support during another long period of gestation. I hope the product is worthy of all these investments.

Saskatoon, Canada,   Ron Fisher
February 1996

Interactive Conflict Resolution

Introduction

Violent Social Conflict: Its Costs and Causes

The world today continues to be besieged by a host of destructive and apparently intractable conflicts between groups, factions, and nations that induce incredible costs in human and material terms and that sap the resources so badly needed for human development. While humankind's technological capacity develops at an incredible pace, our relatively underdeveloped social and political competence sadly determines that we use our increasing physical ability to attain new levels of horror and destruction.

This century has seen two very costly world wars followed by some 150 wars fought on the territory of more than seventy-five countries (Alker & Sherman 1982; Kende 1978; Sivard 1993). These conflagrations have resulted in tens of millions of deaths, and increasingly these have been civilian rather than military casualties, the former constituting ninety percent of war-related deaths in 1990 (Sivard 1991).

In 1993, it was possible to identify thirty-two ongoing armed conflicts that had incurred battle-related deaths of more than a thousand persons (Wallensteen & Axell 1994). Not one of these conflicts was an interstate war, and an increasing number were being fought in Eastern Europe and the former Soviet Union in the wake of the cold war. Of the armed conflicts that ended or became inactive in 1989–93, only one in seven was resolved by a peace agreement.

The economic and social costs of preparing for and waging war are simply incredible. World military expenditures, although falling about ten percent from a 1987 high, still approximate one *trillion* dollars, with many governments spending more on the development and employment of arms than on providing for the good health of their citizens (Sivard 1993). In a related comparison, military expenditures per soldier are twenty-five times higher than the money spent on education for each child in the world.

Comparative and dramatic examples of the forgone opportunity costs of military expenditures are readily identified, but a comprehensive analysis by the World Game Institute (Gabel & Frisch 1991) is even more disturbing (fig. I.1). This analysis compares the cost of world military expenditures with the estimated annual cost of solving in the next decade all of the major health, development, and environmental problems facing the world. These estimates are based on the most reliable sources, including the World Bank and other United Nations intergovernmental organizations. The combined costs of these programs—to eliminate starvation, to provide clean water, to prevent global warming, to stabilize population growth, etc.—amount to only one-quarter of the yearly military expenditure!

What needs to be done to move us toward peace, justice, and a reasonable quality of life for all peoples of the world? In a phrase—a great deal! A recent statement by an esteemed international group, the Stockholm Initiative on Global Security and Governance (1991), outlines proposals in a number of areas for moving toward a new world order. The statement builds on previous international initiatives, including the Independent Commission on Disarmament and Security Issues (1982), which called for the development of *common security* as an alternative to the doctrine of mutual deterrence or mutual-assured destruction. Common security is based on the realization that the nations of the world can achieve political and economic security only through a commitment to joint survival, rather than individually attempting to achieve security through military strength.

The proposals of the Stockholm Initiative include a strengthening of the United Nations in its ability to prevent and manage destructive conflicts and a pledge by governments to reduce military spending and to allocate the "peace dividend" to international cooperation and human development. Most of the savings, which could reach $300 billion annually by the year 2000, would come from the $600 billion a year that was being spent on the cold war—which no longer exists! Even a small slice of the potential dividend would create miracles in a world of poverty, disease, and environmental degradation. Embedded in the Stockholm statement is also the realization that we must develop more effective methods for dealing with the conflicts that wreak havoc in so many areas of the globe.

In the wake of the Gulf War and the flare-up of ethnic conflict in Eastern Europe and the former Soviet Union, the former secretary-general of the United Nations, Boutrous-Ghali, presented a renewed vision, "An Agenda for Peace," which focused on the role of the UN in conflict management (United Nations 1992). Besides many recommendations for strengthening UN peacemaking, peacekeeping, and peace

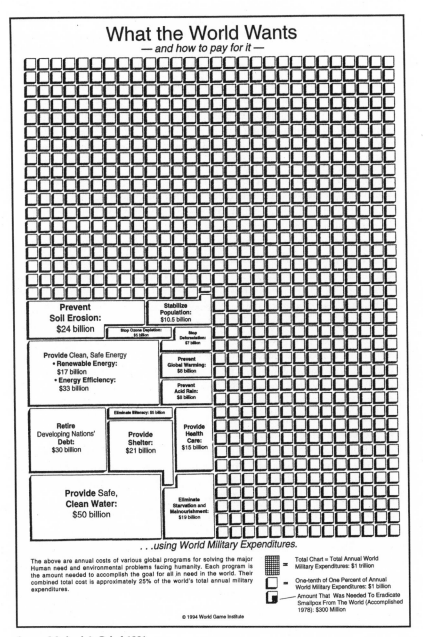

What the World Wants
— and how to pay for it —

Prevent Soil Erosion: $24 billion

Stabilize Population: $10.5 billion

Stop Ozone Depletion: $5 billion

Stop Deforestation: $7 billion

Provide Clean, Safe Energy
• **Renewable Energy:** $17 billion
• **Energy Efficiency:** $33 billion

Prevent Global Warming: $8 billion

Prevent Acid Rain: $8 billion

Eliminate Illiteracy: $5 billion

Retire Developing Nations' Debt: $30 billion

Provide Shelter: $21 billion

Provide Health Care: $15 billion

Provide Safe, Clean Water: $50 billion

Eliminate Starvation and Malnourishment: $19 billion

. . .using World Military Expenditures.

The above are annual costs of various global programs for solving the major Human need and environmental problems facing humanity. Each program is the amount needed to accomplish the goal for all in need in the world. Their combined total cost is approximately 25% of the world's total annual military expenditures.

= Total Chart = Total Annual World Military Expenditures: $1 trillion

= One-tenth of One Percent of Annual World Military Expenditures: $1 billion

— Amount That Was Needed To Eradicate Smallpox From The World (Accomplished 1978): $300 Million

© 1994 World Game Institute

Source: Medard & Gabel 1991.

Fig. I.1. The Costs of War

enforcement, the report calls for increased efforts in preventive diplomacy and postconflict peacebuilding. Preventive diplomacy includes increased use of confidence-building measures, more effective monitoring of trends leading to tensions, better early warning systems for conflict, and the preventive deployment of UN personnel to trouble spots. After successful peacemaking, peacebuilding should be directed toward economic, social, and political development that would support peace in the long term.

Although the former secretary-general's vision is a comprehensive and forward-looking document in some respects, it largely reinforces and extends traditional diplomatic and military approaches to achieving and maintaining peace. It does not include newer, innovative approaches to conflict resolution that might play a useful complementary role in a rapidly changing world.

Many of the world's intense and intractable conflicts occur between different ethnic groups within the same nation. Thus they do not fit the state-versus-state model of conflict built into the UN and other international and regional organizations. In fact, since 1945, most "international conflicts" have pitted state authorities against armed insurgencies by ethnic, religious, or ideological groups seeking autonomy or protection from persecution (Holsti 1992b; Kende 1978). Often these conflicts cut across state borders where the same groups have been separated by accidents of history or the arbitrary demarcation of boundaries during decolonization. A few conflicts (18 of 120 in Kende's analysis) are primarily international conflicts in which states fight across their boundaries, sometimes involving regional powers who are vying for dominance.

Although many conflicts are initiated by disadvantaged groups to gain what they perceive as justice and equity, the overall picture is one of pernicious competition in which the unleashing of the spiral of violence sets in motion a mutual debilitation. In their commitment to unilateral and coercive strategies designed to win, all parties eventually lose, and laudable calls for productive societal change are lost in the process. Thus the world witnesses a continuous parade of tragedies, from Lebanon to Sri Lanka, from Northern Ireland to Angola, from Peru to Afghanistan, from Somalia to former Yugoslavia. Fortunately, from time to time, there are bright spots in which a lengthy conflict appears to be resolved through peaceful social change and to the satisfaction of the parties, often after they have exhausted themselves through military action—Namibia, Nicaragua, Mozambique, Cambodia? The underlying question is whether methods of conflict analysis and resolution might be developed that would allow the parties an earlier opportunity to meet their needs and resolve their differences in a less costly and more effective manner.

In many conflicts, a continuing tension is punctuated by episodes of violent escalation, sometimes ended by stalemate and the imposition of peacekeeping. The UN and other international bodies typically do not take action until large-scale violence has occurred, although the Agenda for Peace does call for the greater use of preventive diplomacy. Existing strategies of conflict management, such as mediation or arbitration, appear to be ineffective and the deeper issues move no closer to resolution. This type of seemingly intractable conflict is gaining increasing attention of social scientists and has recently been defined as "protracted social conflict" by Edward Azar (see chapter 4) and as "deep-rooted conflict" by John Burton (see chapter 1).

Protracted Social Conflicts: Problems Without Solutions?

Azar coined the term *protracted social conflict* to denote the ongoing and apparently irresolvable nature of disputes in locations such as the Middle East, Sri Lanka, Northern Ireland, Cyprus, the Horn of Africa, Cambodia, and Kashmir (Azar 1983, 1990; Azar, Jureidini & McLaurin 1978). According to Azar, the source of these conflicts is not in economics and power, but in the denial of elements necessary to the development of all people, and whose pursuit is therefore a compelling need. These fundamental and universal human needs include security, distinct identity, social recognition of identity, and effective participation in determining development requirements. In addition, protracted social conflict evidences the enduring features of economic underdevelopment, structural inequality, and unintegrated social and political systems. Thus intergroup cleavages are combined with underdevelopment and distributive injustice to make these conflicts particularly resistant to resolution.

It follows that the central unit of analysis in protracted social conflict is the *identity group*, defined in ethnic, racial, religious, linguistic, or other terms, for it is through the identity group that compelling human needs are expressed in social and often political terms. Furthermore, communal identity itself is dependent upon the satisfaction of basic needs for security, recognition, and distributive justice. Thus such conflicts arise when identity groups perceive that they are oppressed and victimized through a denial of recognition, security, equity, and political participation.

Burton (1987, 1990a) uses the term *deep-rooted conflict* to refer to conflicts that are not based on negotiable interests and positions, but on underlying needs that cannot be compromised. Such conflicts can occur in any relationship where inequality exists and basic needs for identity and participation are frustrated, but the most conspicuous are violent conflicts between communities or nations over the preservation of cultures and values. Whether in domestic or international settings, identity groups will pursue their fundamental needs by all possible means, constrained only by the need to maintain valued relationships. Besides the needs for identity and participation, Burton identifies basic needs for consistency, security, recognition, and distributive justice, the latter being linked to underdevelopment and thereby to structural inequality and violence.

According to Burton, conflicts over basic needs must be distinguished from "disputes" about tangible, negotiable interests, and therefore conflict resolution must be distinguished from dispute settlement. Conflicts are situations in both domestic and international arenas that are not subject to negotiated or coerced settlements, and attempts to do so will only prolong and exacerbate the situation. Thus much of the world's machinery for managing conflict is inappropriate and ineffective. Deep-rooted conflicts cannot be contained or suppressed in the long term, but can be prevented or resolved only by the satisfaction of basic needs through conflict resolution. Thus Burton sees conflict as a generic phenomenon, which regardless of the system—ethnic, community, international—involves the same human needs that must be addressed by the same analysis and problem solving. The concepts of protracted social conflict and deep-rooted conflict are compatible with the approach taken to understanding intergroup and international conflict by the interdisciplinary field of applied social psychology (Fisher 1982b, 1990). The humanistic value base of this approach holds that both individuals and groups have undeniable needs for identity, dignity, security, equity, participation in decisions that affect them, and control over their destiny. Frustration of these basic needs along with a denial of related human rights, both individual and collective, becomes a source of social conflict and creates a dynamic for social change that must be considered in any analysis of intergroup and international conflict.

An interdisciplinary approach to understanding and resolving conflict requires the use of multiple levels of analysis and a sensitivity to escalation and de-escalation over time. Accordingly, Fisher (1990) presents an *eclectic model of intergroup conflict,* which sees protracted conflict as rooted in discrepancies in interests, values, needs, or power between groups that are exacerbated by cultural differences and a history of antagonism. The typical competitive orientation taken by conflicting parties fuels the perception of threat and the development of intense ethnocentrism and mistrust, which in combination with human deficiencies in cognitive functioning feed ineffective communication and interaction. Political factors expressed through constituent pressure on representatives also contributes to the escalation that spirals to new levels at each round of destructive interaction.

Once intergroup conflict has escalated to high intensity, it is highly resistant to de-escalation and resolution because of solidifying mechanisms, such as commitments to past actions and structural changes that support coercive strategies. Thus settlement procedures that work with low intensity conflict, such as fact finding or conciliation, are impotent in the face of escalated, protracted conflict. It is therefore essential that innovative, creative means of analysis and resolution be developed and integrated in a complementary way with existing methods of conflict management. That is the main theme of this book.

Interactive Conflict Resolution: Part of a Peaceful Future?

Within the context of these developing realizations, a number of scholar-practitioners based primarily in academic settings began experimenting with small-group discussion methods for resolving protracted international conflict. Foremost among these pioneers in peacebuilding was John Burton, founder of the Centre for the Analysis of Conflict at University College London, who organized "controlled communication" workshops focusing on the Malaysia-Indonesia and Cyprus conflicts during the mid-1960s (see chapter 1). Herbert Kelman of Harvard University was a participant in the Cyprus discussions and subsequently developed his "interactional approach" of the "problem-solving workshop" in collaboration with Stephen Cohen, Edward Azar, and others, focusing mainly on the conflict in the Middle East (see chapter 3). Leonard Doob of Yale University organized "workshops" on the conflicts in the Horn of Africa and in Northern Ireland, which used small-group methods from human relations training (see chapter 2). These pioneering ventures and related initiatives have been captured under the label of "third party consultation" in my work (Fisher 1972, 1983), to emphasize that such discussions are organized and facilitated by scholar-practitioners who provide an essential consulting role as impartial intermediaries and analysts (see chapter 7).

I have recently identified this developing scholarly and professional field as *interactive conflict resolution* to emphasize that effective and constructive face-to-face interaction among representatives of the parties themselves is required to understand and resolve complex intercommunal and international conflicts (Fisher 1993a). In a focused manner, interactive conflict resolution (ICR) is defined as involving small-group, problem-solving discussions between unofficial representatives of identity groups or states engaged in destructive conflict that are facilitated by an impartial third party of social scientist-practitioners. In a broader manner, ICR can be defined as facilitated face-to-face activities in communication, training, education, or consultation that promote collaborative conflict analysis and problem solving among parties engaged in protracted conflict in a manner that addresses basic human needs and promotes the building of peace, justice, and equality. This book will generally follow the focused definition and equate ICR with the implementation of conflict analysis or problem-solving discussions in a workshop format that are directed toward mutual understanding of the conflict and the development of collaborative actions to de-escalate and eventually resolve it.

A central assumption of ICR is that constructive analysis and creative problem solving between antagonists can be most satisfactorily implemented through the assistance of a skilled and knowledgeable third party. The method also takes a social-psychological approach by asserting that relationship issues (misperceptions, unmet basic needs, and so on) must be addressed and that the conflict will be resolved only by mutually acceptable solutions that are developed through joint interaction. The objectives of the discussions, as initially articulated in my model of third party consultation, typically range from individual attitude change, through the generation of innovative, mutually agreeable solutions to the conflict, to improvements in the wider relationship between the parties. "Conflict resolution" therefore is not seen as a single or time-limited outcome, but as a complex process of de-escalation and reconciliation that develops over time to the point where a new qualities and mechanisms exist in the relationship to allow for the constructive settlement of disputes.

The participants in ICR workshops have varied from loyal members of the respective groups or nations, through influential persons who have access to decision makers, to appointed but unofficial representatives who report directly to their leaders. Obviously, the identity of the individual participants will have a major influence on the degree of transfer of outcomes to the wider relationship between the parties in policy formation and implementation (see chapter 9). In all cases, however, ICR provides an informal, unofficial, low-risk forum for the exchange of views and intense dialogue on the basic issues in the conflict. In that vein, it is regarded as an important development in the burgeoning fields of unofficial diplomacy and peacebuilding, and it is in that vein that its potential as a method of intercommunal and international conflict resolution will be explored.

The realization that humankind's repertoire for dealing with intense conflict must be broadened has led to a search for alternate, that is, nonmilitary, means of achieving international security. Stephenson (1982) divides alternative methods into two broad areas: those dealing with organizational initiatives in world law and government, and those involving nonviolent conflict resolution. In the latter area, she identifies two forms of activity: private third party initiatives in conciliation or mediation that address a particular conflict, and regular, often annual, conferences that bring together influential nationals from countries involved in hostile and potentially destructive relations. An exemplar of the former activity are the Quaker efforts in peacemaking (Curle 1971, 1990; Yarrow 1978), while the best-known prototypes of the latter are the Pugwash and Dartmouth conferences (Cousins 1977; Rotblat & Holdren 1989; Stewart 1987).

Most of these methods of nonviolent conflict resolution have also been identified as forms of "unofficial diplomacy" by Berman and Johnson (1977) and more recently as "track two diplomacy" by Montville (1987) to distinguish them from "track one," or official diplomatic, that is, government-to-government interaction (McDonald & Bendahmane 1987). Track two diplomacy denotes various informal, unofficial forms of interaction between members of adversary parties that attempt to influence public opinion, develop strategies, or organize resources toward the resolution of the conflict.

An ambitious attempt to gain a greater sense of order over the rapidly evolving arena of unofficial interaction is represented in a recent conceptualization by Diamond and McDonald (1991) on "multi-track diplomacy." This conceptual framework expands the track one–track two distinction to include nine tracks of activities that contribute to international peacemaking and peacebuilding. Track one remains as diplomatic, governmental activities in peacemaking, while track two is defined more precisely as professional, nongovernmental conflict resolution that works on the analysis, prevention, and resolution of international conflict. The other tracks are defined largely by the actors or channels involved in the interactions (e.g., business people, private citizens, peace activists, religious communities, philanthropic foundations) with the assertion that each can work in its unique ways to foster peaceful relations between adversaries. Diamond and McDonald (1991) point out that each of these tracks is a world unto itself, but that numerous places and opportunities exist for overlapping and complementary activities. Thus they recommend that relationships need to be built among the nine tracks in ways that share knowledge, create new resources, models and institutions, and explore the possibilities for collaboration.

In a comprehensive attempt to chart all avenues for promoting the resolution of international conflict, the United States Institute of Peace (USIP) has completed an intellectual mapping of both traditional and newer approaches to peace (Thompson & Jensen 1991). This ambitious project was carried out through a series of colloquia on different approaches culminating in a major conference involving representatives of all approaches. The resulting typology identifies three traditional approaches that emphasize state-to-state interaction: (1) collective security and deterrence, (2) diplomacy and negotiation, and (3) strategic management and arms control. Newer approaches emphasize interactions among individuals and groupings that cut across state boundaries and include: (1) behavioral approaches, (2) transnationalism, and (3) conflict resolution. Added to these groupings were international law approaches including: (1) the role of law in peace, (2) interstate organizations, and (3) third party dispute settlement, and political systems approaches differentiated into: (1) internal systems that emphasize domestic political arrangements and (2) world systems that focus on broad philosophical views.

Although there are crosscutting interests among many of these approaches, the map elucidates the various ways of working toward a peaceful world. Some of these are complementary; others are in conflict in underlying assumptions, preferred values, chosen methods of influencing others, and definitions of peace. One way of slicing through this complexity and confusion is to use an earlier and simpler typology, which identifies two approaches: (1) *peace through strength*, which relies on armaments, particularly nuclear weapons, to maintain deterrence and facilitate negotiations on arms control, and (2) *peace through cooperation*, which emphasizes conflict resolution methods to reduce tension, build trust, and promote cooperative security (Kimmel 1985). The challenge for the future may lie in some combination of approaches, which while eschewing violence, firmly maintains one party's self-interests while searching for cooperative avenues to meet the other party's self-interests as well (Fisher 1990). This is the challenge for the newer methods of conflict resolution.

A final typology that is useful for understanding the range of pacific methods of dealing with international conflict comes from the distinction among peacemaking, peacekeeping, and peacebuilding first articulated by Galtung (1976). *Peacemaking* attempts to transcend incompatibilities that impede human progress and is typically operationalized through traditional diplomatic activities directed toward reaching a settlement between conflicting parties. The negotiation of treaties, peace conferences to end hostilities, the ongoing diplomatic efforts of the United Nations, particularly the security council and the secretary-general, and the efforts of various mediators in attaining agreements would all come under the rubric of peacemaking.

Peacekeeping involves the intervention of a third party to keep the warring parties apart and maintain an absence of direct violence. Thus it typically requires the agreed-upon imposition of an impartial military force for monitoring a cease-fire, maintaining the separation of the combatants, mediating incidents to prevent escalation, and offering humanitarian assistance to support a return to normalcy for the affected populations (International Peace Academy 1984).

Peacebuilding attempts to create a structure of peace in equity and justice both within and between nations that removes the causes of war and provides alternatives to war. It is the least understood and operationalized of the triumvarate, partly because it alludes to a wide range of less publicized and more innovative activities. On the one hand, reflecting back to Galtung (1976), peacebuilding refers to social change and economic development that reduces inequity and injustice (International Peace Academy 1984). On the other hand, it often refers to efforts for improving the relationship between adversaries toward greater trust and cooperation, more accurate perceptions and attitudes, a more positive climate, and a stronger political will to deal constructively with their differences. I have recently proposed a comprehensive definition of peacebuilding as "developmental and interactive activities, often facilitated by a third party, which are directed toward meeting the basic needs, de-escalating the hostility, and improving the relationship of parties engaged in protracted social conflict" (Fisher 1993b).

Where does all this conceptualizing place the developing field of interactive conflict resolution? Fig. I.2 approximates in spatial terms the conceptual position of ICR in relation to the approaches to peace and conflict management described so far. The space is roughly defined by peace through strength on the left, peace through cooperation on the right, older approaches toward the top, and newer approaches toward the bottom. ICR is placed within the larger space of peacebuilding, in the sense that ICR fosters improved relationships between antagonists through interactive processes. Unofficial diplomacy and tracks two through nine of the multi-track model are also incorporated within peacebuilding. As a scholarly and professional endeavor, ICR is also boxed within the larger domains of conflict resolution and transnationalism, identified as newer approaches by the USIP intellectual map project. *Conflict resolution* is a rapidly evolving field that focuses on the process, including third party involvement, of moving

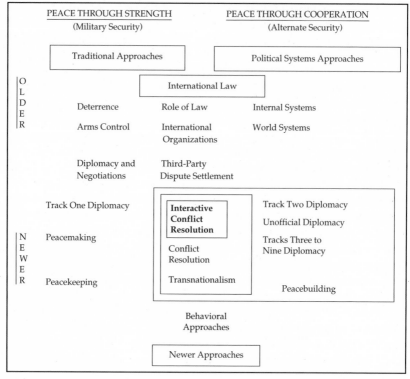

Fig. I.2. The Position of Interactive Conflict Resolution in the Conceptual Domain of Approaches to Peace

conflict presentation and escalation to de-escalation and resolution in ways that are self-sustaining (Laue 1991). *Transnationalism* refers to a host of interactive activities outside of state-to-state interaction that involve various nongovernmental actors in developing peaceful political relationships (Montville 1991).

ICR is also placed close in fig. I.2 to the overlapping approaches of peacemaking, track one diplomacy, diplomacy and negotiation, and third party dispute settlement. This placement is because ICR has the potential of serving as a complementary method to these more traditional methods of peacemaking (see chapter 8). Thus ICR as a method of nonviolent conflict resolution can potentially provide some integration between the often conflicting major strategies of peace through strength and peace through cooperation. This potential is because ICR accepts the importance of power in influencing relationships, appeals to standards of fairness and justice as espoused by international law and world order models, and assumes that a firm and cooperative approach to conflict management will lead to satisfactory outcomes for all parties. This analysis therefore places ICR in a central position for potentially moving intercommunal and international conflict resolution in a more integrated, realistic, collaborative, and ultimately effective direction pointing toward a peaceful future.

Sources of Information and Plan of the Book

The purpose of this book is to provide a description, analysis, and evaluation of interactive conflict resolution and its potential for helping create a peaceful world. Part of this will require looking at possible linkages with official diplomacy and other methods of third party intervention, particularly mediation and prenegotiation. It is hoped that this work will demonstrate the unique ability of ICR to contribute effectively as a form of peacebuilding to the resolution of destructive intercommunal and international conflicts, which will require an assessment of the current state of the method and the critical issues and challenges it faces.

The information on which this work is based has been drawn from a number of sources. First, I have followed the literature in this area from its beginning, with reviews being produced in 1972, 1983, 1986, and 1993. Second, through a research project in 1989–90 funded by the now-defunct Canadian Institute for International Peace and Security (CIIPS), I undertook a number of site visits to locations where leading edge work in international conflict resolution is being carried out. Program documents were reviewed as well as project reports on past and ongoing work. In conjunction with these visits, interviews were held with about twenty-five persons who represent almost all of the senior scholar-practitioners working in the field. In the book, many of the institutional locations will be identified, but the persons will not for confidentiality and anonymity. The interview schedule and some themes from interviewee responses are described in chapter 9.

Besides the site visits, further discussion of issues was facilitated by my participation in a two-day workshop in April 1990 on the current state of the field, which was organized by the Center for Psychological Studies in the Nuclear Age (now the Center for Psychology and Social Change) and which involved about twenty-five scholar-practitioners in both domestic and international conflict resolution. Additional understanding and analysis was provided by my involvement in a series of two-day seminars organized during 1990 by Rutgers University on the interconnections between domestic dispute resolution and international conflict resolution. Finally, the initial results of the research project were presented, discussed, and extended at a one-day working seminar in June 1990 at CIIPS attended by a mix of scholar-practitioners, policy analysts, and diplomats.

Since the completion of the initial project, a continuing series of opportunities have extended the work. At the Annual Scientific Meetings of the International Society of Political Psychology from 1991 to the present, organizing meetings for the field of interactive conflict resolution have been held to discuss the current state of the field and the possibilities for professional networking. Also in June 1992, an intergenerational conversation for dialogue between junior and senior scholar-practitioners was held at the Institute for Conflict Analysis and Resolution at George Mason University. My involvement in planning and participating in these events has provided ongoing opportunities to discuss the major issues facing the field with a widening network of individuals. Thus, from all these activities, a broad range of information was continuously acquired on which to base the description, analysis, and recommendations presented in this book.

The book is divided into three parts. Part 1 presents the contributions of three persons regarded as creative and courageous pioneers in the field: John Burton (chapter 1), Leonard Doob (chapter 2), and Herbert Kelman (chapter 3). Material from various sources will be used to describe the genesis and rationale of their work, applications to specific conflicts, and conceptual contributions in terms of a theory of practice, from their initial thinking to most recent works.

Part 2 provides a sense of the potential of interactive conflict resolution by describing various developments, some of which followed closely on the seminal work of the pioneers and represent major contributions to the development of the field. Particular attention will be given to the work of Edward Azar on problem-solving forums (chapter 4) and Vamik Volkan, Joseph Montville, and Demetrius Julius in developing a psychoanalytically orientated approach (chapter 5). A range of applications at the intercommunal level are highlighted in chapter 6, including dialogue work related to conflicts in the Middle East, Sri Lanka, and Cambodia. Chapter 7 describes the development of a model that sees ICR as a form of professional consultation with applications to the India-Pakistan and Cyprus conflicts. In chapter 8, the potential of ICR is magnified by proposing a contingency model of third party intervention that indicates how different methods might be sequenced and coordinated for maximum utility. This chapter will emphasize the complementarity of ICR and traditional approaches, but also ICR's unique potential for addressing highly escalated and protracted conflicts.

In Part 3, the future prospects for ICR will be elucidated. First, a comparative review of applications will provide an assessment of the field in strengths and weaknesses in theory, research, and practice, and an initial model of transfer effects will be presented (chapter 9). Second, the critical developmental issues facing the field, in training, funding, and institutionalization, will be described as first articulated in the interviews and extended through the conferences and meetings (chapter 10). Then a number of practice and policy prescriptions will be advanced to provide directions to address the issues and move the field forward (chapter 11). The Conclusion will briefly overview ICR, place it in the context of the approaches to peace, and question its cultural generalizability and ultimate efficacy. The unique potential of the method will be underscored by placing it in the context of generic principles for resolving intergroup conflict.

Part One
The Pioneers of Peacebuilding

1

John Burton
Controlled Communication to Analytic Problem Solving

The genesis of interactive conflict resolution is generally attributed to the work of John Burton and his colleagues who founded the Centre for the Analysis of Conflict at University College London in the mid-sixties. John Burton was born in Australia and received his first degree in psychology from the University of Sydney, later obtaining doctoral degrees in economics and international relations from the University of London. He spent his early professional life in a meteoric and at times controversial career with the Australian Foreign Service, culminating in his appointment as permanent head of the Department of External Affairs from 1947 to 1951. Burton was a delegate at the founding Charter Conference of the United Nations in 1945 and at the Paris Peace Conference in 1946. As he shifted into the world of academia, he carried with him a range of real world experiences and a wealth of personal contacts in diplomatic circles and centers of power around the world.

Burton moved to London in the early sixties, having gained notoriety through various speaking and writing activities that challenged conventional thinking. His diplomatic experience had convinced him of the need for an alternative to the power approach that dominated international affairs (Burton 1994). He took an appointment in the Faculty of Laws at University College London to head up a department of international relations. Along with many others, including Anthony (Tony) de Reuck, he worked to initiate a series of conferences of social scientists concerned with international peace and security, modeled on the Pugwash conferences for natural scientists. This initiative was later transformed into the International Peace Research Association, founded in 1964.

Tony de Reuck was deputy director of the Ciba Foundation for medical research, and in that position organized numerous international meetings on a range of health and social issues during the sixties.

In that position, he arranged for facilities and funding to support John Burton's early forays into conflict resolution. A conference sponsored in 1965 brought together an international and multidisciplinary group of social scientists on the topic of "Conflict in Society" (de Reuck & Knight 1966). These developments laid the basis for the genesis of the first form of interactive conflict resolution by Burton and his colleagues.

Conflict and the Creation of Interactive Conflict Resolution

In the early sixties, a serious, escalating conflict was developing in Southeast Asia between Malaysia and Indonesia. The United Kingdom, working to extricate itself from the area as a colonial power, had considered the creation of a Malaysian Federation in 1961, which would unite the territories of Malaya, Singapore, Brunei, Sarawak, and Sabah. This plan was resisted by Indonesia, which had its own territorial ambitions, and by elements within Sarawak and Brunei, both of which erupted in armed rebellion in late 1962. These revolts were crushed and some of the insurgents, including many members of the Chinese resistance in Sarawak, regrouped in Indonesia and with Indonesian support began a guerrilla campaign along the border.

A United Nations mission investigated the situation in Sarawak and Sabah and confirmed that most of the population favored federation as expressed in an earlier election, and the Malaysian Federation was proclaimed in September 1963. However, Indonesia escalated the conflict with Malaysia in both political and military terms, refusing to grant diplomatic recognition and taking a direct role in the guerrilla operations. A cease-fire was brokered by the United States in early 1964, but a meeting of leaders was unable to reach a settlement, and in September 1964, Indonesian paratroopers mounted a serious incursion into Malaysia. The United Nations Security Council was unable to take action because of cold war entrenchment, and in early 1965, Indonesia withdrew from the United Nations to protest the granting of membership to Malaysia.

In London, another conflict was brewing—a conflict much more intellectual than the military clash in Malaysia, and yet one with important practical implications. As Burton developed his teaching and research program at University College London, it became clear that his unconventional thinking about international relations was at odds with the prevalent, traditional perspectives of most of the academic leaders in the field. The traditional approach to international relations emphasized interactions among sovereign states who pursue their national interests by exercising economic and military power through the formation of alliances, the use of deterrence, and at times, adherence to international law. Security is attained through the threat or use of force, and inevitable conflict is managed through compromise or suppression. In contrast to this "realist" approach to international relations, Burton was developing his thinking toward a new "pluralist" paradigm—*the world society perspective*—which emphasized the values and relationships of multiple actors in the global system (Banks 1984). This wider explanatory view of Burton and his colleagues came into conflict with the traditional historical and empirical approach to international relations (Burton 1994).

The intellectual conflict came to a head when different colleges at the University of London—the London School of Economics and University College London—began failing each other's students in shared classes, for the two sets of students were presenting radically different views of international relations on their examination papers. One particularly bitter case ended when the external examiner came down on the side of Burton's school. The conflict seized the agenda at a biannual meeting of British teachers in international relations, and a challenge was thrown down for the new perspective to take a case and demonstrate that their alternative ideas had any validity. The traditionalists suggested the case of Cuba, but this was rejected because the conflict had already been documented and interpreted in the power framework. Burton drew on his diplomatic experience and connections to select and address a serious, ongoing conflict to demonstrate the utility of his ideas—that involving Indonesia, Malaysia, and Singapore, which had become independent of the Malaysian federation.

With the knowledge and approval of the then British prime minister, Harold Wilson, who had tried unsuccessfully to mediate the conflict, Burton sent letters of invitation to the governments concerned, asking them to send representatives for discussions in London. The invitations clearly identified the purpose of the sessions as an academic analysis of the conflict rather than conciliation or mediation directed toward a settlement. The response was positive, and in December 1965, a five-day meeting was held with two nominees from each country and a panel of ten social scientists including John Burton, Fred Emery and David Barkla of the Tavistock Institute in London, Tom Burns of the University of Edinburgh, Roger Fisher from Harvard University, H. M. Lo of the Australian National University, and Roger Holmes, Peter Lyon, and Abraham (Bram) Oppenheim of the London School of Economics. Tony de Reuck arranged for the Ciba Foundation to provide the accommodation, meeting facilities, and travel support necessary for the meeting to take place.

There was confusion and uncertainty among the panel members about how the sessions should be conducted, and there was limited planning time and little sense of a team approach in the beginning. Tony de Reuck hosted the meeting in recognition of his experience in organizing a wide variety of small-group meetings involving international participants. Planning questions arose as to whether there should be an agenda and whether the panel members were conciliators or mediators or academics who should present papers analyzing the case at hand. In the end, de Reuck opened the meeting by indicating that none of the ordinary rules of meetings would apply—there would be no agenda, no minutes, and no agreed-upon statements at the end. The participants were simply invited to discuss the case with the social scientists until all parties were satisfied.

Following introductions, the participants were asked to tell the panel what they thought was the basis of the conflict. Each group of representatives in turn launched into an obligatory presentation of the positions of their respective governments. After this, some free discussion ensued that allowed the panel to provide interpretations of the conflict and draw parallels with other conflicts. However, much to the surprise of the delegates, an intense conflict arose among the panel itself over the degree of structure there should be in the meeting, particularly around whether there should be a detailed agenda and whether the panel should produce a draft agreement as a basis for negotiations. The modal preference was to continue with the analytical discussion approach. This conflict had an unanticipated positive effect on the participants, who now expressed an earlier suspicion that the panel had had some sort of hidden plan and a fear that they would be manipulated in some way. Now they saw that the discussion truly was free and could explore whatever directions were mutually decided upon. The rest of the meeting flowed productively, and the delegates stopped phoning their respective offices every half day to see if they should continue! Interactive conflict resolution was born.

The constructive process of this first workshop may be attributable in part to the modal characteristics of the parties' nominees. They tended to be younger, more flexible, and less orthodox diplomats and bureaucrats with university training in the social and administrative sciences from Western universities. Thus they accepted the relative lack of structure in the sessions, and welcomed the opportunity to take the concepts and models offered by the panel and apply them to their existing situation. They were able, for example, to mutually entertain the question of how the internal relations with minorities were affecting the conflict between their states.

After successfully engaging in mutual analysis of the conflict, the delegates began to develop and entertain options that might help the parties move toward resolution and settlement. The discussion emphasized principles and possibilities rather than positions and demands. Thus the sessions were not negotiations in the usual sense, but would likely be termed prenegotiation in today's terminology (see chapter 8). For the remainder of the meeting, the discussions alternated between analysis and the development of options, moving back and forth when the panel sensed that one "agenda" was likely to be more productive than the other.

After the first meeting of five days, the delegates returned home and their respective governments reestablished diplomatic contact. This became apparent when one delegation requested further meetings and indicated that the other parties favored continuing the process! Five further meetings of shorter duration were held over about the next six months, at some points including representatives of Australia and the United Kingdom at the suggestion of the parties themselves. The alternating mix of analysis and option development continued to characterize these sessions. According to de Reuck (1974), the sessions overall allowed the parties to correct mutual misperceptions, redefine the conflict, reassess the costs of their objectives, and envisage new policy options.

During the meetings, the parties reached a series of understandings, but these were not committed to paper, for the representatives were reluctant to do so and the panel thought it would take time away from the discussions. Nonetheless, it appears that much agreement was reached on the framework of a solution and many of its component parts. At the last meeting in London, the participants were shocked to hear of a coup in Indonesia, and the potential benefit of the sessions was thrown into question. However, the new administration in Indonesia appeared motivated toward peace, and quickly reached an agreement with Malaysia. The accord signed at the Manila peace conference in August 1966 followed closely the lines discussed in the London sessions. Hostilities ceased, full diplomatic relations were restored, and Indonesia rejoined the United Nations.

Burton (1994) indicates that the motive for this first workshop was in response to an academic challenge to test a theoretical approach, rather than to help resolve the conflict. However, the more the panel probed to find out about international relations, the more the delegates discussed their relationship. This mutual analysis provided realizations about the sources of the conflict that enabled them to move toward resolution. The London group had inadvertently started a conflict resolution process through the power of facilitated analysis made possible through academic sponsorship.

It is difficult to judge the influence of the London workshop on the resolution of the Malaysia-Indonesia conflict, for so many processes and factors were in play simultaneously. Nonetheless, the small group of conflict researchers in London were ecstatic and enthusiastic about building on their success to further the development of their new-found methodology. To do this, they established the Centre for the Analysis of Conflict, a concept that had been under discussion for some time and was founded in 1965, although it did not become fully operational until after the Malaysia-Indonesia workshop.

The Centre for the Analysis of Conflict (CAC) was established as a nonprofit institution for social science research in conflict analysis and resolution. A unique aspect of the CAC within academia was its professional practice interest in providing reconciliation services to interested parties engaged in destructive conflict through analytic discussions. On the research side, the CAC was designed to serve as a network of scholars to sponsor seminars and foster interchange on their theoretical and empirical work toward developing a pluralist perspective of international relations to counteract the prevailing realist orientation. John Burton was able to obtain initial funding from a number of sources, and the CAC launched into the demanding world of conflict analysis and resolution. A. J. R. (John) Groom was a founding member of the CAC and along with Burton constituted the primary faculty resources at University College London. A number of faculty from the London School of Economics and Political Science were also involved, as were several research fellows, including Tony de Reuck and Christopher Mitchell.

In 1966, the intercommunal conflict on the small island of Cyprus in the eastern Mediterranean was at an impasse. The Republic of Cyprus had gained independence from Britain in 1960 with the proclamation of a federal constitution that shared power through bicommunal structures and procedures between the larger Greek Cypriot and smaller Turkish Cypriot communities. Unfortunately, each side worked to implement the constitution in ways that protected and furthered its own agenda, resulting in a deadlock and ultimately a breakdown in 1963. Intercommunal violence broke out as the Greek Cypriots continued to press for "enosis," or union with Greece, while the Turkish Cypriots countered with "taksim," or partition. In early 1964, the United Nations established a peacekeeping force on the island, and a UN mediator subsequently produced a report in 1965 that was rejected by both sides. The parties now refused to meet under UN auspices, both insisting on incompatible preconditions before returning to the negotiating table. John Burton saw the significance of dealing with a case using his new methodology that traditional approaches could not address.

The UN was quite concerned about the Cyprus case, and was stymied in bringing the parties together (Burton 1985b). However, when Burton broached his ideas with the secretary-general's office, he was not taken seriously, for the UN officials assumed the parties would refuse to meet. Undaunted, he wrote letters to the two sides and followed up with a visit to Cyprus in mid-1966 for discussions with the leaders of the two communities. Both sides welcomed the opportunity for a discussion of the situation under an academic umbrella, and within a matter of days, each agreed to send delegates to a meeting in London.

The Cyprus meeting took place over five days in October 1966, with two representatives of each community and a larger panel of scholars, mainly from the CAC group (John Burton, Tony de Reuck, Chris Mitchell, Michael Banks, Bram Oppenheim, John Groom, Michael Nicholson, and R. M. Farr), but also including three Americans: Chad Alger, Herbert Kelman, and Robert North. In a planning session before the meeting, disagreement about how to initiate the meeting was followed by a decision to ask each side to first present its case as it wished, in the hope that this would free them up psychologically to listen to the other. Thus, after introductions and some comments by Burton to set the academic tone, each party presented its view of the situation. Unfortunately, after one presentation, a heated discussion ensued, consisting of statements, counterstatements, and accusations in which the parties adopted a legalistic, debating style of interaction.

At the end of the first day, the panel met and after having shared its frustration, agreed that it must intervene somehow at the end of the second presentation to create an academic climate. This was accomplished by a spontaneous conceptual input on the spiral model of conflict escalation, which the delegates then discussed in relation to their situation and which successfully launched the workshop into an analytic mode. Later in the week, the general topic turned to the exploration of probable approaches to the problem that focused on ensuring security and autonomy for the Turkish Cypriot community within an integrated political system. On the final day, the panel produced a summary report, which was amended in response to delegates' comments and which was perceived by them as a basis for future discussions.

Although the Cyprus meeting evidenced some uncertainty and disagreement among the panel and some unevenness in process, it did allow the parties to share their perceptions of one another's actions and goals, their differing definitions of the conflict, and their evaluation of alternative paths toward resolution (Mitchell 1966, 1981). According to Burton (1994), the discovery of important misperceptions and deeprooted, nonnegotiable sentiments, such as the identity and security needs for ethnic autonomy, shifted his approach firmly to analytic, problem-solving. The sessions also allowed the parties to actively explore the possibilities and to build part of the framework for returning to negotiations, including the status of the representatives, the involvement of other parties, and the objective of the negotiations. Essentially the delegates agreed in principle to return to negotiations, which the parties subsequently did under UN auspices. Follow-up investigations by the CAC indicated that some of the insights gained at the London meeting were communicated to the decision-making elites of the two communities and had significantly assisted in the resumption of mediation (Mitchell 1981).

However, the reinvolvement of the UN to some degree precluded further meetings under CAC auspices because of the potential interference of one track with the other. In addition, the members of the centre were uncertain whether this new process was appropriate to the needs of the parties to go beyond an academic analysis toward the settlement of the problem. In addition, as university faculty, they were soon faced with the teaching demands of a new term and on these and other practical grounds had to decline queries by the parties about continuing the process. Nonetheless, this second foray into interactive conflict resolution had again demonstrated the potential of the method as a useful prenegotiation approach. Burton and his colleagues now turned part of their attention to conceptualizing their experience to share it with the scholarly and diplomatic communities.

Developing a Theory of Practice: Controlled Communication

In moving into the arena of conflict analysis and resolution, the CAC group had formed some assumptions and directions, but had not developed in any way a clear and organized theory of practice. The articulation of the method was constructed through the inductive process of theory building, based largely on the Malaysia-Indonesia and Cyprus meetings. John Burton had first used the term "casework approach" to describe the method, and saw it as loosely linked to individual and group casework in psychotherapy and social work and to intergroup problem solving in industrial relations (Blake, Shepard & Mouton 1964; Burton 1967). However, in developing his theory of practice, he coined the term "controlled communication" to capture the approach of bringing together high-level representatives of groups or states involved in violent conflict in private, informal discussions in the presence of an impartial third party panel of social scientists (Burton 1969).

The essential role of the panel is to control communication to create a nonthreatening atmosphere in which the participants can examine their perceptions and misperceptions about the conflict and about each other, and then jointly explore avenues for analyzing and resolving the conflict, partly through the development of common functional interests. Due consideration must be given to the identification of the parties and the issues in the conflict, to the selection of representatives and their relationship with their principals. Burton makes it clear that the first procedures contemplated for the discussions were too rigid, and that the scholars from different disciplines had to relax their usual ways of analyzing and responding to conflict and join with the representatives in mutual analysis. The scholars play a useful role of injecting knowledge regarding conflict processes and in helping the parties stand back from the conflict and see it as a problem to be solved, but the establishment of effective communication between the parties is critical to success.

The role of the third party in controlled communication is therefore radically different from traditional methods of mediation and arbitration that seek to persuade, verify, or judge. In contrast, the panel's role is to help explain the origin and escalation of the conflict through analysis and comparison with other conflicts. However, it is for the representatives themselves to decide which theoretical explanations are useful and which avenues toward resolution have promise. In controlling communication after the first presentation of cases, the third party engages in supportive and facilitative behaviors that parallel those of the nondirective caseworker—seeking clarifications, promoting insight, questioning misperceptions, explaining processes of interaction. Once the parties can see their actions and antagonisms in the analytical framework of interaction processes and conflict escalation, communication becomes effective, the past is reperceived, and the future can be viewed in a less fearful light. Burton suggests that reperception can be introduced through reference to visual illusions, and that effective communication can be maintained by continually introducing appropriate models drawn from the conflict literature.

Successful analysis of the conflict to the mutual satisfaction of the parties paves the way to an exploration of possible solutions in broad terms. Here Burton (1969) places much emphasis on functional cooperation between the parties, particularly in a context of regional cooperation. He also acknowledges that at the stage of constructing administrative arrangements for cooperation, negotiation takes over from controlled communication. A prime function of the method is therefore to prepare the ground for negotiation by establishing the conditions under which it can be successful. Thus, in his earliest work on this new approach, Burton (1969) foresaw the potential prenegotiation role for interactive conflict resolution and the possibility of complementarity among different approaches to conflict management and resolution.

The term "problem solving" did not enter into the lexicon of the London group until after the Cyprus meeting, to help distinguish what was going on in contrast to the processes of diplomatic negotiation. Tony de Reuck applied the term because he saw many parallels between the conflict analysis sessions and earlier problem-solving groups that he had organized and studied through his work with the Ciba Foundation (de Reuck 1974). The term was used in the first instance to identify a third stage in the discussions, where after the first presentation of cases by the delegates and the ensuing analysis stimulated by the panel, the parties moved to consolidate their understandings and explore the possibilities for cooperative solutions. Subsequently the "problem-solving procedure" took over from "controlled communication" in describing and promulgating the work of the Centre for the Analysis of Conflict.

The early work of the London group was not without its critics, given that modal thinking in international relations followed the realist school, and debates about the merits of the new approach raged, both in pubic and in print. Yalem (1971) articulated the general concern about how applicable and effective the new procedures could be in dealing with the complex reality of international conflict. On the theoretical side, he questioned whether altering subjective elements in the minds of a few persons without decision-making responsibility would have any effect on primarily objective incompatibilities between large collectivities driven by power and ideology. He noted that much of the rationale and techniques of controlled communication came from the interpersonal and intergroup levels rather than the international one. In addition, Yalem raised a number of practical questions about the method related to the inhibiting constraints of secrecy and confidentiality, the influence level of the representatives, and the reentry problem of participants retaining perceptual and attitudinal changes in the back-home setting.

In a series of counterarguments to Yalem, Mitchell (1973) deals with most of these concerns by drawing on theoretical considerations as well as his experience in the work of the CAC. In particular, he argues for a complex understanding of the subjectivity of conflict and for the commonality of conflict processes over levels of analysis that makes it possible to transfer techniques of analysis. He also makes it clear that controlled communication is not proposed as a substitute for negotiations in international conflict resolution, but as a preparation or supplement to them. This issue of applicability is complex and pervasive, and needs to be given continuing consideration in attempts to assess the field of interactive conflict resolution (see chapter 9).

After the enthusiasm based on the successes of the Malaysia-Indonesia and Cyprus meetings, the practical work of the CAC went through a period of some difficulty, although the teaching demands on faculty continued to grow. The intention was to organize a series of meetings on different conflicts, but the competing demands of teaching, developing curriculum, and seeking research funds made it hard to concentrate on developing new cases. John Burton explored possibilities in the Middle East, but these were ended by the June 1967 war. Chris Mitchell spent considerable time in the Horn of Africa in 1967, and eventually obtained agreement from the governments of Somalia, Ethiopia, and Kenya to send delegates, but meetings never took place. John Burton began some contacts to interest India and Pakistan in a meeting on the Kashmir conflict, but a change of government in India ended that possibility.

Academic resistance to the new method was also apparent and was partly expressed through difficulties the CAC experienced in obtaining funding to continue its practical research. As a result, a period of reduced activity occurred, with some associates leaving the centre to continue their work elsewhere, including Chris Mitchell and Michael Banks. Tony de Reuck, who was trained as a physicist, completed a graduate degree in economics and political science and went to the University of Surrey as research fellow and later head of international relations. Thus, by the late sixties, the CAC was mainly a research network among members, with the hub in the teaching anchor at University College London, where John Burton and John Groom were on faculty. In the mid-seventies, financial cuts began hitting British universities and rationalization was the order of the day. Partly as a result, the international relations faculty at University College London moved to the new University of Kent in Canterbury and the CAC was reestablished there in 1978.

After the Cyprus meeting, Burton became increasingly concerned that the method should have a firmer theoretical base, before further interventions were undertaken into highly escalated and sensitive situations of intercommunal and international conflict. Thus, after some explorations into other protracted international conflicts, he turned his attention to situations of less intensity and complexity. He consulted on conflict between students and teachers in London schools and on conflict within a consulting firm of industrial relations specialists. This in part led him to intervene in a costly and bitter labor dispute at an automobile manufacturer, which he resolved through consultations with the major players.

Also during this period, Burton continued to develop his thinking about international relations in ways that were compatible with the insights achieved through the first workshops (Burton 1994). In conjunction with ideas derived from general systems theory, the result was *World Society* (1972), which stressed multiple forms of intersocietal interactions in a cobweb model. This work also stressed the role of misperception in conflict, and included a chapter on conflict resolution.

In the late sixties and early seventies, Burton became involved in the conflict in Northern Ireland, at first at the request of the Community Relations Commission established by the government. He was able to help arrange an informal meeting of the leaders of the opposing paramilitaries, and was working to initiate formal meetings on a wider basis between the leadership groups of the Irish Republican Army and the Ulster Defence Forces. However, news of the work was leaked to the press and the initiative had to be ended. A related initiative that was successful involved bringing together representatives of the Catholic and the Protestant trade unions for a meeting designed along the lines of controlled communication. The panel of four included John Burton and Chris Mitchell with two associates from Northern Ireland, while each side was represented by five delegates. The representatives found they had much in common, even though they operated in totally separate "territories." Unfortunately, the work ended when the British government dissolved the Community Relations Commission and told Burton his further involvement was not advisable.

After spending some years at the University of Kent, Burton moved to the United States in the early 1980s, where he held an International Studies Association Fellowship at the University of South Carolina in 1982. He then joined Edward Azar at the University of Maryland, before moving on to George Mason University in 1985. Working with a network of mainly American scholars, Azar and Burton organized problem-solving sessions on the Lebanese, Sri Lankan, and Falklands-Malvinas conflicts. These initiatives are described in chapter 4. Concurrently Burton continued to develop and refine his theory of practice in procedural, methodological, and ethical terms.

Analytic, Problem-Solving Conflict Resolution

Controlled communication was designed to address the subjective nature of conflict as a means toward resolution. By subjective, Burton (1969) was referring to two major elements. One had to do with the perception of the parties, in which the origins of the conflict are pushed into the background as perception and communication escalate the conflict toward a set of changed conditions that then underlie its persistence. The other aspect of subjectivity relates to the differential valuing and costing of objective differences and alternative goals and means over time, such that a conflict that is irresolvable at one point is resolvable at another. The analysis provided by controlled communication allowed the parties to realize the subjective nature of their situation and to develop mutual acceptable alternatives to move out of it.

Over the years, Burton's thinking about the phenomenon moved toward the conceptualization of "deep-rooted conflict" (see the Introduction). This was partly driven by the inductive learnings accruing from what participants said during conflict analysis, and partly through the influence of colleagues such as Edward Azar and Herbert Kelman (see chapter 3). Burton came to see the protracted nature of deep-rooted conflict as due to two sources: the causation of the conflict and the character of the processes traditionally employed to deal with it.

In causation, Burton had long considered protracted conflicts as not negotiable in the usual sense, and more and more came to see them as rooted in underlying, fundamental needs that could not be suppressed or compromised (e.g., Burton 1979, 1987). Although acknowledging the work of early "need theorists," such as the clinical psychologist Abraham Maslow (1970), he placed particular credibility in the work of sociologist Paul Sites (1973), who argued that the real source of power in social life lies in individual needs such as those for consistency, security, recognition, distributive justice, and a sense of control. Burton (1979) argued that these fundamental needs underlie institutions that promote group integrity and identity and promote legitimate and valued relationships with others. Thus, basic needs provide for allegiances to groups and will be pursued by individuals and groups at all costs. The source of protracted conflict therefore lies in the expression of ontological human needs and not in differences over objective interests and misperceptions about them. Deep-rooted conflict therefore requires an analysis that allows the parties to ascertain deeper motivations and to explore means to meet common human needs.

Deep-rooted conflict is also rendered protracted and seemingly intractable by the very methods that are typically employed to address it (Burton 1985a). Traditional means of settlement, such as negotiation, mediation, and arbitration, deal solely or primarily with surface interests and positions and do not directly address underlying needs and values. Attempts to translate needs into interests simply to fit the method of intervention make the situation worse. In addition, traditional methods often employ leverage in its various forms of persuasion, inducement, normative pressures, or coercion in attempts to gain or force a settlement. Under these conditions, not only are settlements difficult to obtain from the parties, but they are also unstable over time. In addition, the traditional methods of conflict management are devoid of the means of deeper analysis on which to base a resolution of the conflict. Thus, although hostilities between the parties might be controlled through the mediation of a cease-fire and the intervention of peacekeeping, the conflict itself moves no closer to resolution and in fact becomes more intractable.

Throughout John Burton's work, distinctions develop between "dispute" and "conflict," "settlement" and "resolution," and then the paired terms "dispute settlement" and "conflict resolution." Disputes refer to differences over negotiable interests, choices and preferences that are found in all human relationships, while conflicts arise out of the frustration of basic human needs that cannot be compromised or suppressed. Settlement refers to the negotiated or arbitrated processes and outcomes of disputes, whereas resolution refers to a transformation process, the outcomes of which satisfy the needs of all parties. Thus it makes sense to speak of *dispute settlement* and *conflict resolution*, but not to mix and confuse the two, even though disputes are sometimes symptoms of conflicts.

The implication of these distinctions is that conflict resolution requires the analysis of the underlying sources of the conflict situation by the parties involved. This can best be accomplished by facilitated, analytic, problem-solving conflict resolution provided by an impartial panel of social scientists. In his 1987 *Handbook,* Burton sets out the parameters and procedures of this method, which thereby extends and explicates his theory of practice. Besides providing for an analysis of the interests, needs, perceptions, tactics, and goals of the parties, the approach allows for the costing of different alternatives and for the deducing of policies and structures that would lead to mutual need fulfilment. The *Handbook* lays out detailed rules for the operationalization of problem-solving conflict resolution and considers the professional and ethical obligations of those who would deem to be facilitators.

Burton (1987) uses the term "rules" to emphasize the importance of acting appropriately in delicate interactions where discussion must be tightly controlled so that dialogue and constructive, innovative outcomes are realized. Rules must be deduced from theory about conflict resolution and also emerge out of the experience of practice. The rigid aspect of the rules is more in relation to the principles on which they are based, rather than their specific application across all conflict situations. The rules are not perfect, but should only be modified carefully in the light of evolving theory and practice. The rules are organized more or less according to the sequence of activities that a problem-solving initiative would follow in actual implementation (Burton 1987).

With regard to the sponsorship of problem-solving discussions, Burton (1987) emphasizes the responsibility of the sponsor, that is, the person or institution that initiates and arranges the process. For example, sponsors should not initiate contact with the parties unless they can provide competent facilitators and guarantee commitment over the long term, that is, until their services are no longer required. In the entry process, Burton's approach requires identical and simultaneous communication with the leaderships of the parties, or at least operating with their knowledge. Representation of all factions should be sought through participants who are not official delegates, but do have easy access to decision makers.

The role of the third party in problem-solving conflict resolution is to place the parties in direct analytical dialogue, to facilitate the clarification of interests, values, needs, goals, and tactics and to help deduce possible outcomes on the basis of this analysis. To accomplish this, the panel needs to be drawn from several disciplines with knowledge of conflict theories and with experience in the facilitation process. The panel should not include individuals whose exclusive specialty is the conflict or region in question, for they may have preconceived views based on their expert knowledge. This would contradict the principle that ultimately the parties are the real experts who must draw on their perceptions and experiences to analyze and resolve the conflict. The panel should be balanced in relevant respects, such as ethnicity, class, and gender, and should be able to prepare, confer, and work effectively as a team.

In preparation for the discussions, Burton provides reasons funding needs to be the responsibility of the sponsor, and indicates that even before approaches are made, adequate funds should be available for a first meeting to reduce uncertainty and anxiety. After the first session, participants are encouraged to meet their own costs if possible, with the sponsor continuing to support the involvement of the panel. For location, the site should be neutral, ideally chosen in consultation with the parties, with due consideration to separate accommodation facilities and appropriate seating arrangements for the discussions. The environment should moderate tension and encourage direct interaction, and participants should be given clear expectations about the sessions.

In the analytical stage of the discussions, much responsibility falls to the panel for setting the expectations, norms, and rules for the interaction and for sequencing the discussions from first perceptions, through clarifications to analysis and evaluation, to an agreed-upon definition of the situation, and finally to the exploration of options that meet the needs of all parties. Although there is no fixed agenda in time or items, the panel must control the substance and the flow of the discussions for the interaction to be successful. Although one member acts as a formal chair, the panel operates as a team, throwing the ball to whoever's specialization or participation is most relevant at the time. Besides facilitating the discussions, the panel brings forward relevant knowledge about conflict for the participants to consider and potentially use in their analysis, in the spirit of an academic research seminar. Later on, the panel identifies the key issues at the heart of the conflict, and prepares a statement of propositions about the conflict, which through further discussion is reduced to an agreed-upon summary of the workshop.

The search for options is unlikely to produce much yield in one workshop, and Burton (1987) envisages a series of seminars, interspersed with back-home discussions, to deduce from the propositions what changes in policies, institutions, and structures are necessary to implement them. At this point, interests will reemerge and resistance to change will become evident. The role of the panel is to press for a balanced assessment of the costs of change versus no change, and to encourage and participate in the creation of a wide range of options, even if they must at first be transition steps toward longer-term solutions.

Throughout the seminar series, the sponsor should provide reports to the leadership of the parties and should be sensitive to the transition stage between these unofficial discussions and official negotiations. A discussion of transitional policies later in the unofficial process might lead to further workshops on specific issues and on particular policies designed to move constructively into the future. In terms of reentry and follow-up, the panel should allow time toward the end of every seminar for a discussion of next steps and the means of continued communication, and must be sensitive to conflict among factions within the parties. Each seminar should build on the last, with appropriate selection of participants, but the panel should always be thinking about the earliest possible termination point so that the process does not become institutionalized.

John Burton draws attention to the ethics of conflict resolution, because he acknowledges that third party intervention is a delicate task, which can easily do more harm than good. His concern is more with functional competence than moral philosophy in that would-be intervenors with experience in conflict management but not resolution or who may be looking for personal or institutional credits are dangerous. The professional in conflict resolution should approach the problem as any other professionals approach their work. This requires strict adherence to principles about confidentiality, the selection of participants and panel members, the need for perceived neutrality, and indeed all matters that are covered in the *Handbook*. The importance of an ethical code of conduct will be discussed further in chapter 7, which sees ICR as a form of professional consultation with all the ethical requirements that this entails.

Conclusion

It is impossible in a short space to do justice to the work of John Burton, including not only the commendations and further considerations but also the reservations and criticisms that could be raised. The range, depth, and creativity of his contributions are truly phenomenal and lie at the heart of the field of conflict resolution. The limited focus here has been on the creation, development, and refinement of his theory of practice and the cases that gave rise to it. Before his practical interventions and at each step in their development, Burton has also provided collateral work on the conceptual understanding of international relations and conflict resolution (e.g., Burton 1965, 1968, 1972, 1979, 1984). The culmination of his work in conflict resolution is presented in a four-volume series, two of which are coedited with Frank Dukes (Burton 1990a, 1990b; Burton & Dukes 1990a, 1990b). This series provides a historical and theoretical perspective of the field, surveys a broad spectrum of contributions, highlights human needs theory as the foundation for conflict analysis and resolution, and overviews and distinguishes practices in the management, settlement, and resolution of conflict.

Burton's work has contributed to the pluralist perspective in international relations and to a proposed paradigm shift from power-based political realism to needs-based functionalism and "behavioral realism." This orientation contains numerous elements and many implications for how conflict is approached, managed, and resolved. Burton has also introduced the concept of "conflict provention" to denote the promotion of the environmental conditions that create harmonious and cooperative relationships, that is, that remove the causes of conflict. In his later work, Burton has presented conflict resolution as a political philosophy and the necessary core of a new political system. That is, conflict resolution addresses how human aspirations can be satisfied in the context of the social good, and as such provides an alternative or at least supplement to authority-based political systems.

Thus the historical significance of problem-solving conflict resolution is not simply as an interactive process dealing with a few special cases, but in providing for a new approach to decision making based on human needs that could underlie a radically different social-political system (Burton 1992). The ultimate challenge is the establishment of institutions that embody a problem-solving rather than an adversarial approach to decision making. A small step in this direction would be the development of institutional bases that would support applied research in ICR, an issue that will be discussed in chapter 10.

John Burton's contributions in conflict resolution and international relations have generated some controversy, although comprehensive, critical reviews of his work are not available. Warfield (1988) takes issue with the presentation of rules in the *Handbook*, finding little justification for rigid adherence to them in Burton's arguments or evidence. He notes the limited sources in social science that Burton draws on to support his propositions, the lack of attention to cognitive processes in problem solving, and the hidden assumptions in Burton's presentation. Warfield (1988) concludes that the *Handbook* is heavily flawed and yet may contain some critical ideas for improving our approach to resolving conflict. Wider reviews of Burton's work might raise similar criticisms, for Burton tends to draw selectively from various disciplines to support conclusions that often appear based more on insight than on the usual rules of scientific inquiry and theory building.

One final consideration of Burton's work relates to the degree of generalizability across different cultures in both the theory and practice of conflict resolution. Burton contends that although intervenors need to be sensitive to cultural elements, the problem-solving approach is rooted in generic concepts and processes that transcend cultural differences. Others disagree. This question of cultural generalizability is of such importance to the entire field of ICR that it will be discussed at length in the Conclusion.

2

Leonard Doob
Human Relations Workshops Applied to Conflict Resolution

Leonard Doob is Sterling Professor Emeritus of Psychology at Yale University, where his distinguished academic career in social psychology has spanned some decades and numerous areas of interest. From classic work on the frustration-aggression hypothesis to his latest book on the guides and perils of intervention, his erudite mind has considered a wide range of questions including morality and ethics, the patterning of time, and the pursuit of peace. On the more applied side, he has spent much time in Africa working on various research projects, particularly in South Africa, and has also been involved in training seminars for diplomats and military personnel sponsored by the International Peace Academy. The interest in this chapter centers on Leonard Doob's creative and controversial application of human-relations training to intergroup and international conflict resolution.

In the summer of 1965, Doob was on one of his many visits to Africa, and had ventured into the Somali bush to study eidetic imagery among the local people, who not having a written language were of particular interest in this regard. After finishing with the research study, Doob had time to reflect on the impoverished lot of the Somali people, at a time when their government was spending more than half of its budget on a seemingly fruitless war over its borders with neighboring Ethiopia and Kenya. His humanitarian concern and compassion led to the question of whether social science had any knowledge or methods to offer that might help such antagonists resolve their mutually destructive conflicts. On his return to Yale, Doob organized a small seminar of interested social scientists to consider what kind of intervention might be useful and how it might be operationalized. The long road from the initial "wild idea" to its full realization is an amazing tale of persistence and ingenuity.

The Fermeda Workshop on the Horn of Africa

In 1960, the colonies of British and Italian Somaliland gained independence as the Republic of Somalia, which continued the historical claim to incorporate areas of Ethiopia and Kenya populated by ethnic Somali majorities. In the early sixties, guerrilla attacks by Somalis in the disputed areas were paralleled by an escalating diplomatic offensive on all sides and eventually armed conflict between regular forces. The conflict continued through the mid- to late sixties, with alternating periods of confrontation and accommodation, but without any resolution of the underlying problems. Somalia continued to press its claims that the borders should be redrawn through self-determination. Ethiopia countered that its composition as a multiracial state was supported by boundaries determined by various treaties valid under international law. Similarly, Kenya continued to claim sovereignty over its northeastern province as essential to its territorial integrity and identity as a multiracial state. In part, the problem also centered in the conflict between the nomadic tradition of the Somalis and the fixed boundaries determined during the decolonization of the Horn. Various mediation initiatives during the sixties by the Organization of African Unity and the United Nations all proved unsuccessful in engendering negotiations or movement toward settlement (Doob 1970).

Against this harsh backdrop, Doob and his colleagues considered how to offer a new approach informed by social science to shed some light on the path toward resolution of the Somalia-Ethiopia-Kenya conflict. Doob had at first deemed that one-time meetings would accomplish little, and that for real progress to occur it would be necessary to take individuals out of the conflict situation for a period of intensive interaction. After learning from their interaction, participants could then apply their insights to the solution of the conflict. Along this line, the Yale group decided that a human relations training workshop would be an appropriate intervention for the conflict in the Horn, partly because such workshops, created in the United States and Britain, had been successfully employed in a number of African countries (see Wickes 1970). The rationale was that participants would learn about themselves and their relations with others, particularly how to communicate effectively with those from different groups, and thereby be able to overcome the usual verbal facades and possibly create innovative solutions to the conflict (Doob 1970).

This rationale is fundamentally different from that adopted by the Burton group in their controlled communication workshops (see chapter 1). The Burton approach was to adapt an open, unstructured seminar discussion to an analysis of the sources and the processes of the conflict, with potential insights offered by the panel of social scientists. The initial learning is in the analysis itself, which then supports the development and consideration of mutually acceptable alternatives. The contrasting assumption in the Doob approach is that general learnings about one's self and about human interaction can be transferred to the creative development of innovative solutions to a specific conflict. In both cases, it is assumed that the development of qualities such as trust and candor in the early interaction will have a salutary effect on the later problem solving.

Specifically the Yale group adopted the small-group method of *sensitivity training,* then popular in North America, to the conflict in the Horn (Doob, Foltz & Stevens 1969). Sensitivity, or T-groups (T for training), involve an intense series of unstructured discussions in which a small group of participants openly share their perceptions, ideas, and feelings about what is happening in the group and about one another. It is a form of experiential learning that is directed toward increased self-awareness, interpersonal effectiveness, and understanding of group processes (Fisher 1982b). The group is usually led by a professional trainer who takes a nondirective and facilitative role that emphasizes a here-and-now focus for understanding the interaction of the participants in processes (how people are behaving) rather than content (what they are saying). Typical norms that develop in T-groups include the candid description of feelings, the giving and receiving of interpersonal feedback (how group members perceive one another), the confrontation of behaviors that affect others negatively, and the making of group decisions by consensus. T-groups generally go through a series of developmental stages from initial confusion, anxiety, and confrontation over the lack of structure, to shared responsibility and cohesion, to learnings about interpersonal and group functioning, and finally to a high level of affection and trust among the members. The method is not without its risks and pitfalls, but it can be a powerful resocialization experience in which participants acquire more productive and respectful ways of relating to others.

It took the Yale group more than three years beginning in 1966 to gain the approval of all three governments simultaneously, to recruit and maintain participants from the three countries, and to acquire funding for what many saw as a courageous but risky enterprise (Doob 1970; Doob et al. 1969). The plan was to invite from each country six academics with an understanding of the situation and an openness to change, who were fluent in English and influential in policymaking circles, but who would not come as official representatives. Recruitment in two countries was achieved primarily through the universities, where Doob had previous contacts, and in the third (which had no uni-

versity) by approaching scholars in various positions. Two governments gave approval readily, but the third was hesitant for well over a
year. When its resistance was finally overcome, the workshop was
scheduled for the summer of 1968. However, the approval of one of the
other governments was then revoked because of a concern about upcoming elections, and the workshop had to be canceled on three
months notice. When approval was reinstituted after the election, there
was a mad rush to restart the process, including the rerecruitment of
participants, the solicitation of trainers, and the selection of an appropriate venue.

The persistence required to obtain funding for the project is a story
in itself, demonstrating why financial support is one of the most difficult issues facing the field of ICR (see chapter 10). Major American
foundations were attracted to the idea, but saw it as unrealistic and
were concerned about political sensitivities. When Doob received tacit
approval from the U.S. State Department to allay their fears, the foundations found other reasons for refusal. Fortunately Yale University
continued to provide operating funds to keep the project alive, and
with the backing of the United Nations Institute for Training and Research, funds became available from two American donors and a British
trust. It is therefore a minor miracle that the eighteen African scholars,
four T-group trainers, and three Yale organizers met one another at the
Rome airport in early August 1969, and traveled twelve more hours by
bus into the mountains of South Tyrol to the Hotel Fermeda, which
Doob had located only days before! There over the next two weeks, the
plan of the workshop unfolded.

Participants were initially divided into two mixed T-groups where
they spent most of their time for the first five days, before a weekend
break. Some time was also devoted to meetings of the total workshop,
dubbed the "General Assembly." The sensitivity training proceeded as
expected, with confusion, anxiety, and anger being expressed at the
lack of structure and the lack of discussion about the conflict itself, followed by movement to profitable discussions without the benefit of
agenda or formal leadership. The training was supplemented by short
lectures, games, and structured exercises designed to increase participants' awareness of human interaction in interpersonal, group, and intergroup situations.

Toward the end of the first week, the focus shifted from sensitivity
training to the substantive issues of the border disputes, with the three
national groups discussing, with some resistance, their country's grievances and the perceived grievances of the other countries. In the second week, the two T-groups moved from discussion of the issues in the
conflict to creating approaches and potential solutions to the conflict.

During this stage, the workshop was managed by a planning group consisting of two participants from each country, two trainers, and one of the organizers.

According to the organizers (Doob, Foltz & Stevens 1969), the first phase of the workshop went well. Cross-national ties were built more quickly than expected, and the two T-groups developed strong loyalty and pride, thus inducing an element of intergroup competition. One group was more effective than the other, which seemed particularly hampered by the erratic and disruptive behavior of one malcontent participant.

The General Assembly in the final week was, however, an exercise in frustration, with unproductive behavior (avoiding, undercutting, intransigence, posturing) being inadequately controlled with an increasingly repressive reliance on parliamentary procedure. The more cooperative orientation and the mutually acceptable proposals developed in the two T-groups could not be transferred to the General Assembly, and the workshop faltered in frustration and factionalism. The planning group attempted to amalgamate the two proposals into an acceptable plan, but the General Assembly session led to acrimonious debate, fragmentation of previous loyalties, and finally to deadlock and defeat. After discussion of reentry and formal good-byes, the weary participants, trainers, and organizers departed in a somber mood (Wickes 1970).

In substance, there were few disagreements over the facts of the situation, but the evaluation of the facts differed markedly, especially around self-determination and sovereignty. Attitudes related to these issues did not change, although participants learned about the details and the resolve of opposing positions. Bargaining between national subgroups was intense in the two T-groups, and yet they were able to develop detailed proposals that were genuinely international. Both proposals called for some form of joint administration and demilitarization of the disputed areas implemented in a staged process within the context of a regional political arrangement. Unfortunately, the quick amalgamation of the two proposals appeared to satisfy no one, as each T-group saw elaborate and hard-won elements of its proposal fall by the wayside or be rejected in the General Assembly. The primary objective of the workshop, in producing an innovative solution to the conflict in the Horn, was therefore not attained. The organizers concluded nonetheless that the training experience did contribute appreciably to breaking down reserve and enhancing communication among participants from the different countries (Doob 1970; Doob et al. 1969).

Appraisals by three of the African participants are mixed at best. A Somali participant (Duhul 1970) observed that prejudices and preconceptions doomed the workshop to failure, even though the procedural aspects were excellent, partly because the unstructured T-groups lent themselves well to a traditional form of Somali discussion. Unfortunately, the two solutions were based on different premises respecting the degree of self-determination allotted to the people of the disputed territories, which along with other factors led to the final fiasco. A Kenyan participant (Okumu 1970) questioned whether small group methods are appropriate to address highly charged issues such as sovereignty or territorial integrity in an international context where no structural or constitutional framework exists. Thus, although the T-group activities involved candor, mutual learning, and creativity, there was little transformation of participants' attitudes and attachments to the problem itself, and the exercise came to naught as national prerogatives asserted themselves. An Ethiopian participant (Eshete 1970) expected a more than superficial dialogue on the conflict, and in the end was disappointed and concluded that such interactions are unlikely to succeed. The broad and uninformative discussions in the T-groups ignored ideological underpinnings, and the attempts at creating solutions to the dispute simply elicited national positions. Thus Eshete regards the psychological approach of the training methods as inapplicable to complex conflicts, which are not simply over the distribution of interests, but the very legitimacy of interests. Taken together, it appears that the African participants questioned the rationale and design of the workshop in terms of the applicability of the training methods to the conflict situation.

In contrast, the rationale for the workshop continued to receive the support of the trainers and organizers in their evaluations. Ferguson (1970) maintains that the T-group method was appropriate to develop collaborative relationships that could sustain the development of solutions to the conflict. He wonders if the trainers worked the process problems in the whole group strongly enough, and he notes that several of the participants recruited at the last minute were either disruptive or ineffective. Nonetheless the two T-groups did develop collaboration and commitment. Unfortunately, there was not the time, the strategy or the effort to develop the total group in a similar manner, and the final product went unrealized.

Walton (1970a, 1970b) presents a comprehensive and systematic analysis and evaluation of the Fermeda design. In support of the design, he notes that participant responses to an evaluation questionnaire generally indicated much mutual education and understanding of others' views, as well as a moderate increase in openness to alternate solutions and an acknowledgment of the innovative ideas produced in the workshop. He attributes the failure of the overall proposal to the shortage of time necessary to develop the total community and to effectively merge the two T-group proposals. Walton and also Crockett (1970) in part attribute the frustration and fiasco of the General Assembly to the disempowering effect of parliamentary procedure on the process interventions of the trainers. In sum, the commentaries of the trainers indicate areas where the design and implementation could have been improved.

In conclusion, the Fermeda experiment produced ambiguous results. The organizers and trainers contend that the rationale of applying sensitivity training methods was sound, but that improvements needed to be made in the design and its execution. The African participants appear less enthusiastic about the rationale, and the failure and frustration of the later sessions likely soured the entire event. In transfer of outcomes to the wider relations between the three countries, little is known. Apparently participants were debriefed by their respective governments, so that elements of the proposals were likely passed on (Walton 1970a). One would also expect that high level influentials, such as the participants, would continue to have an ongoing effect on policy making, depending on their connection to the regime in power. In Somali, for example, in the months after the workshop, there was a coup d'état, which might have precluded the transfer of any ideas, but which also saw two of the participants become ministers in the new government (Duhul 1970). The question of transfer of outcomes, however, seems premature when serious questions have been raised about the workshop design itself.

The Belfast-Stirling Workshop on Northern Ireland

In the early 1970s, Doob and his Yale associates became interested in intervening in the bitter sectarian dispute between Protestants and Catholics in Northern Ireland. During their involvement, the conflict was going through escalation to new levels of destructiveness and intractability (see, for example, Duffy & Frensley 1991). In Belfast and other centers, everyday life for ordinary people was becoming increasingly difficult in the face of shootings, bombings, and other acts of violence associated with the "troubles." In mid-1971, Doob and William Foltz visited Belfast and were encouraged through their meetings with a wide variety of individuals. Through these discussions, a modest objective emerged: to bring together influentials from two strife-torn neighborhoods of Belfast to build mutual trust and work on plans for improving relations (Doob & Foltz 1973). The intervenors further expected that the participants from the two communities would learn about working in collectivities, increase their understanding of each others' attitudes, and discover common interests and ways of cooperating that could be implemented and generalized.

During the next year, the organizers expanded their Yale planning group, acquired funding for the project, and returned for a visit to Belfast. The project scope was expanded to a wider range of areas in Belfast and criteria for participation were established. Recruiting was delegated to two associates, both American scholars who had lived in Belfast for many years and had detailed knowledge of relevant organizations and potential participants. Specifically the participants were to be influential community leaders and members from predominantly grass roots organizations who were emotionally stable and interested in cooperating with the other side.

Doob spent two months close by during this period, so that contact could be maintained with the associates. He also returned to Belfast before to the event and interviewed most of the participants, in part explaining the demands of the training experience. The workshop was described as a training conference in which participants would learn about working in groups in ways that might help them achieve their goals relating to the conflict, with the possible future assistance of the organizers and associates in developing concrete projects in Belfast. The outcome was that fifty-six persons (sixty being the target number), roughly split between the two religious factions, took part in a nine-day workshop held at Stirling University in Scotland in late August 1972.

The design called for an initial five-day immersion in a human relations training approach known as the *Tavistock model*, which focuses on interaction processes in groups, particularly around authority and power issues (Shaffer & Galinsky 1974). The trainers enact a detached and autocratic role, mainly providing comment on how the group is attempting to deal with the various difficulties it finds in organizing itself and studying its own interaction. The aloofness of the trainers extends to the informal time of the workshop as well, so that participants find no direction or support to help deal with the confusion, anxiety, and anger that they typically experience. In the Stirling workshop, the Tavistock design was modified slightly in two ways: introductory and sequential discussion groups were formed on the common social denominators of sex, religion, and age, and at the end of the Tavistock period, application groups with Protestants and Catholics from contiguous areas talked about community development activities.

In the last four days of the workshop, the participants worked mainly in mixed planning groups directed toward community problems. These sessions were supplemented by other human relations training exercises (role plays, simulations) designed primarily to illustrate relations between unequal groups. Questions of reentry into the Belfast environment were also discussed. The demands of the workshop were considerable in the light of the challenging agenda, but also because the original design of two weeks had been compressed into nine days.

The rationale for Stirling was that if participants could learn about the processes occurring within themselves and the various groups in which they interacted, they might be able to apply these learnings to improve such processes within their own communities. Doob and Foltz (1973) contend that much learning occurred about issues of authority, power, and leadership, particularly about the dynamics of powerlessness and ambivalence toward authority. In addition, participants had to confront issues of group identity, boundaries, and loyalty, and the manner in which they typically dealt with cross-conflict relations in Northern Ireland. Finally, participants learned about people from the other side, and worked closely with them to develop plans for community projects involving parallel but also cooperative ventures.

The pressure and tension at Stirling was considerable. Many participants experienced varying levels of disorientation, especially during the Tavistock phase; some withdrew from active participation; one person with a history of instability, who had been sent by an organization without a preworkshop interview, wandered aimlessly between groups; one higher status person was humiliated by a coup against his leadership with a resulting sense of hurt and anger. The two associates, who served as a buffer between the organizers and trainers, and the participants began to question the entire enterprise. They later decided to return the pre- and post-workshop questionnaires to the participants, and some time after returning to Belfast, they broke their association with the project. After the workshop, two participants attacked the project in the Belfast press, and this was followed by rebuttals praising the workshop from six other participants.

Doob and Foltz (1973) indicate that the workshop had positive effects for some participants, including increased self-confidence and greater professional competence. However, they do acknowledge that the informed consent necessary for individuals to take part in such a rigorous and atypical exercise might not have been attained because of faulty communication about the nature of the workshop from the organizers through the associates to the participants. Doob and Foltz (1974) returned to Belfast nine months after the workshop, and were able to interview forty of the participants about longer-term effects.

The unstructured interviews generally affirmed the mixed reactions and outcomes of the workshop, with a somewhat greater preponderance of positive over negative effects. Many participants reported increases in self-confidence and organizational effectiveness, along with a greater appreciation of the diversity on both sides of the conflict. Some, who were strategically placed, apparently brought about changes that may have reduced the incidence of random violence. However, none of the planning groups had been able to implement its project because of practical constraints and social pressures, including intimidating threats of personal violence. Thus, although many participants saw the workshop as a valuable learning experience, the practical gains in intercommunal cooperation were limited.

The generally positive assessment of the workshop came through despite most participants' impressions that they were not adequately informed about its nature. Thus they were surprised by the Tavistock phase, and only after the workshop did they come to see the learning utility of the experience. Many did not think the written outline portrayed the true nature of the workshop, and their limited contact with the associates failed to provide them with a satisfactory understanding. Some had no contact with the associates, for they were simply sent as delegates by their organizations or were last-minute substitutes. Nonetheless, Doob and Foltz (1974) report that there did not appear to be any lasting negative effects on the few participants who were identified as outcasts or casualties. However, it is clear that both procedural and ethical problems arose in the planning and recruitment phases of the enterprise.

A comprehensive, searing critique of the Stirling workshop is offered by the two associates and two of their colleagues familiar with the project and the situation in Northern Ireland (Boehringer et al. 1974). They identify four apparent goals of the intervention: experimentation, education, social innovation, and conflict resolution; and propose that these were improperly articulated, unrelated, and contradictory. The experimental nature of the high stress workshop methods was not articulated, and the associates were therefore unable to secure informed consent or to screen participants, for they themselves did not know what was going to happen in the workshop. With regard to education, participants were informed that they would gain insights into their behavior, but the use of Tavistock techniques, which induce punishing self-analysis, with individuals from a society undergoing severe upheaval is hazardous, irresponsible, and morally unjustifiable. On social innovation, the attempt to develop planning groups was a total failure, and the claims that certain outcomes might have reduced the incidence of violence are extremely difficult to substantiate in a complex and confusing situation. Finally, the implicit goal of conflict resolution was resisted by the associates, who in fact removed the reference to the conflict in Belfast from the workshop announcement. They wanted to reassure participants that this was not a political attempt to get the two sides together, but was a workshop focusing on community problems.

Boehringer et al. also criticized the research methodology as impressionistic and inadequate in assessing processes or outcomes. They therefore found it difficult to see how the organizers could conclude that the conference was worthwhile. On the contrary, a wider consideration of gains and costs indicated that the workshop was harmful to participants and to the community, and engendered considerable suspicion and antagonism toward the Yale group in Northern Ireland.

These criticisms are mirrored in a journalistic analysis of the project by Chinoy (1975), based on interviews with the two associates and others. His account confirms the large misunderstanding that occurred between the Yale group and the associates, who contend that initial resistance to a workshop on the conflict led to the focus on community development. The associates therefore recruited individuals for a low stress conference focusing on community problems that would be identified by participants. As the workshop unfolded, the widely differing expectations became apparent, and the disagreement between the organizers and trainers and the associates escalated to the point of breakup after the return to Belfast.

In a rejoinder, the organizers and trainers attempted to clear up some of the confusion and misunderstanding on intentions and methods (Alevy et al. 1974). The organizers maintained that the workshop was conceived and portrayed as a conference in which participants would learn about their behavior in groups and could take learnings back to their communities for cooperative activities. Contrary to a goal of experimentation, research was subordinated to the training objectives of the workshop. The trainers saw their goal as providing a learning experience on development and change in groups and social systems—a goal that they believe was not accepted by the associates. The training methods employed were educational rather than therapeutic, and having a considerable base in theory and practice, should not be considered experimental. The trainers suggest that in recruiting participants, the associates unfortunately became more concerned about filling the workshop with participants than explaining its nature, thus de-emphasizing the information they had received on the training methods. Even with differing expectations, the goal of the workshop remained the same: to train community leaders in group and intergroup processes so that they could function more effectively in their communities.

Doob and Foltz (1975) returned to Northern Ireland about a year and a half after the Stirling workshop to conduct a weekend follow-up session with some of the participants who had expressed interest during the earlier visit. Rather than a comprehensive description of the session, the organizers rely on the reports of three participants covering their reactions to both workshops. What emerges is a clear contrast between the confusion, tension, and disorientation of Stirling and the clarity, productivity, and usefulness of the follow-up workshop. The latter was planned in relation to the interests and goals of the participants and, drawing in part on the Stirling experience, covered such topics as leadership skills, social change and resistance to it, and women's difficulties in leadership roles. In part, the follow-up session provided some of the answers to Stirling as to how conflict can be transformed through explanation and analysis to cooperation and consensus.

In conclusion, the negative outcomes of Stirling appear primarily owing to the miscommunication regarding goals and methods that occurred between the organizers and their associates. These different members of the workshop team had different understandings and priorities for the event, which were not clarified and resolved during the planning or recruitment phases through continuous monitoring and negotiating. This shortfall produced a gap in expectations between organizers and trainers on the one hand, and the associates and many participants on the other, which led in part to the partial breakdown of the enterprise.

In addition, Stirling did involve the questionable application of a powerful form of human-relations training with participants from a tense, highly charged and fragile situation of intercommunal conflict. It is also possible that the predominantly working-class participants, in comparison to the more typical middle-class professionals who partake in human relations training, may have been less cognitively and socially experienced and adept at responding effectively to such a novel and challenging situation. In any event, it is most unfortunate that the project ended in an exchange of charges and countercharges, ironically illustrating in a microcosm some of the insidious dynamics of destructive conflict.

The Cyprus Initiatives: Aborted and Terminated

After his experiences in the Horn of Africa and Northern Ireland, Leonard Doob turned his attention to the intercommunal and regional conflict gripping the tiny island of Cyprus in the eastern Mediterranean. Through contact with one of the organizers, he was invited in

November 1973 to an informal seminar on the Cyprus conflict sponsored by the Center for Mediterranean Studies in Rome (see Doob 1974b and Talbot 1977). The participants were diplomats with Cyprus experience, a few academics, and the chief negotiators from the Greek and Turkish Cypriot communities who were high level leaders involved in the UN-sponsored intercommunal talks. The purpose was to examine the substance of the negotiations, with the participants suggesting new perspectives or alternative options to assist in movement toward a settlement. During the seminar, Doob described his previous workshop initiatives and was able to talk informally with the two negotiators, who encouraged him to visit Cyprus and explore the possibility of contributing to the reduction of the conflict.

The dispute in Cyprus (noted in chapter 1) has proven to be one of the most intractable interethnic and regional conflicts on the world scene, and at the time of the Rome seminar was at an intermediate stage of escalation. Conquered by successive empires over the centuries, Cyprus's basically Hellenic character was modified by more than three hundred years of Turkish Ottoman rule and close to another hundred of British administration. After five years of guerrilla warfare by the Greek Cypriot majority to throw off British rule and unite the island with Greece, Cyprus was proclaimed as an independent republic in 1960, with its sovereignty guaranteed by Britain, Turkey, and Greece, and with complex power-sharing arrangements between the communities. Unfortunately, three years of political maneuvering and administrative stalemate culminated in a constitutional deadlock and a breakdown in the government apparatus in late 1963. Intercommunal violence, which had first appeared during the war for independence, flared anew, and the Turkish Cypriot minority increasingly withdrew into enclaves. The UN intervened with a peacekeeping force in early 1964, which remains on the island to this day. Mediation efforts, primarily by the UN, were unsuccessful, including the intercommunal talks between the representatives who attended the Rome seminar. In 1974, the situation changed dramatically, with an Athens-sponsored coup d'état by nationalist Greek Cypriots, followed by escalating intercommunal violence, and culminating in a Turkish military intervention that ultimately took control of more than a third of the island. Through the movement of displaced persons and a transfer of populations, the two communities moved to almost complete segregation on either side of a UN buffer zone. Continuing negotiation and mediation efforts have failed to move the conflict toward settlement.

In early 1974, Doob visited Cyprus for four months, and assisted by the two negotiators and two social science associates, one in each community, he was able to meet with a wide range of Cypriots and explore their interest in a workshop (Doob 1974b). Responses were pre-dominantly positive, and Doob received approval from the two ad-ministrations and applied for (and subsequently received) foundation support for the project. It was made clear that participants, whether nominated by the two representatives or by local organizations, would be coming in an unofficial capacity. Potential participants needed to be influential in their communities, emotionally capable of performing under stress, and with independent and creative minds. Doob asked potential participants to consider any risks that their attendance might involve, although he was not sure it was possible to adequately com-municate the nature of the workshop, thus raising again the ethical concern of informed consent.

The goals of the workshop were for the participants to devise ways to diminish misunderstanding and tension between the communities through existing or new associations, and to develop creative ideas that might be useful to the two representatives in the negotiations. The de-sign involved twelve participants from each community taking part in an initial training session for a few days, followed by discussions on the Cyprus conflict for the remainder of the two-week duration. Be-cause Doob wanted to avoid a repetition of the negative reactions to the Tavistock method in the Stirling workshop, he leaned toward the sen-sitivity training approach, and William Foltz therefore recruited two American T-group trainers. Participant lists were finalized through a sequential interview and selection process involving the two asso-ciates and Doob, and the Hotel Fermeda was again reserved for the event.

The participants were to depart Cyprus on July 20, 1974; however, on July 15, the Greek Cypriot nationalist coup against the government began and Cypriots were not allowed to leave the island. After two days of uncertainty, Doob canceled the workshop. Fighting among the Greek Cypriot factions was followed by violence between the two com-munities in various locations. The Turkish military invasion began on the proposed day of departure, July 20, and the face of the Cyprus con-flict was radically altered.

Doob maintained his interest in the Cyprus conflict, visiting in the summer of 1975 to ascertain whether an intervention might be feasible and useful (Doob 1976b). However, in the tragic aftermath of the 1974 war, any involvement by a neutral outsider was regarded as prema-ture, futile, and even dangerous. Not only would the approval of the leaderships not be forthcoming, but Doob judged the intercommu-nal hatred to be too strong to be managed in any intervention. Nonetheless, personal relationships were strengthened, and Doob waited with patience for a future opportunity, visiting the island six times between 1975 and 1985.

In the mid-1980s, the restrictive position of the Greek Cypriot leadership on intercommunal contact began to soften. In 1984, Doob was able to gain the permission of the Turkish Cypriot leadership to hold meetings on the island, but not that of the Greek Cypriot administration (Doob 1987). During his visit in 1985, however, Doob observed that some Greek Cypriots were becoming openly eager to foster contacts with the Turkish Cypriots, although the latter were now generally sceptical about cooperation (Doob 1986). Nonetheless, he was able to gain the approval of both sides and to bring together eight enthusiastic persons from each community for a series of weekly or twice-weekly meetings in a UN-controlled hotel in the buffer zone at Nicosia (Doob 1987). After an official welcome by a supportive UN official, who then departed, Doob turned the meeting over to the Cypriots to use as they saw fit. After some hesitancy, a joke was told to break the tension, and the participants began discussing how to proceed.

The Nicosia meetings, which went on for about three months, were unstructured open discussions directed by the Cypriots themselves, who developed the agenda as they went. After about the first month, Doob returned to begin his teaching duties at Yale, and the Cypriots continued on their own. Apparently they exchanged information about conditions and perspectives on the two sides, and began to plan cross-line visits. At one point in the early going, one Turkish Cypriot participant convinced his leadership that the workshop was against the best interests of their community, and permission was withdrawn. However, Doob and other Turkish Cypriot participants protested and the meetings resumed. Suddenly in October 1985, the Turkish Cypriot leadership withdrew support, and the meetings ended with some negative reaction in the Greek Cypriot press (Doob 1987). Among the reasons eventually proffered was that the workshop was making no progress, and was becoming a "political establishment" that could interfere with official interactions. A press statement by the Greek Cypriot participants indicated that views had been exchanged on various issues, including the fears and concerns of the two communities, and that an atmosphere of goodwill and personal trust had been established (Doob 1987).

In his retrospective evaluation of the Cyprus initiatives, as well as Fermeda and Stirling, Doob (1987) presents a very candid and sober description and analysis of the process and outcomes of the interventions. With regard to the Cyprus meetings, he negatively implicates a few individuals in the difficulties and demise of the project, who while not named are potentially identifiable by knowledgeable readers. Besides compromising anonymity, publication of the details of an unsuccessful intervention could compromise any previous understandings or expectations about confidentiality by the participants or the parties. Although the public candor demonstrated by Doob is useful for the learning of would-be intervenors and the field as a whole, it is not likely to foster or maintain trusting relations with past or future workshop participants or supporters. It also might make it difficult for Doob or other researchers to ascertain through follow-up activities whether the sessions had any useful effects on conflict amelioration. It is unfortunate and disappointing that Leonard Doob's creative forays into conflict resolution ended on such sour notes.

Contributions to a Theory of Practice

Perhaps because of the controversy that his interventions have generated, it seems less well known that Leonard Doob has significantly contributed to developing a theory of practice for ICR. His understanding of the broader context of his interventions is demonstrated in a report on a discussion workshop of scholars and practitioners involved in the analysis and resolution of international disputes (Doob 1974a). Three basic questions on the course of disputes addressed why negotiation is successful or not, how disputes could be prevented, mitigated or resolved, and how skills in conflict analysis and resolution could be improved. The wide gap between scholars and practitioners was explored, and ways of closing the gap were seen as steps toward improving both the theory and practice of conflict resolution.

Doob (1975) considers a number of components involved in unofficial interventions in destructive social conflicts in relation to his work and that of Burton and Wedge, the activities of the Society of Friends, and the annual Pugwash conferences. Juxtaposed with this wide range of "workshops," Doob discusses the characteristics of effective intervenors, the attributes of appropriate participants, the various aspects of the procedure, reentry, and the possible results. He concludes that interventions are a highly risky activity, and that results are difficult to ascertain. One reason is that some of the information on effects is politically sensitive if not classified, and evaluators are reluctant to seek it out. However, Doob (1975) maintains there are enough indications of success to suggest that the work is desirable and useful.

Evaluation is taken up in much greater detail in Doob (1976b). He contends that although this may seem to be a straightforward procedure, the complexities of the processes and potential outcomes of intervention make assessment an immense challenge. Although methods of evaluation need to be adapted to each unique situation of intervention, some standardization among researchers is necessary to cumulate knowledge that could improve practice.

Doob's later theorizing cuts a much wider swath, both in understanding conflict and in considering interventions that may reduce its destructive aspects. In *The Pursuit of Peace,* Doob (1981) presents a comprehensive model of the elements and processes that underlie and affect the conditions of war and peace at the individual, national, and international levels. The analysis culminates in a statement of succinct propositions at each level that cover the existing reality, the ideal of peace, and the ways in which to move from the former to the latter. In asking the question of "international realization," that is, how to improve relations to reduce violent conflict, Doob (1981) considers the role of unofficial diplomacy, including workshops.

Doob (1981) draws on an important distinction between problem-solving and process-promoting workshops articulated earlier by Foltz (1977): the former focusing on possible solutions to the conflict and the latter emphasizing the provision of new abilities and knowledge to the participants that might be useful in helping them function more effectively, particularly in organized groups. The problem-solving type of workshop thus resembles negotiations, but involves the openness to consider radical solutions and must distinguish negotiable issues from the intractable ones. The process-promoting type also relates to the conflict in that some participants will make personal contacts and build trust across the line. The Fermeda and Stirling workshops illustrate the contrast between these two types (Foltz 1977). Doob (1981) also notes the potential of workshops as a useful prelude to negotiation to uncover both emotional issues and possible solutions. And he considers the qualifications of facilitators that would enable them to better enact their intermediary role.

Doob's *Intervention: Guides and Perils* (1993) provides an overview and analysis of intervention in human affairs, broadly conceived as the efforts of an actor to affect other(s) when one or both perceive that a problem needs resolution. Examples include assisting in life-threatening emergencies, providing therapy, and mediating in conflict. Thus many of the illustrations and most of the principles of intervention apply to third party intervenors in situations of two-party conflict. Doob (1993) discusses a wide variety of considerations to be taken into account in the planning, selection, timing, implementation, and evaluation of interventions. He places a special emphasis on considering the morality of interventions, particularly which processes and outcomes should merit our disapproval, such as the use of force, the violation of human rights, or the lack of informed consent. He also discusses again the complex matter of evaluating interventions.

Conclusion

Each of Leonard Doob's forays in ICR was fraught with difficulties and yielded diverging evaluations of outcomes. The Fermeda workshop can be seen as providing encouragement to continue exploring methodologies, even though it cannot be concluded that sensitivity training is applicable to situations of intense international conflict. The difficulty of having to create an intervention within the constraints of simultaneous governmental approval and adequate funding likely predetermined problems to some degree. The push of moving forward at the propitious and unexpected moment meant that there was some poor substitution of participants, inadequate team development and planning time for the organizers and trainers, a loss of implementation control to the workshop planning group, and insufficient time to operationalize the full design. The results can therefore be seen as encouraging at best, and it is unfortunate that no further applications of T-groups to international conflict have occurred, allowing their utility to be better evaluated.

The Stirling workshop is the most controversial of Doob's interventions. Again, the constraints of working in a complex and sensitive environment and the press of time had negative effects on the implementation process. The delegation of recruitment to the associates and the compression of a two-week design into nine days resulted in a gap in expectations and a pressure cooker of interaction that was bound to have negative effects. However, the most questionable aspect of the enterprise was the application of an impactful form of human-relations training (the Tavistock model) to a delicate and volatile intercommunal conflict. Doob himself (1987), while adhering to methodological eclecticism, concludes that there appeared to be no connection between the initial training and the later development of ideas or proposals. This conclusion is rather dismal, given that Doob's critics contend that there were harmful effects both for the participants and the communities in Belfast. In addition, the acrimony surrounding the Northern Ireland work has contributed to scepticism and criticism of unofficial interventions in intense conflicts. How much Doob and his associates were victims of miscommunication and questionable intervention choices versus how much they were pulled into the vortex of dysfunctional relations that surround destructive conflict will never be known.

The planning for the Cyprus workshop overcame some of the

deficiencies in recruitment that attended the earlier efforts, and the choice of sensitivity training as the primary method would probably have worked well. The contrast of no structured intervention in the 1985 Cyprus meetings can be questioned, but it does follow Doob's prescription of adapting the methodology to the situation at hand. The difficulties that Doob experienced in Cyprus, but also in the Horn of Africa and Northern Ireland, demonstrate the need to have a strong institutional base from which to work. With assured funding and competent and knowledgeable staff, consistent long-term efforts could be mounted that would overcome many of the pitfalls that Doob encountered.

In conceptual terms, Leonard Doob rightly places his interventions in much wider fields of thinking and practice. This placement is useful for grasping the full complexity of the work, and for ethically weighing the potential and actual costs and benefits of these interventions. It is also valuable for the agenda of developing a profession of scholar-practitioners who can carry forward the field of interactive conflict resolution.

3

Herbert Kelman
Interactive Problem Solving

Herbert Kelman is the Cabot Professor of Social Ethics in the Department of Psychology at Harvard University, where he has spent most of his academic career, except for several years at the University of Michigan where he was a core contributor to the world's first Center for Research on Conflict Resolution. Besides being the chair of the Middle East Seminar at the Harvard Center for International Affairs, he is also director of the Program on International Conflict Analysis and Resolution. He has served as president of a number of professional associations, including the International Society of Political Psychology, and has received numerous awards for his many and varied contributions to social science. His work demonstrates a lifelong commitment to creating and applying social scientific knowledge for the improvement of human welfare. In particular, his ground-breaking efforts to develop the social psychology of international relations and to apply social-psychological concepts to the analysis and resolution of conflict, have placed him at the center of developments in interactive conflict resolution.

Kelman's early interests in peace and social change drew him to a career in social psychology, because of that discipline's potential for integrating the individual with social institutions in ways that had implications for beneficial applications of knowledge. In the early 1950s, he was involved in the Research Exchange on the Prevention of War, the first organized effort at peace research, and helped establish the *Journal of Conflict Resolution* in 1957 (Kelman 1993b). His pioneering contribution to the social psychology of international relations was expressed through work on various topics including nationalism, public opinion and foreign policy, and linkages between levels of analysis, and culminated in a milestone collection on international behavior (Kelman 1965). A driving theme in Kelman's early work was to make the knowledge and methodology of social science relevant to human problems, especially destructive conflict.

In 1966, Kelman met John Burton, and as Burton talked about his innovative workshop approach, Kelman realized that it was essentially a social-psychological method of intervention, in that changes at the individual level were being linked with policy processes at the macro level. Burton invited Kelman to join the third-party panel for the upcoming Cyprus workshop (see chapter 1), and Kelman enthusiastically agreed. The workshop was not without its shortcomings, but the central outcome for Kelman was that he found an intriguing avenue of application for social-psychological concepts and methods relevant to conflict resolution—a discovery that had a major impact on his ensuing career priorities. "One of the things that I found particularly exciting about the work was that . . . it represented a uniquely social-psychological form of practice. I saw it as a way of translating the social-psychological concepts about international relations that I had been working with into a model of intervention toward the resolution of international conflicts" (Kelman 1993b, 3–4).

In 1967, as Kelman agonized over the Six-Day War between Israel and its Arab neighbors, he realized that the workshop approach might be applicable to this bitter and seemingly intractable conflict. He collaborated with John Burton in putting together a proposal, but support was not forthcoming and the project fizzled out. Nonetheless, Kelman continued to talk with various people about the possible utility of such an initiative, and wrote a comparative analysis of the Burton and Doob approaches, thus laying the groundwork for some of his thinking on the problem-solving workshop (Kelman 1972).

In 1971, Kelman agreed to coteach a graduate seminar on the social psychology of international relations with Stephen Cohen, a recent Harvard graduate and then faculty member, who was also active in holding political meetings on the Middle East conflict. Cohen convinced Kelman that a problem-solving workshop would be an appropriate and useful part of the course, and that first workshop, involving Israeli and Palestinian "preinfluentials" (graduate students and young professionals), became a prototype for many others to follow. The 1973 Arab-Israeli war had a further impact on Kelman, increasing his commitment to the problem-solving approach and leading him to be increasingly involved in its application to the Middle East conflict.

Besides holding further Israeli-Palestinian workshops with Stephen Cohen and others, Kelman acquired increasing substantive knowledge about the Middle East conflict itself. Thus he has been able to integrate an understanding of the content of the conflict with the workshop process to produce policy prescriptions for its resolution. As part of a larger action research initiative, the workshops have identified and helped create the psychological prerequisites for mutual acceptance and the conditions for meaningful negotiations. Hence Kelman has come to see his work more and more as a prenegotiation methodology, and in the present context, as a continuing and supportive parallel track to the peace negotiations themselves.

For his part, Stephen Cohen extended his involvement with the problem-solving approach, at first through collaborating with Edward Azar on the Israeli-Egyptian peace process (see chapter 4). Subsequently Cohen focused on the application of ICR to the diplomatic process, by serving as a third party between Egyptian and Israeli officials and other Arab actors. He has also brought together official representatives of Israel and the Palestine Liberation Organization during both the prenegotiation phase and the peace negotiations (Cohen 1994). These activities serve as important applications of the problem-solving approach to official interactions, but as with these interactions, are not in the public domain.

To acknowledge the fundamental contributions of Herbert Kelman's work to ICR, this chapter will first elucidate the conceptual basis that he has articulated over the past twenty years. Then Kelman's approach of interactive problem solving will be considered as a form of prenegotiation that can influence both the political discourse and the strategic thinking of the parties. Finally, with the advent of the Middle East peace talks and the historic accord between the Israelis and Palestininans, the role of parallel and continuing workshops in the conflict resolution process will be illuminated. The conclusion will affirm that the work of Herbert Kelman has made an important contribution to the search for peace in the Middle East, and has greatly informed our understanding of how ICR can promote the amelioration of international conflict.

The Conceptual Basis of Interactive Problem Solving

For more than twenty years, Kelman has articulated and elaborated the conceptual rationale of the problem-solving workshop, thus affirming his identity as a scholar-practitioner. In his first comparison of Burton and Doob, Kelman (1972) noted several commonalities, including the prestigious yet unofficial participants, the facilitative role of the third party, the informal atmosphere, the relatively unstructured agenda, and the isolated setting. These elements were taken into account by Kelman and Cohen in designing the first pilot workshop on the Israeli-Palestinian conflict (Cohen, Kelman, Miller & Smith 1977), and in providing a description of a hypothetical problem-solving workshop (Kelman & Cohen 1976). A detailed rationale appeared in

Kelman and Cohen (1979, 1986), and has been extended through a number of descriptions of the typical Israeli-Palestinian workshop (Kelman 1979, 1986, 1992).

Kelman sees interactive problem solving as a program of action research that integrates efforts at conflict resolution with opportunities to observe and learn about the Middle East conflict and international conflict in general. The workshops are the action component in that they provide a unique forum for communication and mutual analysis of the conflict, promote a collaborative, problem-solving process, and use social scientist-practitioners in a facilitative third party role (Kelman 1979). Other activities are included, such as widening contacts with decision-making elites, recruiting and training new third party team members, and developing policy analyses. Kelman (1986) notes how the action component requires involvement in a research program to provide rationale and legitimacy, and the research aspect requires involvement in action to learn about the conflict and contribute to its resolution.

The typical workshop brings together unofficial representatives of conflicting parties in a relatively isolated and preferably academic setting to engage in face-to-face communication with the guidance of social scientists who are knowledgeable about conflict theory, group processes, and the region in question. The ideal participants are highly influential within their own communities, but are not in policymaking positions, although they usually participate with the tacit consent of officials to maximize the influence on the policy process. Over the years, the workshops organized by Kelman through his graduate seminar and at the Harvard Center for International Affairs have brought together Israeli and Palestinian preinfluentials (senior graduate students, young professionals), influentials (academics, writers, journalists, former officials), and political actors (party activists, parliamentarians, policy advisers). Recruitment is done on an individual basis with an attempt to build a varied and balanced team, and the purpose, procedures, and ground rules of the workshop are made clear before commitment is sought. Each party is represented by three to six members, along with several third party members. The discussions typically take place in a seminar room around a large round table.

As opposed to a neutral third party national or ethnic identity, Kelman has operated with and argued for an ethnically balanced team. Thus he has sought Arab collaborators to balance his own Jewish identity on the third party panel, and argues that this provides an element of engagement along with impartiality that identity-neutral third parties do not have. Preworkshop sessions are held with the representatives of each party and the third party in which participants discuss their side's views of the conflict and the possibilities for resolving it, and what they see as the needs and positions of the other side. Besides clarifying the discussion format of the workshop, these sessions build familiarity and allow the third party to observe differences within each team.

The workshop itself usually lasts two and one-half days, often over an extended weekend, and the discussions are relatively unstructured, yet guided by the third party. Several aspects of the workshop (setting, norms, ground rules, agenda, procedures, third party interventions) are designed to overcome the usual accusatory, legalistic, and hostile interactions, and replace them with an analytical, task-orientated atmosphere, which has the potential for changing attitudes and creating ideas that can be fed into the policymaking process. The ground rules call for an analytic stance, stress the principles of anonymity and confidentiality, and introduce the role of the third party as a facilitator of communication rather than an audience or adjudicator to be convinced.

The typical agenda begins with each participant describing their view of the conflict and placing themselves on the spectrum of political positions in their own community. Having expressed their substantive perception of the conflict, participants are then free to move into the analytic phase of the workshop by discussing their central concerns, that is, the basic needs and fundamental fears that any agreement would have to address and allay. When both sets of concerns have been expressed and understood by the other side, the discussion moves to an exploration of the overall shape of an acceptable solution. Finally, the participants talk about the psychological and political constraints that hamper implementation of solutions and the ways in which the two sides can support each other in overcoming these. In line with the prenegotiation phase of the Israeli-Palestinian conflict (until peace talks began), Kelman's workshops have been designed to generate ideas that would be useful in bringing the parties to the negotiating table.

The workshop thus casts the third party in a unique role as the facilitator of communication, conflict analysis, and the development of creative solutions. The special status, knowledge, and skills of social scientists allows them to provide an acceptable context with alternate norms, and to structure and intervene in the interaction in ways that facilitate group process and have impact on policy formation (Kelman & Cohen 1979, 1986). The third party carries out a number of functions (Kelman 1986). It provides a framework for parties to talk and listen to each other under a set of norms that encourage open communication and new learning. It selects appropriate participants and briefs them carefully to maximize the usefulness of the workshop. It serves as a repository of trust for the two sides, so that they can move toward developing a "working trust" recognizing common interests despite profound differences. It proposes and guides the participants through a broad and flexible agenda focusing directly on basic concerns and constraints that must be addressed for movement toward a solution. It makes substantive interventions in the form of theoretical inputs about conflict dynamics, content observations about points being made, and process observations that suggest how interactions in the workshop may reflect intergroup relations between the two sides. For all of these functions to occur, it is necessary for the third party to be perceived as knowledgeable, skillful, and objective, and thereby as credible and legitimate.

The problem-solving workshop has the dual purpose of being both *educational*—producing changes in the perceptions, attitudes, and ideas held by the individual participants—and *political*—transferring these changes to the political dialogue and decision making in each community (Kelman 1986). Thus workshops take on a dialectic nature, in which the requirements for maximizing change in individuals may be contradictory or antagonistic to those for maximizing impact on the social system (Kelman 1979; Kelman & Cohen 1979, 1986). This leads to a number of theoretical dialectics related to the major elements of the approach. For example, with respect to the joint goals of change and transfer, providing the freedom for participants to move away from official positions and to mutually explore new ideas with the adversary may be antagonistic to the transfer of any creative thinking back to the official policy process, which is strongly grounded in the current realities. Also, for example, in participants, unofficial representatives are less constrained by public pressure and have more freedom to explore different ideas, but at the same time, they do not have direct, immediate, and strong influence on official decision making. Finally, the workshop setting must have elements of novelty and insulation if participants are to adopt the norms of openness and exploration, and yet an element of realism must be maintained so that an illusory atmosphere of comraderie is not developed in which participants forget about the bitter conflict between their communities. Such dialectics require the third party to work toward balance and integration of contradictory elements in the design and implementation of the workshop so that both the educational and political purposes are achieved.

Kelman (1979) sees the problem-solving workshop as a uniquely social-psychological approach to conflict resolution in that social interaction, which is at the heart of the evolution and resolution of conflict, is the central focus and unique level of analysis of social psychology.

Furthermore, social psychology pays simultaneous attention to psychological and institutional factors whose interplay typically provide for the dynamics of intergroup and international conflict. The social-psychological approach is seen as complementary to political analysis in that while conflict arises out of objective and ideological differences, the escalation and perpetuation of conflict is typically fuelled by psychological factors such as misperception and distrust. Thus overcoming psychological barriers creates new possibilities for negotiation on objective conditions and interests, which is necessary for the resolution of the conflict.

In line with its basic rationale, the social-psychological approach makes unique assumptions about international conflict and its resolution in relation to the structure, the process, and the content of the problem-solving workshop (Kelman 1979, 1992). For example, international conflict is not seen as merely conflict between states, but as conflict between societies, thus underscoring the importance of psychological and cultural factors in the analysis along with military and strategic ones. It follows that third party efforts need to be directed toward a resolution between collectivities rather than simply a settlement between governments. Furthermore, to transform the relationship between the parties, solutions must come from the interaction of the parties and must jointly address their needs. Thus it is assumed that conflict resolution requires direct, bilateral interaction between the central parties, as well as multilateral efforts involving related actors. In addition, this interaction must have an emergent character in which the parties can observe directly their differing perceptions and reactions and in which they can jointly shape new insights and ideas for resolution.

Finally, the substantive content of workshops is informed by assumptions about the importance of human needs, perceptual constraints, and influence processes in situations of conflict. Kelman (1990, 1992) considers the satisfaction of basic human needs as articulated through identity groups as the ultimate criterion of a satisfactory resolution. Only through interaction around needs and related fears can the parties identify actions of mutual reassurance that are essential to deescalate existential conflicts involving identity and security. Similarly, parties must come to understand the constraints on information processing that maintain the conflict and the broader range of influence processes beyond deterrence and compellance that are required to transform it. Thus, in many ways, the social-psychological approach differs from and goes beyond the traditional, realist assumptions that are made about the causation and resolution of international conflict.

The learnings that accrue from the unique forum of the problem-solving workshop stem from the innovative analysis and face-to-face interaction of the participants (Kelman 1979, 1986). First, parties gain new insights into the perspective of each other, particularly in fundamental concerns, priorities, and constraints. Kelman maintains that there is simply no substitute for the immediacy and concreteness of the insights provided by workshop interaction. Second, parties learn about the occurrence of changes in the adversary and the possibility of further change, which in part can be promoted through their own actions. Third, participants gain awareness about the significance of gestures and symbolic acts for indicating a basic human acceptance of the other's identity—gestures that usually can be extended at very little cost and yet may provide considerable reassurance.

For workshop learnings to have significance, they must be fed into the political discourse and the policy process related to the conflict. From his more than twenty years of experience in organizing workshops between influential Israelis and Palestinians, Kelman (1992) identifies specific learnings that participants have communicated to their communities and leadership. These include items such as information on the range of views in the other party, insights into the other side's priorities and rock-bottom requirements, and ideas for ways of moving to the negotiating table.

The relevance of interactive problem solving has never been at doubt for Kelman and his colleagues. Kelman and Cohen (1976) indicated that although workshops are not substitutes for negotiation, the products can be useful inputs into all phases of the negotiation process. In prenegotiation, workshops allow for noncommittal testing of the feasibility of negotiations and for determining the bases on which negotiations could proceed. During negotiations, workshops can provide a forum for working out details and alternatives on issues that are creating blocks to an agreement. Finally, in postnegotiation, workshops allow for considering the future social and economic relations between the two parties that could have impact on the stability of a political settlement. Most of Kelman's work on the Israeli-Palestinian conflict can thus be seen as a contribution to the prenegotiation process in helping create an atmosphere conducive to negotiation and a set of principles that serve as a basis for negotiation (Kelman 1986).

On a broader scale of relevance, Kelman (1992) suggests that interactive problem solving, along with other forms of unofficial diplomacy, should be regarded as an integral element of the larger diplomatic process. Such unofficial interventions make unique contributions, such as the noncommittal exploration of possibilities or alternatives, that official channels can or usually do not. These contributions are most useful in protracted and bitter conflicts between identity groups, in which the simple recognition of common interests is insufficient to overcome the psychological barriers that have been erected. Given the preponderance of such conflicts on the world scene today, Kelman's suggestion and its rationale deserve much attention and support.

Interactive Problem Solving as Prenegotiation: The Israeli-Palestinian Case

Since 1971, Kelman and his associates have held numerous workshops on the Israeli-Palestinian conflict, with increasingly influential participants. Within the context of their action research program on the Middle East, Kelman and his colleagues have engaged in many visits, meetings, and conversations with opinion leaders, decision makers, and policy advisers. Throughout his involvement, Kelman has increasingly come to see the Israeli-Palestinian issue as lying at the heart of the Arab-Israeli conflict (Kelman 1988).

The Israeli-Palestinian conflict, like many protracted social conflicts between identity groups, has a long history and a violent present. For thousands of years, Jews and Arabs coinhabited the land between the Jordan River and the Mediterranean Sea, which came to be known in modern times as Palestine. As with all parts of the Middle East, the area was ruled by a succession of kingdoms and empires, with the Ottoman Turks maintaining control from the early 1500s until the latter days of World War I when the British defeated them with Arab assistance. Britain received a mandate from the League of Nations in 1922 to rule Palestine in a manner compatible with a previous British declaration calling for the establishment of a national homeland for Jews. Political and economic control was increasingly turned over to Zionist organizations, while at the same time the British showed some concern about the interests of Arabs living in Palestine. In the late 1930s, Arab unrest was quashed through combined British and Zionist efforts, and the seeds for Israeli-Palestinian hostility were sown as developments, including Zionist agitation, continued toward the establishment of a Jewish state.

In 1947, the United Nations recommended the partition of Palestine into separate Jewish and Arab states, and in early 1948 the Zionists proclaimed the State of Israel. War immediately broke out between Israel and all surrounding Arab states, and in the fighting, several hundred thousand Palestinian Arabs were displaced from their homes. Jordon secured the part of central Palestine now known as the West Bank, which had been identified as part of a Palestinian state by the United Nations. The intent of the Arab states, however, was simply to stop the creation of Israel. In this they failed as the Israelis gained about three-quarters of Palestine. Armistice agreements were brokered through United Nations mediation in 1949, but the Middle East has been in a state of cold or hot war ever since. Besides 1948, wars have been fought between Israel and its Arab neighbors in 1956, 1967, and 1973, with the Israeli invasion of Lebanon in 1982 constituting another major conflagration. In territorial acquisition, the 1967 war is the most significant, given that Israel gained control of the Sinai Peninsula, the Gaza Strip, the Golan Heights, the West Bank, and East Jerusalem. For the Palestinians, the negative results included hundreds of thousands of additional refugees and Israeli occupation in the West Bank and Gaza.

The United States mediated disengagement agreements between Egypt and Israel after the 1973 war, and in the late seventies managed the peace process that resulted in the signing of the Camp David accords and a historic treaty between the two powers. However, the Palestinian issue was excluded from the process, because it was clear that agreement on it was highly unlikely. Thus the Middle East conflict has moved more and more to relations between Israelis and Palestinians. At the same time, the Palestinian Liberation Organization (PLO), which began largely as a guerrilla movement against Israel, has come to be the primary political representative of the Palestinian people, operating as a government in exile. Palestinian resistance in the occupied territories entered a more active phase with the initiation of the intifada in the late 1980s.

In the aftermath of the Gulf War in 1991, the United States and Russia were able to initiate formal peace negotiations between Israel and its Arab neighbors. These talks also included an Israeli-Palestinian table, in which the PLO was not formally included, but was clearly the behind-the-scenes voice of the Palestinian people. Unfortunately the formal talks yielded little progress after almost two years of jockeying for position on various matters. However, this lack of progress was dramatically altered in 1993 through back-channel negotiations mediated by Norwegian academics and officials. These talks produced an in-principle agreement on a transition toward self-rule for Palestinians in the West Bank and Gaza, and also resulted in the breakthrough of mutual recognition by the Israeli government and the PLO. The latter agreement includes Palestinian recognition of the right of Israel to exist in peace and security and Israeli recognition of the PLO as the legitimate representative of the Palestinian people. The declaration of principles for Palestinian self-rule proclaims a five-year interim period and leaves a number of central issues unresolved, including the status of Jerusalem, the question of Israeli settlements in the occupied territories, and the right of return for almost a million Palestinian refugees.

In addressing the Israeli-Palestinian conflict, Kelman has consistently maintained that problem-solving workshops are not a substitute for diplomatic negotiations, but an unofficial approach that can prepare the way for, supplement, and feed into negotiations (Kelman 1991b). Thus workshops and related activities can gradually help provide the atmosphere of mutual reassurance conducive to negotiations or by providing parties with an opportunity to work out elements of a solution that can then be fed into the formal process.

Based on Kelman's work, it appears that the influence of the problem-solving workshops (and the wider action research program) on the negotiating atmosphere can occur in two ways. First are the transfer effects engendered by workshop participants and other contacts who experience changes in their thinking and inject these new ideas into the political discourse in their community and into the policymaking of their leadership. Second, there is a role for the third party in providing policy analyses and positions, both formally and informally, that may influence the thinking of the two sides. This role goes beyond the usual functions of ICR scholar-practitioners, who generally do not provide comment on the substance of the dispute. However, Herbert Kelman has broken new ground in the field by increasingly approaching the Israeli-Palestinian conflict in both a facilitative and a substantive manner. Specifically he has provided an analysis of the psychological prerequisites for mutual acceptance, has conceptualized a prenegotiation process involving successive approximations toward mutual reassurance, and has articulated ways of overcoming the barriers to a negotiated solution. Based on his workshop experiences and other interactions with the two sides, he has integrated the perspectives of both Israelis and Palestinians with his analysis of the conflict, thus providing a balanced and powerful statement of the requisite directions for movement toward settlement and resolution.

In his first policy-relevant analysis of the conflict, Kelman (1978) contended that a lasting settlement had to be responsive to the needs and fears of both parties, and it was therefore essential to understand the two perspectives and to confront the differences between them. He maintained that any solution had to come from the parties themselves, and he advocated no particular solution or action. However, his value commitment was to a peaceful solution achieved through dialogue and responsive to concerns for justice on both sides.

According to Kelman in 1978, the core element of the conflict between the nationalist movements was the mutual denial of the adversary's national identity, when in his view, any realistic policy had to be based on an awareness by each side that its adversary constituted a nation. Resistance to this stemmed from each side's concern that acceptance of the other's nationhood undermined its own claim to the land of historic Palestine. Furthermore, each side was deeply fearful of its continuing national existence and believed the other side to be intent on destroying it. Thus the fulfillment of the other's national identity meant the destruction of one's own identity, and in this situation, neither side was prepared to accept the other unless its own existence was first assured.

In the late 1970s, there were no indications of either Israeli or Palestinian readiness to offer acceptance to the other side, and the conflict appeared intractable. The way out of the deadlock, according to Kelman (1978), was to work toward the psychological prerequisites for mutual acceptance, which required complementary and reciprocal actions by the two parties. Not surprisingly, these conditions for acceptance bore similarities to the learnings that could be acquired from problem-solving workshops, with each involving both psychological and objective changes. First, the two sides had to acquire insight into each other's perspective so that they could understand the resistances to acceptance. Second, each side had to see that there were reasonable people on the other side and that there were issues to talk about, rather than that the two sets of demands were mutually exclusive. Third, each side had to distinguish the ideological dreams and rhetoric from the operational programs of the other. Israelis had to be persuaded that the Palestinian dream of a united Palestine did not preclude the acceptance of the State of Israel and a stable peace with it. Palestinians had to be persuaded that the Zionist dream of the ingathering of exiles did not necessitate expansionist policies of annexation and settlement. Fourth, both sides had to see that mutual concessions could bring about change leading toward resolution. Fifth, each side had to believe that leadership changes conducive to a stable peace could take place in the other side. Israelis had to be convinced that the PLO was being transformed from a terrorist organization to a political one, and that moderate elements would remain in control. Palestinians had to be convinced that the hard-line policies of the then-current Israeli government could be transformed or that a more conciliatory leadership could take power. Sixth and finally, each side had to see a responsiveness to its human psychological needs by the other through symbolic gestures. Kelman (1978) concluded that the conditions for mutual acceptance could best be created through direct interaction between the parties—interaction that confronted mutual concerns, tried out possible gestures, and jointly redefined issues in ways amenable to resolution. Thus preparatory discussions could pave the way toward negotiations and the official, simultaneous recognition of each side by the other.

Based on his continuing analysis, Kelman (1982) described a prenegotiation process that could bring about the psychological and political conditions necessary to start negotiations. In the wake of the Egyptian-Israeli peace agreement of 1979, the centrality of the Israeli-Palestinian issue to the Arab-Israeli conflict became increasingly clear to all. Thus Kelman spelled out a number of assumptions that had to be considered for negotiations to result in a stable peace, based on the premise that talks should aim for resolution, that is, a mutually acceptable outcome responsive to each side's needs and minimally consistent with each side's sense of justice. First, negotiations had to be directly between Israeli and Palestinian representatives so that mutual redefinition of the conflict could occur and agreements responsive to mutual concerns were achieved. Second, the talks had to focus on ways of sharing the land of Palestine between the peoples in a manner that met basic concerns for justice, identity, and security. Thus the continued existence of Israel had to be accepted at the same time that the Palestinian people had to have ownership over a share of the land and were able to express their national identity within it. Third, the negotiations had to allow both parties to benefit from the international legitimacy they had achieved. For Israel, this meant accepting that the Palestinian representatives in the negotiations either be the PLO or derive their legitimacy from the PLO. For the Palestinians, this meant accepting the Egyptian-Israeli peace process and the legitimacy that Israel gained from it.

In 1982, Kelman saw little possibility that negotiations would proceed on these bases because of powerful resistances on both sides. However, within the context of a constantly changing situation, he also perceived pronegotiation tendencies and incentives that were shared by important elements in each community and that gave some cause for hope. Unfortunately any move toward negotiations immediately confronted a perplexing dilemma rooted in the zero-sum character of the conflict, that is, any acceptance of the identity, legitimacy, or rights of the other party was profoundly threatening to one's own identity, legitimacy, and rights.

In such a situation, Kelman (1982) maintained that the only way to move toward negotiations was through successive approximations to overcome the barriers and to slowly create adequate mutual reassurance. This process could begin with unofficial communication without commitment or recognition and gradually move toward official negotiations leading to formal recognition and a binding agreement. This communication would follow a problem-solving approach allowing for the emergence of new ideas and mutual trust and leading to the increased reassurance necessary for negotiations to begin. This procedure would work toward creating an understanding that would be the basis for starting official negotiations and that would meet several criteria, including a clear distinction between the start of negotiations, where full explicit recognition is not necessary, and the conclusion of negotiations where it is. The understanding would avoid the language of rights, but would use in a transformed manner the symbols of legitimacy important to both sides. For example, the negotiations could be seen as extending the Egyptian-Israeli peace process to the Palestinian issue, and the Palestinian representatives could be designated by and remain in close consultation with the PLO. Clearly, the understanding should contribute toward mutual trust in the seriousness of the other party's intentions, so that it could effectively serve as a framework for starting official negotiations. In line with earlier statements, Kelman (1982) proposed that the problem-solving workshop was a useful format for such a prenegotiation process.

Kelman (1987) carried his analysis further by proposing that Israeli-Palestinian negotiations were possible in a framework of mutual recognition in which recognition of the other's rights represents assertion rather than abandonment of one's own rights. He outlined several assumptions that represent the basic requirements for a resolution to occur. These included the proposition that both Israelis and Palestinians are nations that must share some part of the land to express their national identity. Both groups must maintain relations and serve the interests of their members in the diaspora and must be represented in negotiations by leaders that they consider legitimate. In contrast to previous analyses, Kelman (1987) perceived strong interest within both communities for a negotiated solution, partly based on a concern in each that continuation of the status quo was dangerous.

Unfortunately the zero-sum core of the conflict with its mutual denial of identity continued to lead each side to delegitimize and dehumanize the other, thus blocking the path to negotiations. This dilemma could be broken only through the mutual recognition of each other's right to self-determination in the land that they must share. Thus Kelman (1987) proposed a prenegotiation process to produce a mutual differentiation of the enemy image in a number of respects. He maintained that his conversations with Yasser Arafat convinced him that the PLO chairman had a differentiated view of the Israelis and their government, and more important, was potentially available for negotiations (Kelman 1983). By penetrating each other's perspective through prenegotation, both Israelis and Palestinians could move to the possibility of developing a future common vision involving mutual fulfillment in the land they share.

From Prenegotiation to Paranegotiation:
A Continuing Contribution

Kelman's work has made a continuing contribution to peace in the Middle East, and in 1990 took on a new dimension in response to dramatic developments in the conflict, including the intifada and shifts in official positions of the Palestinian movement (Kelman 1993a). He decided to organize a continuing workshop in which the same participants would come together regularly for meetings of three to five days over a long period. In collaboration with Nadim Rouhana, and with Christopher Mitchell and Harold Saunders joining the third party panel, Kelman began a series of sessions and adapted their nature to ongoing events in the Israeli-Palestinian conflict (Kelman 1992; Rouhana & Kelman 1994).

The rationale embodies a number of advantages over single workshops and indicates the unique contributions that can be made to the resolution of protracted conflicts (Kelman 1993a; Rouhana & Kelman 1994). First, a continuing workshop allows for a sustained effort to address concrete issues, thus pushing the process beyond the sharing of perspectives to the joint production of creative ideas. Second, the continuing nature allows for an iterative and cumulative process, wherein participants can seek feedback on ideas from their communities and return to the next workshop with suggestions for improvement. Third, participants can communicate either within or between groups to work interactively on ideas to be brought back to the next workshop. Fourth, participants can better address the dissemination of ideas and proposals developed at the sessions. Thus the meetings provide a rare and unique chance for adversaries to jointly create new ideas that can be immediately tested and improved to enhance their acceptability and utility. According to Kelman, the continuing workshop represents an opportunity to maximize the potential of interactive problem solving and also provides for a more effective test of its utility. On the practical side, workshops become more geared to building pronegotiation coalitions across conflict lines, a process that Kelman sees as essential for deescalation and resolution (Kelman 1993a).

The first meeting of the continuing workshop, in November 1990, brought together six Palestinians and six Israelis (each with four men and two women) who were highly influential in their respective communities in positions (the media, academic or policy institutions, and political organizations) that allowed them to influence both public discourse and political decisions. Although representing significant political segments in each community, they were generally within the mainstream of political thinking. The agenda was influenced by the escalating violence in Israel and the occupied territories and the deteriorating relationship between Palestinians and Israelis, and also by the Iraqi invasion of Kuwait. The discussions focused primarily on the fundamental concerns and needs that each side wanted addressed in a settlement and on the constraints that were impeding movement toward negotiations.

The second meeting, in June 1991, took place in even worse Israeli-Palestinian relations after the Gulf War. Nonetheless, the participants began joint exploration of new ideas to address the basic needs and concerns that were articulated in the first session. This shift toward joint thinking was extremely difficult, and required a sense of timing and steady pressure from the third party to allay anxieties and overcome resistances to best use the opportunity (Rouhana & Kelman 1994). The third meeting, in August 1991, occurred during the groundwork phase of U.S.-brokered peace talks, and moved the participants toward the joint formulation of mutually acceptable approaches to very difficult issues—the meaning of Palestinian nationhood and self-determination, the Israeli settlements, the finality of a settlement, and the Palestinian right of return. The third party facilitated joint thinking through techniques such as brainstorming, single-text drafts, and the use of subgroups to formulate agreements after discussion by the total workshop. The participants achieved consensus on three of the issues, and came close on the fourth, with final agreement precluded by a lack of time.

When the official peace talks started in October 1991, the workshop participants had already expressed an interest in maintaining the process, but the focus now shifted from prenegotiation to what could be termed "paranegotiation." Rouhana and Kelman (1994) note that although it had always been assumed that interactive problem solving could make useful contributions during the negotiation phase, the methods, functions, and goals of the continuing workshop had to be readjusted. The close relation that the work had established between the unofficial and official processes was highlighted by the fact that most of the Palestinian participants were now negotiators or advisers in the formal negotiations. Hence a series of consultation meetings was held with subgroups of participants to plan how to best restart the continuing workshop.

A fourth meeting was held in July 1992, with four participants from each side. This session focused on the outcomes and implications of the recent Israeli election in relation to the peace talks, particularly on the ideas for self-government in the West Bank and Gaza. The Israelis wanted to continue the forum, but the Palestinians were ambivalent because of their direct role in the peace talks. Parenthetically, after the election, some of the Israeli participants had also become directly involved in the formal negotiations. In response to participant wishes to continue the process, Kelman and Rouhana decided to reconstitute the workshop in a manner congruent with the ongoing negotiations. The general position was that the workshop process can contribute to negotiations by exploring obstacles to progress and helping create a favorable political environment (Kelman 1993b). Thus the continuing workshop was reconvened in August 1993, with a change in about two-thirds of the participants, and with a strong emphasis on the mutual reassurance necessary for movement toward peace.

Graduates of Kelman's workshops were also involved in the back-channel talks in Norway that broke the logjam in the public negotiations in late 1993. According to Kelman (1993b), at a point before the Norwegian meetings became known, the public talks had not developed momentum and were constantly on the verge of breaking down, with U.S. pressure and inducements constantly required to bring the parties back to the table. In part, the Norway talks produced the exploratory process necessary to develop a set of shared principles, which Kelman saw as essential for negotiations to make progress. In this way, the back-channel talks were the culmination of numerous unofficial interactions over the past two decades that articulated the human dimension of the conflict (Rothman 1993). When these insights were incorporated into the process along with direct PLO involvement, a breakthrough was achieved. The group meeting under Norwegian auspices generated ideas that were fed back to the political leaders and a dramatic realignment of the conflict occurred (Rothman 1993).

Kelman's focus has now shifted to a joint working group, meeting on a continuing basis, with facilitation provided by a third party team (Kelman, Rouhana, and Eileen Babbitt). The emphasis in this process is on an exploration of difficult political issues (e.g., the Jewish settlements, Palestinian self-determination) in preparation for the final-status negotiations (Kelman 1995). In concert with earlier efforts, this work continues to contribute to the Israeli-Palestinian peace process. Kelman (1995) categorizes these as substantive inputs into political thinking in the two communities, an influence on a political atmosphere conducive to negotiations and to the evolution of a new relationship, and the development of cadres who play important roles in negotiating and implementing agreements. Thus Kelman rightly concludes that his work has made unique and substantial contributions to the peace process in the context of other unofficial activities.

Conclusion: More Than a Sideshow

The work of Herbert Kelman on interactive problem solving encompasses a comprehensive and compelling blend of theory, research, and practice in applied social science. At first in collaboration with Stephen Cohen, Kelman has produced a solid conceptual base, grounded in accepted principles of human social behavior. This foundation was articulated before practice was under way, thus providing a theoretical guide for intervention covering all elements of the practice—the mark of a professional scholar-practitioner. The conceptual base has also been constantly elaborated and extended by Kelman in conjunction with his practice endeavors and research evaluations. This action research approach, with its constant interplay of theory, research, and practice, is the most challenging form and highest level of applied social science (Fisher 1982b).

Kelman's theorizing is grounded primarily in his discipline of social psychology, and thus may have limitations in relation to macro-level theories from political science and international relations. In some ways, Kelman's approach offers competing assumptions and principles to those of traditional international relations, for example, in proposing that conflicts are between societies rather than states. Kelman's thinking is compatible with the pluralist paradigm of international relations articulated by John Burton and his colleagues (see Fisher 1990), and thus provides a further challenge to the realist school, which emphasizes state sovereignty and the threat and use of force to protect it.

From the beginning, Kelman has taken the transfer process seriously, thus addressing one of the most serious questions about the utility of ICR (see chapter 9). However, his considerations focus on general processes and possibilities in the manner and substance of how official policymaking might be influenced. For both ethical and practical reasons, Kelman and his colleagues have not tracked and articulated the specific linkages between workshop participants and decision makers that may have helped alter the face of the Israeli-Palestinian conflict. Not only are prenegotiation individuals constantly under personal risk from hardliners in their communities, but the research task of documenting the transfer process is daunting.

Kelman's contributions to ICR are unique in that they provide a long-term demonstration of the power of combining process interventions with substantive analyses in a mutually informing and reinforcing manner. His policy prescriptions not only arose out of the authentic interactions of Israelis and Palestinians in the workshops but are also informed by Kelman's knowledge as a social scientist and his peace-orientated values as a human being. The start of formal negotiations provided Kelman with a unique opportunity to maintain the parallel track of a continuing workshop and now an ongoing working group to sustain pronegotiation coalitions across conflict lines. His policy analyses over the last two decades have most likely helped pave the way for, and in substance presaged, the breakthrough agreement between Israel and the PLO. In essence, Kelman deduced the principles and understandings that were necessary for the conflict to begin moving toward resolution. Furthermore, the ongoing unofficial interaction was likely an important influence on the secret talks that led to the mutual recognition that Kelman had prescribed more than a decade before.

Despite these influences, however, Kelman has never suggested that interactive problem solving could become a substitute for official diplomacy or that it can operate outside national interests shaped by political processes (Kelman 1993b). However, he does maintain that the contribution of unofficial processes, while only part of the picture, are potentially significant, and should thus be seen as part of diplomatic processes rather than as a "sideshow" to the "real work."

In conclusion, although we should recognize John Burton as the innovator who lit the torch of interactive conflict resolution, Herbert Kelman is the master contributor who has carried it a long way forward. By doing so, he has illuminated the path toward peace in both a theoretical and practical manner with such compelling detail and comprehensiveness that it is a much easier task for other scholar-practitioners to follow. His careful and credible work has also been instrumental in slowly helping the field gain the recognition and legitimacy in traditional academic and diplomatic circles that it deserves.

Part Two
The Potential for the Field

4

Edward Azar
Protracted Social Conflicts and Problem-Solving Forums

Edward Azar (1938–91) was an American political scientist who was born and educated in Lebanon and came to the United States for graduate study with an interest in international relations. His early career was distinguished by work on quantitative international relations, particularly on how interstate crises and conflict episodes were reflected in measures of interstate interactions. He developed a data base, the Conflict and Peace Data Bank (COPDAB), at the University of North Carolina, which included measures on international and domestic events at the level of states and international organizations (Azar 1980). Using COPDAB, Azar was able to assess the degree of hostility versus friendliness in interactions and to track the frequency and nature of violent conflict in the world over time (e.g., Azar 1970; Azar & Eckhardt 1978). He was also able to provide analyses of conflict escalation and reduction in specific situations, such as the Suez crisis of 1956 (Azar 1972). In specific conflicts, much of Azar's early focus was on the Middle East, but as the civil war in his homeland unfolded, he increasingly turned his attention to Lebanon, and then beyond to other destructive intercommunal and international conflicts.

Azar's analyses of international conflict indicated that since World War II almost all conflicts had occurred in the Third World, and many were ethnic rather than strategic conflicts. Moreover, during the cold war, interventions by the United States and the Soviet Union, as well as by their allies, tended to exacerbate these conflicts. These results convinced Azar that a shift in focus in international relations was necessary, from a "superpower bias" with its emphasis on strategic interaction, deterrence, crisis management, and violence containment to an acknowledgment that two-thirds of the world's states are small, poorly defined, destitute, and highly vulnerable to both ethnic cleavages and negative international influences (Azar 1983).

This realization, clearly ahead of its time, led Azar to coin the term "protracted social conflict" (PSC) and to develop a model that captured the reality of most violent and apparently intractable conflicts in the world (Azar & Farah 1981; Azar, Jureidini & McLaurin 1978; Azar 1983). Azar (1978) thus sought to change the approach of international relations from strategic to humanistic, proposing that security and stability are linked to human dignity, quality of life, and true peace, rather than to military power and the threat of force.

The practitioner side of Azar's professional identity was stimulated through his participation in numerous conferences and discussions on the Middle East conflict in the late sixties and early seventies. However, it was his involvement as a member of the third party team in one of the early problem-solving workshops organized by Herbert Kelman and Stephen Cohen that placed him firmly on the track of a scholar-practitioner in ICR. After this experience, Azar worked closely with the Harvard team, and particularly with Cohen, to undertake action research activities in the Middle East and to provide analyses relevant to conflict reduction. Of note is a 1979 workshop organized by Cohen and Azar (1981), which brought together Egyptian and Israel influentials during an important phase in the peace process.

In the mid-1980s, Azar moved to the University of Maryland where he founded in collaboration with John Burton the Center for International Development and Conflict Management (CIDCM) in 1985. This unique institutional initiative drew on Azar's combined interests in development needs and conflict resolution, and brought in Burton's experience with the problem-solving approach. Also in the 1980s, Azar turned more of his attention from the Arab-Israeli conflict to the civil war in Lebanon. Besides publishing analyses of this tragic conflict, Azar served for a time as an adviser to the Lebanese government at the presidential level.

CIDCM was concerned with general theory building as well as regional studies in selected areas, but its specialty soon became applied conflict resolution as problem-solving workshops or "forums" focusing on PSCs. For a brief period, CIDCM became a leading light in the ICR field, holding a rapid succession of problem-solving forums on the Falklands-Malvinas dispute, the Lebanese conflict, and the civil strife in Sri Lanka. However, after a brief period, Burton and Azar parted ways, and Burton moved on to George Mason University. Azar continued his work at CIDCM with an emphasis on his PSC model until his untimely death in 1991. CIDCM thus lost its ability to organize and implement problem-solving forums, but continues to sponsor useful activities in international development and conflict resolution.

This chapter will describe Azar's contributions to ICR in a largely chronological order. His work on the Arab-Israeli peace process with

Stephen Cohen and Herbert Kelman will be regarded as a foundation process leading to Azar's realization of the importance of basic human needs in the formation of PSCs. His developing model of protracted social conflict will be described as it evolved over nearly a decade of work, culminating in his 1990 book. Concurrently, the problem-solving forums held at Maryland are seen as both based in the model and as furthering Azar's understanding of the phenomenon, as well as providing another useful theory of practice for ICR. The legacy of Edward Azar's career will be identified as the creative fusion between conflict analysis and resolution and the needs and requirements for domestic and international development.

The Arab-Israeli Peace Process

In the late 1970s, Azar's research agenda shifted from providing analyses of interstate interactions using events data to focusing on the formation and characteristics of PSCs. Azar, Jureidini, and McLaurin (1978) provided a sobering analysis of the Middle East conflict and articulated an initial definition and description of PSCs, which further explicated the conflict. They pointed out that the conflict had been analyzed using a host of social scientific concepts, all of which assumed that causation of the conflict lay in regional and international interactions. These approaches were congruent with the superpower bias in international relations research, which assumed that a focus on superpower politics and its linkages to regional and local situations would explain all manner of interactions. In contrast, Azar and his colleagues suggested looking at social structural properties of conflicts at the local level. Until this was done, they proposed that interventions that were inspired by the superpower approach would continue to be unsuccessful in de-escalating the conflict. These contentions were supported by Azar's analysis of international conflicts over a thirty-year period demonstrating that ninety percent had taken place in the Third World, and that by 1970 most had been the focus of unsuccessful superpower interventions.

Protracted social conflicts are defined in the first instance as "hostile interactions which extend over long periods of time with sporadic outbreaks of open warfare fluctuating in frequency and intensity" (Azar et al. 1978, 50). These conflicts define the scope of national identity and social solidarity, and as such have a strong tendency to grow and to spill over into all domains. Because they tend to be a mixture of socioethnic and interstate conflicts, PSCs are difficult to settle in the usual way and generate a host of perceptions, feelings, and interactions that further exacerbate the situation. Issues that are marginal at one time have a way of becoming central problems at a later point. Furthermore, various domestic and international forces keep the conflict at a moderate intensity, so that crises of war *or of peace* tend to be managed so as to restore the status quo. Thus it is very difficult to deal with fundamental grievances, and PSCs thus involve the absence of a distinct termination.

The implications of seeing the Middle East as a PSC were clear to Azar and his colleagues. First, strong equilibrating forces will operate to undermine attempts at settlement, partly because of vested interests, but also because the unpredictable nature of a possible termination threatens personal, social, and national identities. Because struggles for recognition and acceptance, which are a major part of the conflict, cannot be won or lost through typical PSC behavior, the approach of gradualism in conflict reduction and peacebuilding is necessary. Meanwhile the appalling absorptive capacity of PSCs is demonstrated through the enormous human and material resources that are consumed by the conflict. Finally, the protractedness of the conflict will be reinforced by the tendency of decision makers to use the conflict as an excuse for inaction on pressing problems, such as the place of ethnic minorities, the distribution of income and services, and societal mobility. Such inaction may be excused as caution, indecision, or as cunning, but the outcome is that fundamental needs for development are ignored in the face of the conflict.

By making these points, Azar et al. (1978) provided a penetrating, and in retrospect, valid analysis of the Middle East conflict, and also demonstrated how the application of the PSC concept resulted in an evenhanded treatment of a highly controversial situation. In addition, the presentation showed a linkage and thereby a transition from quantitative analyses of international conflict to a penetrating case study using the emerging PSC model. Embedded in the analysis were also implications for addressing PSCs that constituted a radical departure from the usual realist or power politics model with its attendant superpower bias.

Ways of understanding and approaching destructive and protracted intercommunal conflicts were part of the developing methodology of problem-solving workshops as practiced by John Burton, Herbert Kelman, and others. Edward Azar's involvement in one of the early Kelman-Cohen workshops on the Israeli-Palestinian conflict provided his first exposure to a methodology wherein social scientists could both extend their analysis of such conflicts and provide a useful practice intervention for the parties. After this involvement, Azar worked closely with Kelman and Cohen on the Middle East conflict throughout the seventies, visiting the region, talking with both official and unofficial influentials, and working to understand and articulate the perspectives of the different sides.

One important event was a three-day conference in Cairo in late 1976, which brought together the leading political and social scientists in Egypt with the Kelman group for discussions on Egypt's relationship with Israel, in the present *and* in a possible postsettlement future. It appeared that these Egyptian influentials were not only working to understand Israel at a deeper level but also developing a policy of rapprochement toward their former enemy—a policy that was dramatically demonstrated by President Sadat's visit to Israel in 1977. The meetings, discussions, and related exchanges of information by the Kelman group likely played a useful role in the peace process between Egypt and Israel that culminated in the Camp David Accords of September 1978 and the peace treaty of March 1979.

In a more systematic vein, Cohen and Azar started a comprehensive action research project on the Middle East in 1976, which involved in-depth interviews with selected elites, the analysis of documents, and the holding of meetings with various influentials. In May 1979, Cohen and Azar served as third party facilitators in a problem-solving workshop for about a dozen Israeli and Egyptian intellectuals (Cohen & Azar 1981). This workshop was the first unofficial meeting between influential Egyptians and Israelis in the wake of the Camp David Accords designed to consider the full range of issues stemming from the agreement. In other words, the workshop focused on issues that had to be addressed to build a peaceful and enduring relationship between the two societies, with the peace treaty serving as the legal framework. Thus this workshop serves as a rare example of a postnegotiation intervention in ICR, designed to foster peacebuilding in the wake of successful peacemaking.

The two-day workshop was organized with the support of the Egyptian government, and the participants were carefully selected on the basis of their influential positions in sociopolitical networks and for the representativeness of their views overall. At the same time, the participants generally represented those who were willing to participate in the transition toward peace, with extremists holding polarized and rejectionist attitudes being excluded. The discussions focused on contrasting views of the present situation, and the central issues in the coming transition. The Israelis emphasized the importance of capitalizing on Sadat's visit by accelerating the normalization of relations to convince people in their society of the sincerity of Egypt's desire for peace. The Egyptians emphasized the importance of Israeli moves that would match the Sadat visit, particularly by involving the Palestinians in the peace process. These points led to discussions of the basic issues of security and acceptance, within which there was agreement on the principle of self-determination for the Palestinians, but not on how to implement it. This issue produced the most discordant moments in the workshop, especially when the discussion moved to historical and moral questions rather than pragmatic ones. Cohen and Azar (1981) point out the advantage of problem-solving workshops in being able to move into typically taboo areas involving moral and ideological concerns.

Cohen and Azar (1981) combined the ideas from the workshop with the results of interviews and documentary evidence to provide an articulation of the major issues facing the peace process between Egypt and Israel at that time. The issues of security, interaction, and acceptance were addressed from both points of view as interpreted by the third party. This analysis is useful for the parties and also enables the third party to see the kinds of issues that lie at the heart of intractable conflicts. For Azar, it is likely that the emphasis given to issues such as security, identity, and recognition in problem-solving workshops led in part to a realization of the importance of basic human needs and the role that their frustration plays in PSCs.

The Model of Protracted Social Conflict

A powerful element in Azar's work is the integration of theory, research, and practice. Thus, as he developed his model of protracted social conflict, based on various empirical data, the implications for conflict resolution were immediately articulated. It is therefore useful to understand Azar's model as it unfolded to appreciate his approach to the practice of ICR.

After the initial definition of PSC in 1978, Azar and his colleagues provided a series of expositions in which the concept was clarified and extended, particularly in causative factors and escalatory processes. Azar and Farah (1981) amplified the 1978 definition by noting that deep-seated racial, ethnic, and religious hatreds generate immense hostility, and that these hatreds distinguish PSCs from other international conflicts that do not involve group or national identities and the rights associated with them. However, they also point out that although PSCs express themselves in struggles for group identity, ethnicity alone is not the causative factor.

In a further move away from the superpower bias and the realist approach of power politics, Azar and Farah (1981) posited that structural inequalities and differential political power lie at the heart of

PSCs. When these inequalities and power differences are expressed through distributional inequalities, such that certain social groups get more or less of a society's rewards, the seeds for a PSC are sown. In the relatively disadvantaged Third World, international inequalities tend to reinforce internal inequalities in that more powerful groups will acquire more of the limited resources, partly through their international connections to richer states. Thus the benefits of development are unequally distributed according to group identity, thereby exacerbating the situation.

Azar (1983) extended the argument of how PSCs are linked to a structural relationship between conflict and international stratification, that is, to the inequitable distribution of resources between and within societies. He argued that it is necessary to explore the relationship between conflict and development factors including structural inequality, resource maldistribution, population dynamics, ineffective development projects, and ethnic struggles within the postcolonial context. Thus the interplay of a number of variables is critical to explaining the occurrence and intractability of PSCs. The outcome is that social, political, and economic inequalities are expressed in the domination by one group over another or others. Inequality is therefore linked to ethnic discrimination and victimization, and group identities and PSCs are thereby inextricably connected. Ethnicity becomes a driving force in the conflict through the coloring of all interactions and attributions to the point where intercommunal hatred is passed on through socialization from one generation to the next. The dynamic complexity of all these factors leads to the intractability of PSCs.

A reinterpretation of development factors into a basic human needs analysis took place in Azar's thinking about the time of his collaborative efforts with John Burton, who was also exploring the power of a needs analysis (see chapter 1). In an article listing ten propositions about PSCs, Azar (1985) noted that the enduring features of underdevelopment and unintegrated social and political systems account for the prolonged nature of PSCs. However, causation is directly related to a needs interpretation.

> We are led to the hypothesis that the source of protracted social conflict is the denial of those elements required in the development of all people and societies, and whose pursuit is a compelling need in all. These are *security, distinctive identity, social recognition of identity,* and *effective participation* in the processes that determine conditions of security and identity, and other such developmental requirements. The real source of conflict is the denial of those human needs that are common to all and whose pursuit is an ontological drive in all. (60)

It follows that PSCs arise when attempts by a disadvantaged group are taken to combat conditions of perceived discrimination that come from the denial of identity, an absence of security of culture and valued relationships, and an absence of political participation to remedy this victimization. Azar also articulated the implication that the most useful unit of analysis in PSCs is the identity group—defined in racial, religious, ethnic, cultural, or other terms—and not the unit chosen by traditional analyses, that is, the nation-state, most of which are unintegrated, artificially bounded, and incapable of inspiring national loyalty or a common culture.

The complex interplay among underdevelopment, structural deprivation, communal cleavages, and international linkages in PSCs is further explicated by Azar and Moon (1986), but the most systematic and comprehensive statement of Azar's model occurs in his 1990 book, *The Management of Protracted Social Conflict*. This exposition specifies the variables and the relationships among them that explain the genesis, the process dynamics, and the outcomes of PSCs.

The genesis of PSCs is found in a set of four clusters of variables that work to transform a nonconflictual situation into a conflictual one: communal content, human needs, the state's role, and international linkages (fig. 4.1). In many multiethnic societies, identity groups or communities are typically placed in conflictual relationships through both historical rivalries and a colonial policy of divide and rule. Thus

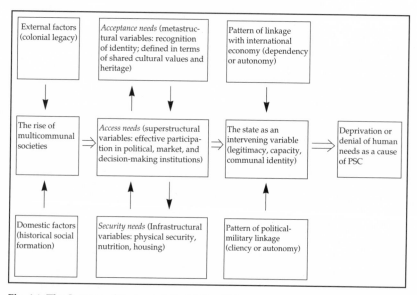

Fig. 4.1. The Sources of Protracted Social Conflict

many emerging states in the Third World are dominated by a single communal group or coalition of groups that ignore the needs of other groups, thereby breeding frustration and fragmentation. Because individuals strive to fulfill their needs through their identity group, grievances stemming from need deprivation are expressed collectively. In addition, a lack of effective participation and economic imbalances among groups resulting from rapid development strategies leads to the marginalization of particular communities, especially minorities. In these cases, the deprivation of needs and denial of access are often rooted in a refusal to even recognize or accept the identity of the disadvantaged group.

The level of need satisfaction is typically mediated by the state, and unfortunately many states experiencing PSCs are governed by regimes that are parochial, incompetent, fragile, and autocratic. Political authority is monopolized by a dominant community or coalition who maximize their interests at the expense of marginalized groups. The policy capacity of the state is limited by a rigid authority structure, which responds to the dominant groups rather than the needs of all constituents. The modes of governance are distorted to limit institutional access by excluded groups, and crises of legitimacy are thereby precipitated. These result in additional developmental problems and further diminish the state's ability to address basic needs. International linkages play an important role through both economic dependency on rich nations and political and military client relationships with strong states. The autonomy of the state is compromised, political and economic development is distorted, and policies are pursued that may be contradictory to the needs of the public. All of these factors deepen intercommunal cleavages and contribute to the causation of PSCs.

Given the above preconditions, the activation of PSC depends on three additional clusters of variables: communal strategies and actions, state actions and strategies, and built-in properties of conflict (fig. 4.2). Within the environment of mutual distrust between groups, a triggering event, which may seem trivial, marks a turning point at which individual grievances become collectively recognized. This leads to collective protest, which is typically met with suppression, thus increasing tension and resulting in a proliferation of issues around security, acceptance, and access needs. Communal mobilization moves to diverse strategies potentially involving civil disobedience, guerrilla activity, or secessionist movements. Calls for greater autonomy by minority groups typically result in coercive responses, and the weaker party seeks external assistance, usually from ethnic kin in neighboring countries. Thus the conflict is regionalized.

The state apparatus could respond to collective grievances with ac-

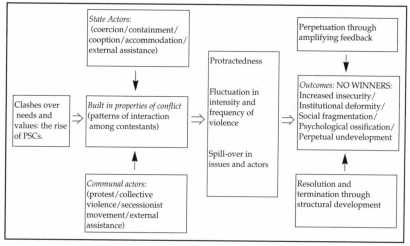

Fig. 4.2. The Processes and Outcomes of Protracted Social Conflict

commodation, thus satisfying needs to an adequate degree and keeping the PSC latent. However, the common state response follows a win-lose approach involving cooptation or repression, neither of which deals satisfactorily with the conflict. Often states adopt a hard-line policy, which simply invites a militant response from the marginalized groups. Failure of cooptation and initial repression justify more coercive measures, which are responded to in kind. The state attempts to contain the conflict by cutting off the protesting group from outside supports, and when this fails the state often seeks outside assistance, thus increasing dependency and inviting external intervention.

The reciprocal dynamic of unilateral, coercive moves is augmented by additional mechanisms of conflict that induce further escalation. PSCs typically involve an enduring set of antagonistic perceptions and interactions between communal groups and the state. Negative attributions of motivations and reciprocal negative images perpetuate the antagonisms and solidify the conflict. The stress of conflict induces close-mindedness and rarely proposed political solutions are rejected simply as power moves. The conflict spiral gains velocity as basic needs are further deprived and reciprocal hostility is institutionalized, thereby rendering the conflict intractable.

The innate behavioral properties of PSCs result in negative sum, that is, lose-lose outcomes. All parties become victimized in a process that has no end and becomes part of the culture of the society. The most obvious outcome is the deterioration of physical security, not simply because of violence, but the very destruction of physical and social infrastructures. Development programs fall victim to excessive military expenditures and a vicious cycle of underdevelopment affects all. Institutional deformity occurs through the paralysis of political bodies that perform regulatory functions and the degeneration of social and economic units that mediate communal relations. The social fabric of society thus becomes fragmented and communal cleavages become petrified.

Psychological ossification of perceptions, cognitions, and attitudes results from the vicious cycle of fear and hostility and contributes to a war culture in which meaningful communication among antagonists is nonexistent. Finally, both communal groups and the state experience increased dependency and cliency as they seek outside support, and as a result, both are further weakened and marginalized. Given these pervasive and extreme outcomes, it is not surprising that Azar (1990) concludes that PSCs present "the most severe challenge to those concerned with peace-building" (17).

What are the implications of the PSC model for conflict management and resolution? The most immediate one that Azar has identified is that traditional approaches simply will not work. Management strategies based in conventional thinking deal only with the symptoms of overt conflict and fail to address the more difficult problems of structural inequity and need deprivation, which drive PSCs (Azar 1983, 1990). Rather than focusing only on violent crisis, the PSC approach brings attention to the perpetual crisis in which the continuous and cumulative effects of victimization are paramount, and which can only be addressed by continuous action leading to transformation. Thus PSCs are seen as societal problems requiring ongoing structural development to redress inequities.

Azar and Moon (1986) identify the bureaucratic-managerial and legal-formalist approaches, both of which make traditional assumptions about conflict and how to handle it. The legal-formalist approach seeks to reduce behavioral violence (through mediation or judicial settlement), and a change in the conflict system (through direct bargaining, conciliation, mediation, arbitration, or legal decisions). Unfortunately both approaches are mainly interested in a containment of the conflict and a settlement that involves a win-lose or compromise outcome. This can produce only a temporary peace in PSCs, for such a conflict controlled at one time typically flares up with greater intensity and violence at the next point, because of unattended grievances held by victimized communal groups.

The alternative proposed by the PSC perspective is to combine short-term interventions to address crises with long-term efforts to transform the conflict situation (Azar & Moon 1986; Azar 1990). The

PSC has to be defined as a societal problem for all parties involved and a dual approach needs to be taken. This approach includes facilitation to create breakthroughs through problem-solving workshops, and development diplomacy to promote structural development by addressing basic needs and communal imbalances.

A further implication of the PSC model is that conflict intervenors must deal with identity groups, for power finally rests with identity groups (Azar 1985). In addition, it is essential to have face-to-face interaction among representatives of identity groups to mutually explore the needs of all parties and the means for satisfying them. This analytical phase of need identification is essential to the resolution process and must precede negotiation over interests or other settlement processes. Given these implications for conflict analysis and resolution, it is understandable why Azar was attracted to the problem-solving method and developed his unique variant of it.

The Maryland Problem-Solving Forums

From his theorizing on PSCs and his experience in working with Herbert Kelman, Stephen Cohen, and particularly John Burton, Edward Azar came to see the power of the problem-solving approach and to articulate his own model. At first, he used the term "facilitation" to refer to the use of problem-solving workshops to produce breakthroughs in PSCs (e.g., Azar & Moon 1986). According to Azar, the workshop format allows the parties to discuss their grievances with the immediate goal of assessing what is at issue and to differentiate needs from interests. The identification of needs initiates a constructive accommodation, which prepares the way for future negotiations.

Azar (1990) places the problem-solving approach clearly in the domain of "track two diplomacy" as defined by Montville (1987; see chapter 5), which involves unofficial efforts in the promotion of peaceful relations between warring parties. He acknowledges the seminal contributions of Burton, Doob, and Kelman, and adopts the term "third party consultation" following Fisher (1972, 1983; see chapter 8). He then places the use of workshops within a four-step process for the management of PSCs that includes: (1) tracking the conflict, (2) facilitating breakthroughs through workshops, (3) promoting structural development within the society, and (4) adopting development diplomacy to alleviate external barriers to resolution.

Azar (1990) coins the term "problem-solving forum" to denote his model of the workshop approach. He emphasizes the importance of creating the proper environment in which representatives of the parties can analyze their identity-related needs through effective communication, leading to the mutual discovery of breakthroughs and to consensus on the compatibility of competing goals. Thus each party must come to recognize the legitimate needs and aspirations of the other, the third party providing impartial facilitation.

Tracking the conflict dynamics is essential to the preparation for holding forums, for it provides information on the nature and trends of a conflict and indicates when a conflict may be ripe for facilitative intervention. Beyond that, Azar (1990) wisely acknowledges that preparation for even a single forum is a major piece of work that must cover physical logistics, interactive elements, and psychological aspects. It is essential to provide a setting where participants feel at ease and that has a sense of neutrality, such as a university. In Azar's experience, a forum should last at least four days if not five, so that participants can accustom themselves to the process and make the essential shift from a bargaining mode to an analytic one. Azar emphasizes how the *interactive process* is critical to induce the participants to make the journey from bargaining over interests to discussing needs, and finally to understanding the sources of the conflict. In addition, he notes that a series of workshops will likely be necessary to have an impact on any PSC.

For forums to be maximally useful in addressing PSCs, participants should be close to and able to influence the key decision makers. They should also be able to explore alternatives without being afraid of political repercussions. Such influential nondecision makers carry advantages in comparison to decision makers as participants. They can more likely break away from the bargaining mode, including previous positions, and do not risk any political capital by interacting with the enemy. In practical terms, nondecision makers generally have more flexible schedules, can avoid publicity, and can have their participation officially disavowed in case of failure. Although the ideal participants have connections with decision makers, others who do not, such as scholars, journalists, and intellectuals, can be useful participants, for they have influence through writing and commentary on both decision making and public opinion.

The panel of facilitators is integral to the forum model (Azar 1990). In line with the general understanding of third party consultation, the facilitators must be objective, knowledgeable, and skilled, and need to be trusted by the parties and able to engender mutual understanding between them. They must be cognizant of the sources of conflict and the processes of analysis and resolution, although they do not need to be full-fledged authorities on the specific conflict. Azar (1990), however, does go farther than most ICR scholar-practitioners by contending that facilitators should have detailed knowledge of the history and issues of the conflict, so that they can point out similarities with other PSCs and can also appreciate the emotional aspects of the conflict.

In addition, Azar (1990) notes that facilitators are chosen precisely because they possess skills that are different from those of the traditional conflict manager. Facilitators require understanding of PSCs, especially their social-psychological aspects, and experience and sensitivity in cross-cultural relations. They carry prestige not because of their organizational affiliation, but because their knowledge and expertise leads participants to see them as independent, unbiased, and helpful. They must also be seen as honest brokers who do not have their own agenda.

In operational terms, the panel is a small group of colleagues from various disciplines who are involved in tracking PSCs. Because they interact extensively among themselves, the facilitators need to be chosen carefully and must work to develop relationships of trust and respect to continuously reassess the dynamics of the forum. Professional qualities of objectivity, confidentiality, and impartiality are essential, so that the recognition and trust that the facilitators accord to the parties transfers to the participants' interaction. These qualities also place the third party in a good position to maintain an ongoing relationship with the parties, so that follow-up activities can be instituted to assist the parties and to evaluate the model.

The Falklands-Malvinas Forums

The first set of problem-solving forums organized at Maryland by Ed Azar and John Burton focused on the conflict between Argentina and the United Kingdom over the ownership of the Falklands-Malvinas islands. This small set of islands off the eastern tip of South America has been a British colony for more than 150 years with Argentina continuously disputing that claim.

An Argentine appeal to the UN and ensuing negotiations throughout the sixties and seventies failed to resolve the dispute. Argentina clearly wanted sovereignty over the Islas Malvinas while Britain maintained its right to protect the interests of the Falkland Islanders, who were predominantly of British descent and had voted in a referendum to remain with Britain. After ominous warnings in early 1982, Argentina invaded the islands at the beginning of April and seized control. The international community generally rejected this use of force, and the United Kingdom dispatched a large military operation to the islands. Serious air and sea battles began in early May, and a three-week ground offensive by British troops culminated in an Argentine surrender by mid-June. Although more than several thousand troops were involved on each side, the combined casualties were fortunately less than a thousand. The captured Argentine troops were returned after a brief period, and the situation basically returned to the previously held positions.

The Falklands-Malvinas forums in 1983–85 thus took place in the climate of hostility and mistrust generated by almost twenty years of inconclusive negotiations and the bitter events of 1982. According to Azar and Pickering (in Azar 1990), the Falklands-Malvinas dispute evidences many characteristics of a PSC (stereotyping, ethnocentrism, concern with national identity), even though it is also an international conflict in the classic sense. Therefore it is amenable to the problem-solving approach. The intractable nature of the conflict, for example, is demonstrated by the failure of official efforts at reconciliation after the 1982 war. Official contact did not occur until early 1984, and the talks that were convened that July broke down after only one day over the question of sovereignty. At the same time, Argentina refused to declare an end to the hostilities, and the United Kingdom declared a 150-mile military exclusion zone around the islands.

The first forum, in September 1983, brought together British academics and parliamentarians (on the House of Commons Foreign Affairs Committee) with political influentials (academics and former officials) from Argentina (Azar 1991; Azar & Pickering 1990; Burton 1985a; Little & Mitchell 1989). Among the objectives of the four-day session was the establishment of informal communications to reduce tensions and address the official impasse, an analysis of the means for returning to negotiations and reaching agreement, a search for possible solutions, and the dissemination of any useful information back to policy makers. One creative outcome of the discussions was an innovative potential solution in which Argentine titular sovereignty (displaying the flag, maintaining an official presence, providing limited services) would be combined with self-government for the islanders (with representation in the Argentine Congress). The participants agreed that the status quo was unacceptable, and returned home to set up new organizations for maintaining contact and working toward further workshops with more influential participants.

The second forum, in April 1984, brought mainly the same participants back with additional parliamentarians from both countries. Organizationally, the forum involved the Argentine Council for International Relations and the British South Atlantic Council (which had been formed after the 1983 forum). The main objectives of the session included reporting on responses to the first forum, searching for long-term solutions, and investigating short-term methods of tension reduction. One realization was that the Argentine conception of sovereignty was different from the British one in that a distinction was made between sovereignty over people and sovereignty over territory. Given that the latter was much more important to the Argentines, a solution balancing Argentine titular sovereignty with self-determination for the islanders seemed more plausible. The forum also created ideas for simultaneous tension reduction measures. The forum ended with an agreement to meet again and to assist in a visit to Buenos Aires by British parliamentarians, which was later reciprocated by a visit of Argentine parliamentarians to London. These tangible outcomes likely would not have accrued if the interaction between the countries had remained solely at the official level.

In February 1985, the third forum convened with the broader participation of higher ranking politicians from both countries and a representative of the islanders. The purposes included a more substantive coverage of alternative conceptions of sovereignty and ways that formal negotiations could be initiated. The most tangible outcome of the forum was a set of twelve principles geared toward breaking the impasse and pointing directions toward renewed talks at the official level. The primary themes in this declaration were that (1) all aspects of the future of the islands must be discussed, (2) the wishes of the islanders must be respected, and (3) there are a number of possible options for dealing with the issue of sovereignty. These propositions addressed the primary concerns of both governments and as such went forward to joint meetings of parliamentarians and meetings of British political party leaders with the president of Argentina, and found expression in the communiqués from these meetings. Little and Mitchell (1989) note this outcome and also point to their edited collection of papers as a direct product of the forums. However, it was also a conclusion of the forums that neither government was in a hurry to resolve the dispute and that each believes time is on its side (Azar 1990, 1991). The forum process was also apparently damaged by a premature statement about the process by a British parliamentarian and a resulting disavowal of the meetings by the British government. Thus it is not surprising that the impasse continues, even though there are positive signs of progress from time to time.

The Problem-Solving Forums on Lebanon

During 1984, two four-day forums were held at CIDCM focusing on the bitter and protracted conflict in Lebanon. In May and again in

October, Lebanese influentials nominated by community leaders came to Maryland to discuss the origins and dynamics of the conflict and possible paths to resolution (Azar 1986, 1990, 1991).

Lebanon is a small country on the eastern edge of the Mediterranean, surrounded by Syria and bordering on Israel in the south. An Arab country of about three million people, Lebanon is distinguished by a large Christian population of somewhat less than half the total, a legacy of the Byzantine Empire. Besides Arabic, French and English are common languages among the relatively well-educated population. After domination by a succession of empires, Lebanon came under French rule through a League of Nations mandate after World War I, and finally gained its independence in 1943.

The most striking and significant feature of Lebanon is its religious and cultural diversity. According to Azar (1990), religious identity is valued as a source of personal security and also plays a crucial role in political action. The primary communities include the Sunni Moslems (now the largest community), the Maronite Christians, the Druze, the Shi'a Moslems, and the Melchite Christians. Intercommunal relations among these groups generally have been difficult, with deep distrust and strong fears going back hundreds of years. Given this situation, Azar notes that Lebanon has been unable to establish the mechanism of a strong state to provide physical and economic security for its diverse population.

The 1943 National Pact, which established modern Lebanon, was an attempt to protect religious identity and encourage political compromise and integration. Power sharing was institutionalized in a complex manner along religious or "confessional" lines, based on each group's proportion of the 1932 census population. However, as the majority shifted from a Christian to a Muslim one and as external forces impinged upon the country, the Lebanese state failed to deliver fair and efficient government. The potential for effective democracy is also complicated by a tradition of loyalty to one's family and leading figures within one's religious group, rather than to the nation.

Tensions reached the boiling point in 1958 with an outbreak of violence, which was overcome partly through an American military presence. The government brought in some minor reforms, but major political and military events in the Middle East conflict continued to buffet Lebanon and further divide its population. Full-scale civil war broke out in 1975 and continued until the late 1980s along varying intergroup cleavages and with various external interventions, all of which brought horrendous human and economic costs to the country.

Amid the chaos of ongoing civil war, the first forum brought together several scholars, political advisers, and consultants to represent the views of the various factions. Because of the restrictions of war, the participants had not been able to meet or communicate for some time, even though they knew about one another and their work. Nonetheless, the formal discussion began with each participant setting out the views of their community and the conditions under which they came to the meeting. Discussion then moved to the main focus of whether a united Lebanon was desired by the different communities. Tensions ran high, strong emotions were expressed, and deadlocks occurred around some of the issues. The interchange revealed a number of common needs and values including security, identity, equality, participation and control, and freedom. In addition, conflicting interests were identified in areas such as property rights, economic privileges, and leadership roles. Nonetheless, the clear conclusion was that all communities desired a united, independent and multireligious Lebanon with a national culture that identifies with both Christian and Islamic civilizations. The final day of discussion was characterized by concern about returning home with concrete accomplishments and about the true intentions of one another. At the same time, many positive statements were made, and participants expressed the desire to maintain contacts.

The second forum again brought together several community representatives, with some overlap from the first meeting, and focused on what kind of Lebanon the parties wanted. This question was discussed in the light of the first forum's conclusion that previous political institutions had not dealt effectively with communal needs and grievances. The dynamics of this forum paralleled the first in that after initial statements, difficult discussion ensued, which ended on a mixed note of concern and hope. The primary product was a set of twenty-two principles on how to move toward the Lebanon that all desired in both the short and long terms.

According to Azar (1990), the forums achieved greater understanding and respect among the parties and demonstrated a commonality of concerns and perspectives, including a shared definition of Lebanon's identity and agreement on the type of society that the country should work to develop. Hence the forums initiated a unique exploration on strategies for consensus building and rehabilitation at the same time as the war continued. Subsequently, the participants established a larger, informal network for the ongoing discussion of issues among the communities. In 1988, this network produced a statement, the "National Covenant Document," proposing principles and steps for the reunification of the country. This statement was integrated into the 1989 Taif Accords among the various parties, which finally brought peace to Lebanon.

The Maryland Forum and Seminars on Sri Lanka

In the mid-eighties, CIDCM also turned its attention to the escalating intercommunal conflict in Sri Lanka, a small country off the southeastern coast of India. Sri Lanka was at first called Ceylon after gaining its independence from Britain in 1948, but chose its present name along with a new constitution in 1972. Although Sri Lanka includes several ethnic groups, the Buddhist Sinhalese constitute about three-quarters of the population of about thirteen million, while the Hindu Tamils make up slightly less than twenty percent.

Interethnic rivalry between Sinhalese and Tamils has a long history, but first erupted in the new state in 1956 over a law that made Sinhalese the official language. Various disturbances fuelled by extremist positions on both sides escalated the conflict especially during the seventies. The onset of civil war began in 1983, with Tamil guerrilla forces fighting for a separate state against the largely Sinhalese government. According to Azar (1990), Sri Lanka constitutes a PSC in which a complex set of unresolved grievances eventually festered and erupted into systematic violence and widespread repression. The colonial legacy of an unintegrated society and unmet needs for cultural identity, communal security, and effective participation have combined with external interventions to produce a complex, tragic, and seemingly intractable situation.

In collaboration with the International Center for Ethnic Studies in Sri Lanka, CIDCM sponsored a problem-solving forum in December 1985 (Azar 1990, 1991). The participants were influential representatives of their communities at the highest levels of leadership and government. The forum agenda was divided into four distinct sections: (1) an analysis of Sri Lankan society and the conflict in terms of religions, ethnicity, and demographics, (2) economic aspects of the conflict, (3) political issues including ethnic politics and decentralization, and (4) mechanisms for resolution.

A summary of the points made by the Tamil and Sinhalese participants makes it clear that each side came with viewpoints that were hotly contested by the other (Azar 1990). Gradually over three days, adversarial debate gave way to a realization that neither side was totally right and that a degree of pluralism existed in both communities. Thus even though more time was required for an adequate analysis (Azar 1991), each side emerged with an increased understanding of the other's views and a sense that winning the debate was impossible and would not resolve the conflict (Azar 1990). Some limitations of the Sri Lankan forum, such as having participants who were too close to the leadership and therefore overly politically sensitive, are enumerated by

Azar (1991). Nonetheless, both sides agreed to maintain contact and to work toward tension-reducing and confidence-building measures back home. Subsequent activities included exchanges among participants and members of the two communities in Sri Lanka.

A genuine desire for follow-up by forum participants on both sides led to the organization of two further seminars in 1986 and 1987. This design option was chosen in the light of the limited resources of the center and with the intention of allowing observation by nonpartici-pants to promote the development of a network of interested scholars. Thus the seminars allowed follow-up contact by some participants and provided for the further analysis of specific issues in the light of chang-ing events. Azar (1990) presents a summary of the main points of the seminars, and concludes that they were productive sessions despite their brief one-and-a-half-day duration. Points of tension occurred but were channeled in substantive directions by the facilitators leading to some fresh insights and positive conclusions. This outcome leads Azar to conclude that the seminars were a useful form of interaction and learning and as such can be included in the broader spectrum of track two diplomacy.

Azar (1990) provides a candid appraisal of the Maryland forums in their achievements and limitations. He also provides a critique of track two diplomacy, geared to fine tuning an approach he believed had already proven its usefulness. On a broader scale, Azar and Burton (1986) edited a collection that places the forum process and the problem-solving approach in the context of international conflict resolution. They note the changes that have taken place in conflict resolution at all levels, and they suggest that there is an emerging breakthrough toward resolving protracted conflicts as opposed to managing or containing them. As this breakthrough hopefully occurs, it will be based in no small way on the theoretical and practical contributions of Ed Azar.

The Legacy of Edward Azar

Edward Azar was not only one of the first international relations scholars to shift the attention of the field from the power politics of the cold war to the host of destructive conflicts gripping the Third World but was also a trailblazer in linking conflict analysis and resolution with economic, political, and social development. He proposed that the most important intellectual challenge for students of PSCs was the re-lationship between conflict theory and development theory, and he brought forward ideas to meet this challenge (Azar 1979, 1983). Be-cause PSCs are in part characterized by poverty and inequality, the core goal of development should be to reduce inequality rather than simply stimulate economic growth. This goal is necessary to remove the structural victimization based on group identities, which lies at the heart of PSCs. In fact, Azar concluded that in situations of protracted conflict, "trying to resolve conflict without dealing with underdevelopment is futile" (1985, 69).

Azar (1990, 1991) outlined the steps of structural development and development diplomacy that must flow from and complement the forum process to resolve PSCs. Structural development involves a balanced internal development strategy that addresses the distorted patterns of development that are linked to communal cleavages and discrimination. Structural development that ensures communal, sectoral, and regional balances at the same time it preserves ecological integrity can be achieved only through sociopolitical reforms that include consensus building within and between communities.

To complement internal policy changes, interventions should take the form of development diplomacy, operationalized as a pattern of assistance to reduce structural victimization. This approach requires a careful analysis of the society to identify how current economic growth policies contribute to structural victimization. External assistance should then be geared to reforms in political institutions and changes in structural inequities that will address the roots of PSCs. Traditional development with its patron-client relationships should be replaced by support for domestic institution building and responsiveness to the needs of all communal groups. Fragmented, short-term economic and military assistance should be replaced with balanced, redistributive, and participative development strategies that would address long-term needs as well as short-term requirements.

In conclusion, Azar's position was that PSCs cannot be managed or resolved without addressing issues of economic development and communal pluralism (Azar 1990). Although problem-solving forums are necessary to achieve short-term breakthroughs, long-term development is essential to address fundamental causes. Thus studying protracted social conflict led Azar to conclude that "peace is development in the broadest sense of the term" (1985, 69).

5

The Psychodynamic Approach and Unofficial Diplomacy

Bryant Wedge and Other Unofficial Diplomats

Bryant Wedge (1921–87) was an American psychiatrist with wide ranging interests in mental health and social policy. During 1958–59 he was an Eisenhower Exchange Fellow, visiting fifteen countries. He was surprised that in each one, his discussions with the American ambassador centered primarily on serious problems of misunderstanding and conflict among states and peoples. Wedge was struck by the similarities in attitudes of the parties across a number of smoldering international conflicts, and by the limitations of diplomacy and power to deal with these conflicts.

Wedge concluded that international relations are unstable and dangerous, that psychological elements are a major source of unpredictability, and that psychological science could increase predictability and thereby reduce dangerousness. He saw the possibilities of a "psychiatry of international affairs" that could help understand and ameliorate the irrational elements of destructive conflict, but found that few of his colleagues were interested in this (Wedge 1967, 1983). In 1965, Wedge's involvement took a very practical turn when he was hired by the U.S. State Department to intervene as an unofficial mediator in a violent crisis in a small Caribbean nation (Wedge 1970).

The Dominican Republic occupies two-thirds of the island of Hispaniola and for most of its recorded history has been a Spanish colony. After independence in 1865, the country experienced an almost constant stream of dictatorships and revolts, the longest period of control being under Trujillo from 1930 to 1961. Subsequent constitutional reform and elections led to a popular government, which was overthrown in a 1963 military coup followed by a period of instability. In 1965, a group of young officers attempted a further coup and were joined by thousands of young revolutionaries supporting the previously elected president. The government and senior military moved to repress the revolution, several hundred people were killed, and the country was on the verge of civil war. At this point, the United States intervened militarily to restore order, although hostilities continued for a time (Wedge 1970).

Wedge received a request from a State Department official in the capital of Santa Domingo, asking if he would intervene to establish communication with the young revolutionaries and help reduce the violence. Wedge agreed to operate as an independent and unofficial consultant who would work to establish dialogue between the hostile groups, the primary ones being the Revolutionary Dominican Youth Movement and the American Embassy.

The youth movement had coalesced around the uprising, and while including Communists, was representative of young Dominicans who supported democratic reforms in opposition to the privileged oligarchy and corrupt military. The movement included virtually all of the rising young leaders in the Republic. Its members were hostile toward the United States, seeing the military intervention as stopping the revolution, and resenting the Americans' imputation of a Communist character to them. While they were frustrated with their inability to communicate with the American embassy, their hostility and distrust stopped them from making contact. For their part, the embassy staff had gone through a traumatic experience, operating in a crisis mode with criticism coming from many directions, and now realizing that the future leadership of the country, including the university community, was associated with the youth movement. If democratic institutions were to be built, the involvement of the youth movement was essential.

Wedge arrived in Santa Domingo, entered the area controlled by the revolutionaries, and explained his role as a psychiatrist interested in the political psychology of revolutions. He was impressed with the openness of the young people and their dedication to democratic reform. As Wedge's dialogue with the movement expanded, he was constantly tested to see if he could appreciate their social concerns and aspirations. He found that almost all were interested not in class warfare but in reforming existing institutions toward greater social justice. His credibility was constantly challenged, and while Wedge maintained he was an independent scholar, he did indicate that he was having discussions with the U.S. Mission. This usually elicited stereotyped views of the mission, but also increased the revolutionaries' interest in conveying their views to the U.S. government.

Wedge's contact with the U.S. Embassy took a formal and systematic approach. After a briefing with the ambassador, he met with every section related to youth affairs to communicate his credentials and to indicate understanding of their difficult role. His ongoing contact with the revolutionaries provided an immediate stimulus for discussion about the movement. It was clear that considerable stereotyping was taking place, particularly on the role of Communists in the movement.

Wedge's strategy was not to challenge stereotypes, for this simply diminished his credibility. Each side held hostile images of the enemy, but each also expressed an interest in the other providing some limited assistance. The Mission knew that the involvement of the young intellectuals was essential to U.S. assistance in building democratic institutions, but could not support Communist elements. The revolutionaries knew that U.S. assistance was needed, but were wary of compromising Dominican independence. A key institution in this process was the Autonomous University of Santa Domingo, which had the confidence and involvement of the youth movement.

As Wedge continued his contacts, each side increased its interest in cooperating, but would not meet directly because of the political ramifications of such recognition. Wedge provided a report outlining the development of the youth movement's political culture and emphasizing the importance of establishing communication. He recommended programs to provide contact between the young Dominicans and nonpolitical American groups, and emphasized the central role of the university in reform activities. This led to a program of development assistance to the university, involving visits by expert consultants identified by the university and supported by the United States.

This program provided the opportunity to bring members of the two sides together at a luncheon for the external consultants, attended by twenty members of the embassy, twenty members of the university, and a number of neutral persons. The participants spontaneously paired off into intense minidialogues, with Wedge and the other neutrals serving as intermediaries. The effect was quite dramatic, in that participants now saw that members of the other side were approachable individuals dedicated to the development of a better society. Wedge followed up with a party for some of the same participants augmented by officials from the university and the mission more directly involved in program administration. This gathering resulted in a pragmatic discussion of program development possibilities, which were soon carried forward through direct contact between the university and U.S. officials and agencies. Wedge now ended his consultation, for further third party involvement would be superfluous. The development programs that were instituted faced attacks on a number of fronts, but continued to function for years afterward.

Wedge's (1970) assessment of his intervention was based on three hypotheses, which were generally supported. First, communication between the groups in conflict did alter intergroup images in a favorable direction, particularly in judgments about each other. Second, programs of cooperation toward partial superordinate goals resulted in additional reductions in hostile intergroup images. The third hypothesis, that favorable changes in images and cooperation would reduce the degree of violence, was difficult to assess, because the primary interface of hostilities was between the Dominican factions, rather than the youth movement and the Americans. Nonetheless, it appears that the reduction of the alienation experienced by the youth movement through its contact with the U.S. Mission did contribute to domestic peace. Also, the mission became less anxious about the political dangers of the movement, thus contributing to a lessening of tension.

From this experience and others, Wedge developed a general model of third party intercession, consisting of five stages (Wedge 1970): (1) the intercessor establishes contact with each side as an interested outsider and initiates a process of dialogue. This stage is accomplished by understanding individuals and groups on their own terms without agreeing or disagreeing, much like the psychiatrist does in establishing communication with an alienated person; (2) each side's interests are defined and mutual interests are identified, some of which can be satisfied only by communication between the two parties; (3) members of the two sides are brought together on neutral ground to establish contact. However, the purposes are not directly related to the conflict, and no agenda is provided, for it is assumed that the identified common interests will assert themselves. Although this interaction does not allow for either group to penetrate the cultural identity of the other, some members of each group come to envision the possibility of working cooperatively on issues of mutual concern; (4) assistance is provided to the parties in considering programs of cooperation; and (5) intercession is ended once cooperative programs have been established. Wedge (1970) sees success of the model as based on a careful accommodation of techniques to the actual flow of events and the nature of the groups guided by ongoing dialogue.

Wedge's experience, along with his knowledge of the pioneering work of Burton, Doob, and others, led him to be optimistic that a "science of peacemaking" could be established (Wedge 1970). This new approach would be based on theoretical understanding of conflict from which the development of procedures would be derived. Wedge (1979) maintained that honest brokers who can help hostile groups articulate their concerns and move toward negotiation are largely absent on the world scene and require independent institutional bases. Wedge worked to help establish a science of peacemaking in various ways, and he came to see this interdisciplinary field as going far beyond the profession of psychiatry (Wedge 1983). Rather than as a psychiatrist concerned with international affairs, he came to see himself as a peacemaker who happened to be a psychiatrist. In retrospect, he saw little of psychiatry in his intercession in the Dominican Republic, and suggested that psychiatrists needed to take on broader roles in public policy if they wished to be involved in the peacemaking process.

As a policy advocate, Wedge was a cofounder of the National Peace Academy Campaign, which led to the establishment of the United States Institute of Peace in 1984. He was also the founder of the Center for Conflict Resolution at George Mason University, which pioneered teaching and research in the field, and established the first graduate program in conflict management in 1982 (Sandole 1991). Wedge (1983) saw this development as the first step in establishing a new profession of conflict management in concert with exciting developments in many areas, including divorce mediation, community relations, and environmental disputes.

Unfortunately Wedge (1983) was less optimistic about the receptivity of the international system to the emerging field of conflict resolution, for the international system is fundamentally based in power relations. He notes that his intervention in the Dominican Republic contributed to resolving the civil war and in extricating U.S. troops from a costly and embarrassing situation. However, the U.S. government classified Wedge's reports and required his public silence, apparently because this new approach did not fit with traditional thinking and its success was an embarrassment to the existing system. It was clear to Wedge that the development of new, catalytic roles was required to change the system, and he devoted the remainder of his life to that goal.

Wedge's interventions can be grouped with various informal activities carried out by "unofficial diplomats" to ease tensions and improve relations in international conflicts (Berman & Johnson 1977). Wedge (1987) saw the importance of linking unofficial mediation efforts with the functions of official diplomacy—a rare event in his experience. Two of the common activities in *unofficial diplomacy* are the informal involvement of nongovernmental organizations or private individuals as conciliators or mediators in specific conflicts and the holding of regular conferences that bring together citizens from adversarial countries to discuss topical issues.

The intermediary activities of the Quakers or Society of Friends is one prominent example of unofficial diplomacy, as exemplified in the work of Quakers such as Adam Curle (1971, 1986). Curle (1990) regards "mediation" as an attempt to change violent, suspicious, and unproductive relationships into cooperative, friendly, and constructive ones. It thus is a psychological effort to change perceptions of both the enemy and the conflict so that the parties see some hope of resolution and thereby become prepared to negotiate. The mediator works individually with decision makers on each side to eradicate misconceptions and exaggerated fears that prevent the opponents from coming together. In this sense, Quaker mediation can be seen as a form of prenegotiation, which blends elements of conciliation and consultation (see chapter 8). It would not, however, be seen as a form of ICR, because representatives of the parties do not come together in face-to-face, facilitated interaction with third party assistance.

Based on his experience with the American Friends Service Committee, Mike Yarrow has provided a description and analysis of the Quaker approach to international conciliation (Yarrow 1978, 1982). His treatment is based on three major case studies, including the Quaker intervention in the Nigerian Civil War, wherein Adam Curle played a useful mediation role. Yarrow sees unofficial efforts as subordinate and auxiliary to official negotiations, but notes a number of advantages, including the ability to approach unrecognized parties, for example, the Palestine Liberation Organization. Pettigrew (1991) provides an overview and evaluation of Quaker mediation, noting the consistent theme of faithfulness to the religious tradition of seeking peace through justice. His assessment is that most efforts have had useful effects, and can be categorized as partial successes. He indicates that an increasing emphasis on selection and training will improve the usefulness of mediation in complex and challenging situations of conflict.

In regular meetings, the Dartmouth Conference stands as a prime example, with the Pugwash Conference and the dialogue meetings organized by the United Nations Association also deserving mention. Pugwash began in 1957 as a result of a manifesto, signed by Albert Einstein, Bertrand Russell, Linus Pauling, Joseph Rotblat, and others calling on the world's natural scientists to meet and work on ways of avoiding nuclear war (Kaplan 1984; Rotblat 1972). The conference was supported by Cyrus Eaton, a wealthy industrialist, who was born in the small, Nova Scotia village where the first conferences were held and from which the series takes its name. Well over a hundred conferences, symposia, and workshops have taken place, bringing together scientists from East and West, North and South, to engage in open and unofficial discussions of world issues, the results of which have been communicated back to government leaders and policy makers. Pugwash claims to have influenced a number of important developments in controlling and ending the cold war, including the Nuclear Test Ban Treaty, the Anti-Ballistic Missile Agreement, and the policies of *pere-*

stroika and *glasnost*, which transformed the Soviet Union and U.S.-
Soviet Union relations (Kaplan 1984, Rotblat & Holdren 1989). In 1995,
the Pugwash Conference and the sole surviving signatory of the 1955
manifesto, Joseph Rotblat, were awarded the Nobel Peace Prize for
their long-term protest against nuclear weapons.

The Dartmouth Conference was initiated by Norman Cousins at
the request of President Eisenhower to establish citizen-to-citizen discussion of difficult issues in American-Soviet relations (Cousins 1977;
Stewart 1987). Beginning in 1960 at Dartmouth College, meetings have
been held on a regular basis, bringing together influential professionals selected by each side to exchange and analyze perspectives on topics of current concern. In the 1980s, the conference established smaller
working groups in areas of mutual interest, including regional conflict
management, arms control, and political relations. Delegates are chosen not simply for their substantive knowledge, but also for their political credibility with the current administrations.

The Dartmouth Conference has been through a number of crisis
points, for example, following the U.S. blockade of Cuba in 1962, but it
persevered to become a very important unofficial link in U.S.-Soviet
Union relations. Besides creating new policy options for official consideration, it has served as a channel for important signals on serious
issues and has provided for visionary thinking on issues not yet on the
official agenda (Stewart 1987). The aspects of the Dartmouth Conference that can be regarded as ICR will be discussed below in considering the work of Harold Saunders, who has served as cochair of the
regional conflict task force since 1982. The distinctions and complementarity between unofficial and official diplomacy are also relevant to
the work of Vamik Volkan, who has played a central role in developing
an approach to ICR based in a psychodynamic analysis of intergroup
conflict.

Vamik Volkan: The Psychodynamic Approach

Vamik Volkan is an American psychiatrist of Turkish-Cypriot origin who has searched for ways to understand and ameliorate destructive and protracted intercommunal conflicts such as the one that grips
his homeland of Cyprus. From a psychoanalytic base, he has drawn
concepts to help explain such conflicts, and he has developed interactive methods for addressing it. Since the early 1980s, Volkan has also
worked closely with Harold Saunders and Joseph Montville, among
others, and the resulting workshop methodology is thereby an interdisciplinary one. Volkan is currently a professor of psychiatry and di-

rector of the Center for the Study of the Mind and Human Interaction at the University of Virginia Medical School.

Volkan (1991a) classifies his work as unofficial diplomacy, and distinguishes it from *official diplomacy*—an art in which the professional diplomat blends personal style with government policies and international protocol. Drawing on Barston (1988), Volkan identifies a number of functions of official diplomacy such as providing formal representation, reducing friction and managing change caused by conflict, and creating the norms and regulations that structure the international system. In all these endeavors, diplomats pursue a highly rational and ritualized approach that downplays the significant role of emotions and does not acknowledge or understand deeper psychological processes of intergroup conflict. This makes official diplomacy inadequate to address intense conflicts, which are partly fueled by processes such as projection and victimization, and in which emotional and psychological elements need to be managed along with political and economic ones. It follows that the complementary role of unofficial diplomacy is to humanize the conflict and build confidence between the parties so that they can overcome hatred and move toward negotiation (Volkan 1991a).

Although Volkan identifies a number of variants of unofficial diplomacy, his definition is very comparable to those of interactive conflict resolution and third party consultation (see Introduction chap. 7). In "unofficial diplomacy," a neutral third party acting as a team brings together politically influential citizens of two opposing countries for a series of meetings to become acquainted, establish workable relationships, and exchange options (Volkan 1991a). The role of the third party, or "catalyst group," is essential to this process. The connection between unofficial and official diplomacy is made through the concept of "critical juncture" in which the insights and options generated in unofficial diplomacy are communicated to and considered by official diplomacy. This procedure may be accomplished by reports from unofficial participants to governments or by involving official diplomats in the sessions in an unofficial capacity. Volkan (1991a) hopes that work in unofficial diplomacy will lead diplomats to give more attention to psychological barriers and deeper processes operating in long-standing conflicts, rather than following "realpolitik" and engaging in short-term crisis intervention.

The first major application of the psychodynamic approach was a series of workshops sponsored by the American Psychiatric Association from 1979 to 1984, which brought together Egyptians, Israelis, and later Palestinians to explore the psychological aspects of the Middle East conflict (Julius 1991; Volkan 1988). Vamik Volkan, Demetrius Julius, and Joseph Montville served as the core of the third party team, who organized and facilitated six major sessions and many minor meetings over the five-year period. About eight participants came from each party, including psychiatrists, journalists, historians, politicians, ambassadors, and retired generals, and each workshop involved both new members and old, core members to provide continuity. Julius (1991) describes and analyzes the experience in organizing principles, applications, and theoretical formulations.

The first of the five-day workshops brought together Israelis and Egyptians in interaction that surfaced the stereotypes each group held of the other and began to replace these with the individualized reality of the other. The second conference was marked by heightened distrust induced by the Israeli bombing of an Iraqi nuclear reactor. Fortunately the core group of participants was able to rebuild adequate trust to address some of the difficult issues raised in the first session. The third meeting spent considerable time discussing the process itself and a new level of group consolidation was reached. Small discussion groups were utilized for the first time, allowing for the airing of more emotional aspects without disrupting the full plenary sessions. Topics identified on the first day were chosen for small-group discussions, and the results were reported back to the total session for synthesis. In representation, the participants resolved to seek Palestinian participants for the next meeting.

The fourth meeting was influenced greatly by the Palestinian delegation, whose presence produced a feeling of accomplishment but also a sense of regression. New members vented their emotions through responses to grievances, accusations of dehumanization, and cries of victimization, all of which old members were able to absorb without counterattacking, because of the understanding and trust that had been built up. The fifth meeting brought a higher level of political representation and a more pragmatic bent to involve more influential persons and disseminate information more widely. As with every meeting, there was a reworking of previous conflict stages and a further development of group process. The final meeting did include more high level participants, but severely tested the group process because of the diverse levels of previous experience. Julius (1991) describes the group at this meeting as "out of sync" and indicates that the limits of the absorptive capacity of the group became apparent. It appeared that the process had reached a new and more complicated level, even as the project ended.

In goals, Julius maintains that the healing approach of psychiatry was intended to allow participants to discuss painful conflicts in an atmosphere conducive to working out problems rather than perpetuating them. It was hoped that conflicts would be discussed from a psychological as well as political standpoint, discovering new psychological formulations to help participants and others understand international conflict. To work toward the goals, questions of organization had to be answered and principles of implementation had to be developed. For example, it was found useful to identify one person as the leader for each national group at each meeting, with these persons forming a steering committee for the entire process.

In outcomes, Volkan (1988) and Julius (1991) cite several practical eventualities that can be attributed to the workshops. For example, an Israeli academic center was established in Cairo, collaboration among scholars from the three national groups was initiated at an Israeli university, and a project was launched to examine and revise Arab images in Israeli textbooks. On a methodological note, the meetings established an interaction that encouraged familiarity and trust that held through some very serious crises, such as the Israeli invasion of Lebanon in 1982. Follow-up indicated that participants continued to see the value of the experience, and that an important and influential network had been established among the opposing parties (Volkan 1988).

Volkan founded the Center for the Study of the Mind and Human Interaction (CSMHI) in 1988 at the University of Virginia, with a focus on understanding the psychological factors in interactions between ethnic or national groups and on practical applications to address intergroup conflicts. Thus a primary activity of CSMHI is organizing conferences and workshops that bring together various professionals from parties engaged in destructive conflict to explore means of breaking down barriers and developing cooperative activities. One such early initiative by CSMHI in April 1989 brought together a small group from the Soviet Union and the United States to examine the psychological aspects of interaction between the nations and the potential of unofficial diplomacy. This conference and related contacts ultimately led to an ongoing collaboration between CSMHI and the Institute of Psychology of the Russian Academy of Sciences and the Russian Diplomatic Academy. Part of this was a study of ethnicity, nationalism, and political change, which led Volkan into a series of workshops focusing on conflict between Russia and the Baltic republics.

The Baltic republics of Estonia, Latvia, and Lithuania are on the eastern shore of the Baltic Sea, and as small national entities, have generally been ruled by a succession of foreign powers. With the fall of the Russian Empire at the end of the First World War, the Baltic republics gained their independence for a brief period before being incorporated into the Soviet Union during the Second World War. Although the three republics evidence historical, cultural, religious, and linguistic differences, this incorporation created a similarity in their multiethnic character—the presence of a sizable Russian minority who came in to serve industrial, administrative, and military functions. The size of this ethnic Russian minority ranges from nine percent in Lithuania, to thirty in Estonia, and thirty-four in Latvia. Although these estimates are somewhat misleading owing to intermarriage among ethnic groups, the fact remains that a major ethnic fault line exists between ethnic Russians and the indigenous populations of the three republics. As the Soviet Union dissolved and the three republics declared their independence during 1990, tensions increased considerably.

Volkan and his colleagues have organized a series of workshops bringing together influential representatives from the different Baltic states and Russia. The first four-day session was held in Lithuania in 1992 to examine the relationship between Russia and the Baltics, which soon included a focus on intergroup tensions involving the ethnic Russian minorities (Volkan & Harris 1992). The fifteen participants were primarily academics and officials (in unofficial capacity) from Lithuania and Russia with single representatives from Latvia, Estonia, and Byelorussia. The American third party team included members experienced in the Arab-Israeli conferences as well as new associates of CSMHI.

Volkan and Harris (1992) present some of the psychoanalytic underpinnings of their approach and provide a description of the discussions. Expressions of historical grievances and competing claims of victimization were followed by alternating exchanges of hostility and empathy among the group representatives. With third party assistance, the participants moved from analysis to possible solutions and formed small groups to develop ideas for confidence-building measures, such as how to deal with the continuing presence of the Soviet army. The proposals were distilled into a list of action possibilities divided into an international category (relations between Russia and the Baltic republics) and an internal one (ethnic relations within the republics). Because many of the delegates held official positions, "critical junctures" could be explored immediately, for example, the establishment of a permanent unofficial negotiating network. Volkan and Harris (1992) conclude that the workshop initiated a process that would improve the chances of a peaceful separation between the Baltic republics and Russia.

The second workshop in Latvia, in 1993, brought together fifty persons, including twelve on the third party team (Volkan & Harris 1993). The larger group enabled better representation of each of the Baltic republics and Russia, and also allowed for more high level policy makers to strengthen possible critical junctures. In preparation, the third party distributed reports of the previous session and also a paper on the ethnic mix and the historical traumas, current wounds, and fears of the parties in each situation. The larger numbers necessitated a design emphasizing small-group discussions on each day sandwiched between plenary sessions. In addition, the catalyst group provided questions to guide the discussions from a focus on own group analysis, to other group understanding, and finally to ways of improving relations among groups.

Volkan and Harris (1993) illustrate the intensity and the utility of the sessions by describing the psychological processes that played out in the discussions of one small group. As with the previous workshop, a list of action possibilities was produced, covering a range of official and unofficial activities. The organizers point out that such action possibilities emerge only when identity issues, historical grievances, and strong emotions have been considered and empathic communication has been established. This second meeting clearly established CSMHI as an accepted third party in helping facilitate a peaceful separation between Russia and the Baltic republics.

Third and fourth meetings were held in 1994, both focusing primarily on relations among Estonia, Russia, and the Russian-speaking minority in Estonia (CSMHI 1995b). Similar agendas and procedures were used as with the earlier workshops, and similarly positive outcomes accrued in greater understanding by the parties of some of the core issues and the means of addressing these. This result is compatible with the goal of the Baltics project to increase mutual understanding of views, concerns, and hopes among influential leaders so that political agreements will address emotional as well as practical elements and will therefore be enduring. Furthermore, Volkan and his colleagues are now working to link the reduction of ethnic tensions with broader democratization and institution building (CSMHI 1995a; Volkan 1995). This plan involves organizing a series of workshops, establishing a local contact group, influencing decision makers, and engaging experts in concrete projects to promote a peaceful and civil society.

The psychodynamic analysis underlying the work of Vamik Volkan and his colleagues draws on both psychoanalytic concepts to understand the conflict and techniques of psychoanalytic therapy to guide the third party. With regard to understanding, Volkan and Harris (1993) state:

> We remain constantly alert for those conscious and, more importantly, unconscious psychological factors which may render political processes unworkable and even malignant. We have found that large groups are profoundly affected by such factors as ethnic or national

pride, and by mental representations of historical grievances and triumphs which are transmitted, with their accompanying defenses and adaptations, from generation to generation. Underlying these factors is a shared need to belong to a large group and to have a cohesive group identity. Such factors function as "unseen powers" in relationships between groups. CSMHI's aim is to shed light on these unseen powers, and to relate our findings to official decision makers so that they may deal with real world issues in a more adaptive way. (170–71)

With regard to the practice implications, Volkan and Harris (1992) identify four concepts from psychoanalytic psychotherapy that are relevant.

(1) the awareness that events have more than one meaning and that sometimes a hidden meaning is more important than a surface one; (2) that all interactions, whether they take the form of overt or concealed actions, verbal or non-verbal statements, formal or informal gatherings, are meaningful and analyzable; (3) that the initiation of a process in which problems become the "shared problems" of opposing parties is more essential than the formulation of "logical" or "quick" answers; and (4) that the creation of an atmosphere in which the expression of emotions is acceptable can lead to the recognition of underlying resistances to change. (24)

These assumptions flow easily into the third party role of the catalyst group, that is, to create an environment in which psychological barriers impeding official diplomacy can be discussed openly and can then be taken into account in negotiations. In such an environment, the conflicting groups themselves often propose measures and solutions that can be taken into official interaction when the time is ripe.

The psychodynamic approach rests in part on the application of psychoanalytic defense mechanisms, including externalization, projection, and identification, that individuals are seen as using to protect themselves from perceived psychological danger (Volkan 1988, 1990). Such individual functioning and development are seen to play a role in intergroup relations, especially in prejudice, discrimination, and conflict. Externalization involves transferring some negative aspect of oneself to an ethnic outgroup. Projection more broadly involves projecting unconscious and unacceptable impulses, thoughts, and characteristics onto a denigrated outgroup so that the individual can maintain an acceptable and cohesive sense of self. Members of one's own group, particularly parents and leaders, help determine what outgroups are the targets. Identification is an unconscious process by which one assimilates the images of another with oneself, in this case, the ethnic group to which one belongs, thus differentiating it from all other groups. The outcome is that the identity of one's group and the identity of its enemies are based respectively on the loved or unwanted projected aspects of group members, and that prejudice functions to retain group identity, which in turn supports individual self-esteem (Volkan 1992).

In a similar vein, Volkan (1985, 1988) maintains that humans need to determine who their friends and enemies are to establish their own group identity. Thus a feature of normal development is that human beings possess an inherent need to have both enemies and allies. This need necessitates intergroup interactions involving the flow of love and aggression and thereby contaminates diplomatic crises that may be essentially economic or political (Volkan 1991a). However, without understanding and dealing with the psychodynamic factors, such conflicts cannot be resolved.

Volkan and his colleagues have similarly used concepts from psychoanalysis to explain the dynamics that they perceive as occurring in workshops (Volkan 1988, 1991b, 1992). Three examples will illustrate this interpretation. Often near the beginning of a workshop, a "miniconflict" occurs over some minor aspect of the arrangements that challenges the leader of the catalyst group. The mechanism of displacement allows the aggression and hostility that relate to the major ethnic conflict to be displaced to and absorbed by the miniconflict in a safer way that still supports group identity. At the same time, the management of the miniconflict initiates and bestows leadership on the chair of the catalyst group.

A second illustration involves the "accordion phenomenon," which is expressed in alternating periods of closeness and separation between the antagonistic groups, driven by derivatives of aggressive emotions. At first, the groups will be distant as a defensive maneuver to keep aggression in check. However, representatives must tame their feelings of hostility and aggression to work together toward peace. But soon this togetherness becomes oppressive, if not threatening, and distance is reestablished—the accordion keeps playing.

A final illustration, which Volkan regards as the most important of such phenomena, is that of mourning. Intergroup conflict typically involves losses for both parties, which must be mourned and accepted before the groups can move on to altered positions. If a group sees what has been lost as too valuable to give up, they will constantly invest in attempting to recover it, and the relationship with the enemy cannot change. The role of the catalyst group is to help representatives express the emotions pertaining to mourning and clarify these for both groups so that they can move on to a changed relationship.

It must be noted that the psychoanalytic base on which Volkan builds his understanding and practice is not universally accepted as a theory of personality development or functioning in other professional and scientific circles. The extension of these concepts from the individual to the collective level, while not the only source of psychodynamic theorizing about intergroup conflict, must therefore be questioned. Competing and more parsimonious explanations for intergroup conflict and workshop methods for addressing it can be found in other fields, particularly social psychology and political science. One observation, however, is that the psychodynamic approach shares with other workshop methods a number of commonalities, regardless of theoretical base, for example, the importance of group identity in ethnic conflicts and of some form of reconciliation for de-escalation.

Thus the utility of the psychodynamic approach lies not so much in its theoretical interpretations, but in the commonalities that its methodology shares with other forms of ICR. Volkan and his colleagues have developed a workshop design that allows representatives from hostile groups to build a climate of cooperation, to enter into dialogue and mutual analysis, and to create effective ideas for addressing their conflict. The role of the catalyst group members, regardless of their psychoanalytic interpretations, is very comparable to that of third party consultants in general. The successes in process and outcomes that Volkan and his colleagues have engendered are a testimony to the careful and systematic development of their methodology over more than a decade of sustained effort.

Harold Saunders: Changing Conflictual Relationships

Harold Saunders is one of a few bureaucrats and diplomats who has had the courage and the vision to break away from the world of realpolitik and move toward new ways of thinking about how nations relate (Saunders 1991a). Saunders served on the National Security Council in the White House and in the State Department, concluding his career as an assistant secretary of state. He was involved in the Kissinger shuttle diplomacy in the Middle East and was a member of the Camp David team that brought about the peace treaty between Egypt and Israel. On the unofficial side, Saunders attended one of the Arab-Israeli workshops organized by Volkan and his colleagues, and has been heavily involved in the Baltics project of CSMHI. He has also has been a member of the third party team in some of the Israeli-Palestinian workshops led by Herbert Kelman. However, his most significant involvement has been as a participant in the Dartmouth

Conference, which brings together Soviet (now Russian) and American influentials, primarily foreign-policy specialists, to engage in citizen-to-citizen dialogue on superpower relations.

Saunders (1991b) notes that while the Dartmouth Conference is unofficial, it is policy relevant in that participants, though speaking as individuals, do discuss issues between their countries and often have experience in policymaking or are close to policymakers or both. A strength of the conference is its continuity, which builds cumulative dialogue and results in an ongoing communication among participants. Effort is made to discuss issues analytically without polemics and to approach difficulties as shared problems that require mutually acceptable scenarios for their resolution. An important element of Dartmouth is joint ownership, with sponsors from both countries sharing the responsibility for organizing the meetings (Saunders 1991b). This is a rare occurrence in ICR—the parties themselves sharing what is typically the role of an outside impartial facilitator.

In the early 1980s, relations between the U.S. and the Soviet Union were at a low point, and consequently the conference formed two task forces in areas where détente had broken down—arms control and regional conflict. Saunders was asked to cochair the latter along with a Soviet colleague, at first Evgeny Primakov and later Gennady Chufrin (Chufrin & Saunders 1993). Since 1981, the regional conflict task force has met more than twenty times (for three to four days) to analyze U.S.-Soviet interaction in situations such as Afghanistan, Central America, and the Middle East, and has shared its insights with official decision makers. The dialogue came to focus not just on substantive issues between the two countries, but also on the nature of the relationship between them. The analysis went beyond stated interests to probe the deeper motivations behind each side's actions, and to ascertain in greater depth how each side perceived the other.

In the late 1980s, the new thinking about American-Soviet relations articulated by Mikhail Gorbachev had some of it roots in policy papers written by veterans of Dartmouth who served as advisers to the Soviet leader (see, for example, Kingston 1988). According to Chufrin and Saunders (1993), these ideas were not born in academic isolation, but were forged over time in dialogue sessions and were offered at the right time as part of a profound change, that is, the demise of the cold war.

Chufrin and Saunders (1993) describe elements of the task force that provided for its unique functioning and apparent success. First, the conference helped create a public space in which citizens from the two countries could discuss how to creatively change relations between their bodies politic, even when official interactions were stalled.

Second, the discussions focused on gaining insight into the whole relationship between the superpowers in interests, motivations, and perceptions. Third, the dialogue led to a mutual understanding of the political environment in each country and the political instruments that can bring about change. Fourth, maintaining communication links between the public dialogue and government was essential to successfully influence policymaking. Fifth, the continuity of the discussions and the cumulative agenda allowed for a deeper probing over time that created ideas and indeed helped bring about fundamental changes in the basic relationship between the countries.

Saunders and his colleagues have articulated a five-stage developmental sequence, which they believe captures the unofficial dialogue between conflicting groups (Chufrin & Saunders 1993; Saunders 1992; Saunders & Slim 1994a). Dialogue groups will move at different rates through the stages, and may even move back and forth as they deepen the dialogue or encounter new problems. However, toward the end of each stage, a critical point of transition is reached by which to judge if the group is ready to move on.

Stage 1—Deciding to Engage. The initial challenges are identifying individuals willing to risk interacting with the enemy, gaining official approval for the initiative, and creating a safe public space for the meetings. Some intragroup interaction may be useful before engaging the other side, and some substantive starting points for the agenda need to be identified. The transition occurs through the decision process to engage and the stage ends with a specific agreement to meet.

Stage 2—Mapping the Relationship Together. Participants need to learn to talk analytically, not polemically or positionally, about the relationship in underlying interests and emotions. Topics need to be discussed in their own right but also as vehicles for understanding the dynamics of the relationship. The ultimate purpose is a stocktaking in difficulties, capacities, and potential, and the transition involves overcoming resistances to a deeper and systematic analysis of sensitive problems.

Stage 3—Probing the Dynamics of the Relationship. Participants now need to listen with greater sensitivity to the other side's hopes and fears to understand how the other's mind works. The focus shifts to how the elements of the relationship interact over time, and the challenge becomes an ability to imagine a constructive relationship. The transition is signaled when the groups are ready and able to begin thinking together—a condition that can be tested by breaking down into smaller, mixed working groups with assigned tasks.

Stage 4—Experiencing the Relationship by Thinking Together. The challenge is to have the group experience how to generate change in the relationship by becoming a microcosm of it. This requires thinking together about how to deal with a particular problem, which is best addressed through a task of scenario building within smaller working groups. These groups identify obstacles, steps to deal with them, and a sequence of actions to enact the desired change. This experiencing of the relationship generates insights, and the transition is reached when the group asks what actions flow from their discussions.

Stage 5—Acting Together. The purpose is to develop practical ways to implement the scenarios so as to have a concrete impact on the relationship. Participants reflect on what is possible for them and choose one of a number of options: sharing their scenarios with others, becoming an action group, inviting individuals with an action ability to join the dialogue, or expanding the meetings to include officials. In all cases, working together on implementation strategies over time will further deepen the group's understanding of the relationship and their ability to help change it constructively.

Using the five-stage model, Saunders and colleague Randa Slim of the Kettering Foundation have collaborated with three Russian members of the Dartmouth Regional Conflicts Task Force to institute a dialogue process on the conflict in Tajikistan (Saunders 1995; Saunders & Slim 1994b; Slim 1995). This former Soviet republic, which became independent in 1991, has experienced internal conflict, primarily between government and opposition groups throughout the 1990s. This extension of activities by the task force was possible owing to the knowledge and contacts of the Russian members. The first session was held in Moscow in March 1993, and meetings have been held about every two months since then, the twelfth one in June 1995. Concurrently, in April 1994, three members of the dialogue group became delegates on the nongovernment side to the formal UN-sponsored negotiations designed to end the civil war.

The first stage was implemented through visits by Russian members of the facilitation team to Tajikistan to enlist participants, seek tacit official approval, and communicate the ground rules of the dialogue. The membership of the resulting group has evidenced continuity, with five of seven original influentials still involved, as well as flexibility, with three new members coming in to provide wider representation. Stage two focused on broad diagnostic questions, such as the causes of the civil war and the interests of the various parties. In the same sessions, questions were also asked regarding the possible ways out of the conflict and about the kind of country that the participants wanted to develop. This analysis led to a consensus on a number of points, including the need to stop the violence and the importance of defining how a unified, democratic, and secular Tajikistan would function. The outcome was an agreement to focus on how to begin negotiations to create the conditions for the return of refugees.

The third stage centered on how to organize negotiations, with a new coordination of opposition forces outside the meetings providing a basis for establishing a workable relationship between government and opposition participants within the meetings. Changes in positions were discussed and the conclusion was reached that negotiations were possible. The facilitators assisted the process by distilling a joint picture of the perceptions and fears that each side held of the other, as well as a list of points representing a common ground from which to begin negotiations. The fourth stage of scenario building was operationalized by participants creating a joint memorandum on a negotiating process, which the facilitators assisted using a reiterative single text procedure. During this same period, the UN envoy made progress toward convening official negotiations between the government and opposition groups. Later in this stage, participants identified the obstacles to normalizing political conditions and produced a memorandum on national reconciliation (Slim 1995).

In the final stage of acting together, the participants carried their two memorandums to officials in Tajikistan. They also gave attention to future issues that would arise in negotiations and in the implementation of any agreement. Thus, although the dialogue process served a highly complementary role to official interaction, the group chose not to deal with the same issues as negotiations. Their broader concern of how to help create a civil society in Tajikistan is an ongoing and difficult challenge and a number of ideas have been generated (Slim 1995). Saunders and Slim (1994b) conclude that a well-functioning dialogue group with the ability to produce common ground has been established, and that it should be able to serve various objectives to help develop a democratic society in Tajikistan. Saunders (1995) describes how the dialogue has recycled through stages to contribute to the negotiation process and to transfer their insights to the political discourse.

Harold Saunders's work in unofficial diplomacy has taken place in the context of a historic challenge in rethinking how nations relate (Saunders 1991a). He believes that we need a more complete and realistic conceptual framework for understanding and conducting international relations. This framework would not simply focus on transactions among states, but would emphasize the total relationship between whole societies as a continuous interaction involving policymaking and policy influencing. Thinking in relationships draws in a wider range of actors and expands nations' abilities for generating change peacefully. Unofficial dialogue can play an important role by providing a forum for critiquing the present relationship, generating alternative ideas, and bringing about a changed relationship in which the parties think and work together (Saunders 1991b).

Montville, McDonald, and Diamond: From Track Two to Multi-Track Diplomacy

The complementarity between official and unofficial diplomacy has been nurtured by a number of creative persons. Joseph Montville, a former U.S. Foreign Service officer now at the Center for Strategic and International Studies in Washington, D.C., coined the term "track two diplomacy" to denote unofficial, nonstructured interaction between members of adversarial groups or nations that is directed toward conflict resolution through addressing psychological factors (Davidson & Montville 1981–82). As compared with "track one," or official, diplomacy, the work of scholar-practitioners such as Herbert Kelman and Vamik Volkan is seen as illustrative of a track two process that is an essential supplement to official interaction.

Montville (1987) broadened his definition to include interactions that develop strategies, affect public opinion, or mobilize resources to support conflict resolution. He thus identified three distinct and yet interrelated processes that constitute track two: (1) the problem-solving workshop, which brings together unofficial representatives to understand each other's perspective and develop joint strategies to address their shared problem, (2) the influencing of public opinion to reduce the sense of victimhood, to rehumanize the image of the adversary, and to support leaders in making conciliatory moves, and (3) cooperative economic activities to provide incentives and continuity to conflict resolution. Montville (1987) provides real world examples of each of these processes, thus making a convincing case for the relevance and utility of track two diplomacy. In underlying theory, Montville supports the psychodynamic approach to understanding and ameliorating destructive conflict between identity groups (Montville 1990; Volkan, Julius & Montville 1991).

John McDonald is a primary contributor to track two and other unofficial processes, and has played a key role in increasing the awareness of track one officials about the potential utility of these complementary methods. McDonald concluded a distinguished diplomatic career, including a number of ambassadorial appointments, with a position at the U.S. Foreign Service Institute's Center for the Study of Foreign Affairs, where he was instrumental in organizing numerous conferences focusing in part on the interface between official and unofficial diplomacy (McDonald & Bendahmane 1987). Subsequently McDonald spent three years as the first president of the Iowa Peace Institute. In the late 1980s, he observed that the concept of track two was proliferating and thus creating confusion about its meaning and usage (McDonald 1991). Thus he proposed a new conceptualization of "multi-track diplomacy," which acknowledged track one and subdivided track two into four different tracks.

Tracks two through five all involve unofficial or citizen diplomacy directed toward helping to de-escalate and resolve international conflict, but track two is now reserved for analytical problem-solving efforts by skilled and informed private citizens (equivalent to ICR). McDonald (1991) provides positive examples of track two: the Dartmouth Conference, the joint meetings of the United Nations Associations in the United States and Soviet Union, and the problem-solving workshops of John Burton and Edward Azar. He points out how the examples demonstrate both the diversity of track two and its potential for positive contributions to track one.

Track three denotes interactions between individuals or corporations in the business field. McDonald contends that the private sector has been overlooked as an instrument of conflict resolution and peacebuilding, and yet the examples he provides indicate the positive role that business can play in establishing mutually beneficial relations. Track four refers to citizen-to-citizen exchange programs in all fields, including cultural, scientific, educational, sports, etc. Examples include the Fulbright exchange program and more recent examples of American-Soviet exchanges sponsored by the Iowa Peace Institute, which were successful in countering the negative image of the enemy. Track five involves efforts of the media in two conflicting countries to educate the public about the culture, needs, and philosophy of the other. The intention is to humanize the enemy and reduce distrust and hostility so that other tracks can build on a new base of understanding. Although track five is a slow process, McDonald (1991) maintains that it is the foundation stone for citizen diplomacy.

In 1991, John McDonald teamed up with Louise Diamond to produce a major study of multi-track diplomacy (Diamond & McDonald 1991). Louise Diamond is a human-relations trainer and organizational consultant with the NTL Institute and at the time of the study was director of PeaceWorks, a Washington-based institute for peace research, education, and training. The work was based on an analysis of written materials, interviews with more than a hundred individuals engaged in various forms of unofficial diplomacy, and attendance at several conferences relevant to one or more tracks. The outcome is a systems view of multi-track diplomacy, the expansion of the model to include nine tracks, and a set of conclusions and recommendations about the system and ways to strengthen it.

For each of the nine tracks, Diamond and McDonald (1991) identify its primary purpose, its various parts and activities of each, its culture and main issues such as self-regulation, and its place and role in the broader field of peacemaking. Tracks two, three, and four remain essentially the same as defined by McDonald (1991) while five becomes a new track nine involving peacemaking through communication and the shaping of public opinion through the media. Track five now becomes peacemaking through the development and exchange of information in research, training, and education. Track six covers peace and environmental activism or advocacy on issues such as human rights, social and economic justice, and disarmament. Track seven captures the religious aspect of peacemaking through the activities of religious communities and morality-based movements such as nonviolence and pacifism. Track eight incorporates the activities of the funding community—the philanthropists and foundations who provide the financial support for activities in many of the other tracks.

Diamond and McDonald's results indicated that each of the tracks represents a world unto itself, with its own culture, assumptions, methods, language, issues, and membership. Although there are numerous points of overlap among the tracks, actors within each generally do not have a systems orientation that encourages mutual learning, sharing resources, and building cooperative networks. Furthermore, the multitrack system as a whole is faced with a number of challenging issues, both internally and externally, such as professional development and funding. Thus, although the system is at the leading edge of addressing many of the world's challenges, it typically lacks the resources to move flexibly and thoroughly. Unofficial peacemaking and conflict resolution is generally not valued in the official policy or public arenas, and the resources to address its needs go to other priorities.

Consequently Diamond and McDonald (1991) make several recommendations. They challenge those working in the nine tracks to build relationships among themselves and to work on their own internal conflicts using the concepts and methods of the field. They challenge unofficial actors to share their knowledge, to explore the potential of systematic, coordinated peacemaking among the tracks, and to create new resources to support their work. They also see the importance of legitimating the field and of creating new multitrack institutions that take a system perspective and engage in collaborative activities.

In 1992, McDonald and Diamond took their own advice and founded the Institute for Multi-Track Diplomacy in Washington, D.C., a not-for-profit organization dedicated to the nonviolent resolution of ethnic and regional conflict through collaborative projects in peacebuilding and peacemaking. Since its inception, IMTD has initiated various networking, training, and dialogue activities, and has actively been involved in a number of conflicts, including the Middle East, Tibet, Liberia, Ethiopia, and Cyprus. At first in partnership with the NTL Institute and later joined by the Conflict Management Group of Cambridge, Massachusetts, IMTD has carried out a major, bicommunal training project on Cyprus, bringing together members of the two divided communities for conflict resolution workshops. Thus the efforts of these two represent the leading edge of developments in unofficial diplomacy.

Conclusion

Work in unofficial diplomacy shows a diversity of models and activities, the core of which is compatible with ICR. There is no obvious reason why unofficial diplomacy and the psychodynamic approach should be intertwined; this situation has come about simply through the efforts of individuals who connect both fields, such as Vamik Volkan and Joseph Montville. The message of psychiatrists such as Volkan is the importance of psychological factors in intergroup conflict, a message that has been brought forward by members of other disciplines, such as Herbert Kelman (a social psychologist), based on different psychological concepts and theories. To argue which theory provides a more valid base for ICR is probably a waste of time, with a predictable outcome like that in psychotherapy, where each school goes in its own direction convinced of the validity of its model.

A more useful focus is on the interactive methods that constitute ICR in practice, and here there is considerable commonality in workshop design and implementation. Practitioners from many different disciplines have operated effectively as third party consultants regardless of their theoretical baggage. Thus the field should build on these commonalities to chart a professional practice that is effective, rather than bickering about whose mental representations are correct. The resistance to unofficial efforts that Bryant Wedge perceived is declining, and it will be further eroded by a common front of success in practical applications. When the field is established and able to mount more sophisticated and comparative evaluations of its various models, it will then be in a position to examine what theoretical underpinnings provide the more valid bases for practice. In the meantime, there is much good work to be done.

6

Intercommunal Dialogue

A common response to destructive conflict between groups is to call for *dialogue*, defined by Webster's dictionary as an "interchange and discussion of ideas, especially when open and frank, as in seeking mutual understanding or harmony." This strategy acknowledges that misunderstanding is often a source of conflict or its escalation or both, and that improved communication and understanding is one of the first steps in de-escalation and resolution. Thus numerous interventions described as dialogues can be considered applications of interactive conflict resolution.

Dialogue interventions come under the broader definition of ICR, in that they are facilitated face-to-face activities in communication designed to promote conflict analysis among parties engaged in protracted conflict. Unlike the more focused forms of ICR, such as problem-solving workshops, dialogue interventions tend to involve not influential, informal representatives of the parties, but simply ordinary members of the antagonistic groups. Furthermore, dialogue is primarily directed toward increased understanding and trust among the participants with some eventual positive effects on public opinion, rather than the creation of alternative solutions to the conflict. Nonetheless, dialogues sometimes produce ideas that can fruitfully be fed into the policymaking process. In addition, some interventions follow a problem-solving agenda even though the participants are simply interested members of their groups.

Thus there is some blurring of the distinctions between the focused and broader forms of ICR, and among dialogue, conflict analysis, and problem solving. At the same time, many of the common characteristics of ICR apply to dialogue interventions, so that these can be distinguished from other forms of intergroup contact, such as professional conferences or citizen exchanges. Therefore much dialogue work is relevant to the development of the generic methodology of ICR.

Projects in intercommunal dialogue have adapted various interactive methodologies to their objectives of increased understanding and trust. These include sensitivity training, family therapy, academic seminars, decision-making seminars, reconciliation meetings, and problem-solving workshops. Also, some dialogue interventions have involved members of the conflicting identity groups while others have dealt with members of diasporas or allies. Although this variety is healthy for the development of the field, it demonstrates there is no generally accepted model for instituting dialogue.

In developing dialogue methodology, it should be noted that many interventions go unreported, partly because of concerns about risks to participants and organizers, but also because many of the intervenors are primarily practitioners without the position or the proclivity to publish their work. Thus the interventions described here must be seen as an incidental sample that is merely illustrative of the wide range of work that is likely going on in many parts of the world, carried out by religious bodies, nongovernmental organizations, professional associations, educational institutions, and others. Nonetheless, it is hoped that these illustrations provide a sense of the variety and the vitality of dialogue interventions as an important component of ICR.

Dialogues on the Middle East Conflict

The conflict in the Middle East between Israelis and their Arab neighbors has captured the attention of the region and the world for almost fifty years. The conflict is of grave concern to Jews and Arabs throughout the world, but particularly in the United States, which has evidenced a high degree of involvement in the conflict. Given also that ICR is developing primarily in the United States, it is understandable that dialogue interventions on the Arab-Israeli conflict have often involved Jewish Americans as organizers and facilitators. Some of these have involved Israelis and Arabs from the region, while others have focused on members of the diasporas or affiliated groupings, such as Jews and Palestinians living in the United States. Illustrative interventions have employed a range of methodologies and have claimed various positive outcomes.

One of the first illustrations of dialogue work using the methodology of sensitivity training (see chapter 2) is found in an intervention by Lakin, Lomranz, and Lieberman (1969), which brought together Jews and Arabs living in Israel. The question was whether a human-relations approach, which usually increases mutual understanding and acceptance among participants, would lead to improved communication and a reduction of suspicion between persons from these conflicting groups.

Two workshops were held, one in Jerusalem and one in Haifa, each involving about a dozen participants balanced between the communities. The design included a pretraining assessment, sensitivity training or the "dialogue group" as the primary forum of interaction, supplemental skill-training exercises in empathy and feedback, mixed teams for developing project proposals to improve Arab-Jewish relations, and a posttraining assessment.

In the dialogue groups, the approach of the trainer was to encourage the participants to assess the effects of their own communications, and in particular to distinguish debate from discussion. The richness of the interaction is illustrated through verbatim excerpts that demonstrate the authenticity of the interchange and the difficult grappling with central issues such as trust, equality, and identity. The project teams were not without their difficulties, particularly personal rivalries, but in each case they produced some useful and innovative ideas for improving Arab-Jewish relations in Israeli.

The workshop assessment package was extensive and multimethod. The pretraining questionnaire included open questions on expectations and incomplete sentences on intergroup perceptions. During the workshop, observations of activities, tallies of key behaviors and topics, and sociometric ratings by participants were completed. Besides the use of a projective test, posttraining interviews centered on the evaluations of participants.

Overall the assessment provided mildly positive indicators for both process and outcomes. Although it was difficult to overcome the polemical style of debate, affection appeared to increase while hostility and suspicion decreased over the course of the workshops. Excerpts from posttraining interviews demonstrated that small but important changes in participants' attitudes and outlook occurred, primarily in increased understanding of the other group and the mutual problem the two share. At the same time, the participants resisted a number of the activities and assessment methods, including the skill training, the sociometric ratings, the questionnaires, and the interviews. The depth of the resistance and its apparently greater strength among Arab participants would lead an outside observer with the advantage of hindsight to question the cultural appropriateness of these methods. The facilitators concluded that the achievements in conflict reduction were limited. This is true, but it should be noted that the project stands as a well-documented, professional demonstration of inducing dialogue in a highly polarized environment.

Another illustration of dialogue involving Israeli Jews and Arabs is a series of problem-solving workshops organized by Levi and Benjamin in the mid-1970s. These sessions brought together Arab and Jewish college students, and followed a systematic, iterative model of conflict resolution. Thus, although they are considered dialogues in terms of participants, the design of the sessions goes beyond dialogue to problem solving, thereby indicating the overlap between these different forms of ICR.

Levi and Benjamin (1976) provide an initial description of their model based on two, two-day workshops that brought together small, mixed groups of Arabs and Jews interested in reaching a mutually acceptable resolution of the Middle East conflict. The model is further explicated in Levi and Benjamin (1977), after the completion of six workshops, in which the authors make a strong case that conflict resolution must go beyond simply dealing with process problems to the substance of the issues between the parties.

The typical workshop begins with a getting acquainted exercise, after which the facilitators discuss their psychological contract with the workshop participants, asking each one to adopt an open and honest problem-solving orientation and to safeguard the confidentiality of others' comments. The first step of the model involves defining the conflict by having each group define its preferred solution, which is of course not preferred by the opposing group. To assess the degree of conflict, participants are asked to rate the opposing solutions on a scale from -10 to $+10$, and the cumulative group ratings and the difference between them then serve as an initial point of reference for later progress toward joint satisfaction. To increase total satisfaction with solutions, participants are encouraged to work to understand each other and to discover solutions that satisfy everyone. Thus the next step involves participants gathering information to clarify why each side prefers its solution. The sharing of reasons for preferred solutions leads to the discovery of the basis for the conflict.

At this point, the facilitators provide options to the participants for proceeding, that is, redefining the conflict, gathering more information, engaging in influence attempts, or creating new solutions. This reiterative process proceeds uniquely in each workshop to the point where participants are ready to move into creating new solutions. The facilitators do not recommend moving into influence attempts, for this typically involves sterile debate and argument; however, this can be useful in some situations to let off steam and to demonstrate the futility of adversarial behaviors.

Creating new solutions shifts the process from a "focus" function, which has pinpointed the crucial elements of the conflict, to a "flexibility" function, which brings in variety and creativity—both being required for conflict resolution (Levi & Benjamin 1977). In the different workshops, the facilitators have used variations of the technique of brainstorming to increase creativity. The new solutions are then subjected to the rating process, and if satisfaction is inadequate, the conflict is redefined and the process continues until a mutually acceptable resolution is reached. In one workshop, for example, participants reached agreement on a solution involving a Palestinian state in the West Bank and Gaza that would formally recognize Israel and share control over a binational Jerusalem (Benjamin & Levi 1979). The analysis of this workshop also makes the point that the facilitators need to deal with various process issues for the model to work in practice. Levi and Benjamin (1977) stress that their model provides greater flexibility than the common linear model of problem solving, and as such it is more suited to both the task and process requirements of conflict resolution.

The final illustration of intercommunal dialogue between Arabs and Jews in Israel comes from the long-term development and application of conflict management workshops at the mixed village of Neve Shalom near Jerusalem ("Wahat Al-Salam" in Arabic and "Oasis of Peace" in English). Neve Shalom is a unique model for cooperation and integration between the cultural groups based on trust and equality, while at the same time encouraging each group to maintain its separate and distinct identity (Bargal & Bar 1988, 1992; Shipler 1986). Within Neve Shalom is the School for Peace, an autonomous educational institution, which conducts conflict management workshops for Jewish and Arab young people age sixteen to seventeen. Since its inception, the School for Peace has involved more than six-thousand students in its workshops with the objectives of encouraging interaction between the national groups, changing intergroup stereotypes and prejudiced attitudes toward an impartial orientation, increasing awareness of the complexity of the Arab-Jewish conflict, and imparting basic skills in conflict management.

The training program and the school itself have undergone a constant process of organizational development that evidences a high degree of professionalism. Through continuous analysis and planning, the design of the workshops has changed from a single session of several hours, to a five-day event, to a three-day meeting with preworkshop uni-national sessions and postworkshop interactions over the subsequent twelve months. In addition, the effects of the training workshops on the participants have been rigorously evaluated over a number of years. The School for Peace thus stands as an innovative demonstration project in the systematic implementation and assessment of a carefully designed, large-scale program of intercommunal dialogue. The description of the workshops here is drawn primarily from Bargal and Bar (1992); further description and rationale is available in Bargal (1992) and Bargal and Bar (1994).

Participants are selected on the basis of favorable attitudes toward the encounter and sociometric ratings that indicate they are influential with their school classmates. The participants are mixed into small working groups of about a dozen, and each group is led by a Jewish and an Arab trainer working as a team. The first day of the workshop involves a warm-up and contracting session in which participants share their expectations and fantasies about the workshop and a responsive and realistic program is worked out with the trainers. The second day emphasizes intercultural understanding in which participants become familiar with the ways that common relationships and interactions are managed in the two different cultures. The third day considers a number of topics including the question of identity formation in which social and political elements of self-identity are discussed. This leads to a confrontation of intergroup prejudice and discrimination in which distorted attitudes and behaviors can be examined and modified. Other topics deal with major elements in the conflict, such as the question of legitimacy of each party's existence. The final agenda item is a political discourse wherein each participant describes his or her beliefs about the Arab-Jewish conflict, and the merits of a democratic, humanistic outlook are discussed. The workshop ends with sharing impressions in relation to expectations, providing feedback and support, and preparing for reentry to the home situation, which is often antagonistic to the outcomes of the experience.

In workshop evaluation, attitudinal changes among several hundred participants were assessed in comparison to a larger group of similar nonparticipants over the four-year period from 1985 to 1988 (Bargal & Bar 1992). Attitudes were measured using pre- and post-questionnaires focusing on three areas: inclinations appropriate to the intervention (e.g., sensitivity to the other group); readiness for contact with the other group (e.g., willingness to host other group members in my home); and awareness of the complexities of the Arab-Jewish conflict (e.g., the other group accepts my attitudes). The changes for the intervention and comparison cohorts for each national group were compared over each of the four years. The Arab participants generally showed favorable attitude changes over the four years, mainly in readiness for contact and awareness of the conflict. The Jewish participants showed strong positive changes in some years but less in others. Thus both groups benefited from the intervention, but the two groups were differentially affected by developing events, such as the onset of the intifada, in the external sociopolitical reality. In-depth case studies of former participants also indicated that many members of both national groups have altered their intergroup perceptions. This dialogue program thus stands as a laudable illustration of action research in the service of intercommunal understanding and conflict resolution.

Outside the Middle East, various dialogue projects have involved Arab and Jewish individuals who identify with the conflict and are willing to work toward understanding the other point of view. Reena Bernards provided the initial coordination for a project bringing together Jewish and Palestinian American women, which held three workshops in the 1989 to 1991 period. The initiative began in response to the intifada which signaled a new and more destructive phase in intercommunal violence in Israel, the West Bank, and Gaza. A group of American-Jewish women from leading Jewish organizations decided to undertake several projects to support the Middle East peace process, one of which was to explore the possibility of dialogue with Palestinian-American women. The outcome was a joint planning committee of women leaders from both communities who organized the workshops with the goals of exploring issues and avenues toward resolution and of examining areas of agreement and disagreement, based on a mutual commitment to a peaceful outcome respecting the needs and rights of both parties.

The first workshop brought together twenty Palestinian and Jewish women for three days of intense discussion as individuals rather than as leaders of their respective organizations (Dialogue Conference Between Jewish and Palestinian American Women, 1989). Besides the general goals, the conference was geared to help the participants get to know one another and their concerns, to build relationships for future work, and to discuss possible actions to support the peace process. Participants were carefully selected for their position in their communities, but also for an ability to listen to the other side. Each party also invited one woman living in the Middle East to add an element of ongoing involvement in the conflict. The workshop was facilitated by a balanced team of third party consultants consisting of one woman from each community and a third neutral facilitator, all with training and experience in conflict resolution.

The structured agenda for the workshop first set the stage for dialogue and then moved to carefully designed presentations and a discussion of history to clarify painful disagreements and understand the other side's perspective. Group caucuses then addressed the future of the conflict by developing principles and strategies for moving the peace process forward. Areas of agreement and disagreement were identified, and joint working groups developed ideas for future projects both within and between the communities. Evaluations of the conference were moderately positive, even though there was tense debate and disagreement on many issues. The commonality of women working together appeared to aid understanding, because emotional expression was included with political discussion, and because as women the participants shared similar values and goals. A clear outcome was to expand the dialogue process into the organizations and communities of the participants.

The second dialogue conference again involved twenty women leaders from the two communities, with new participants being integrated with a number from the first workshop (Dialogue Project Between American Jewish and Palestinian Women, 1990). This three-day session began with separate orientation and goal-setting caucuses for Palestinian and Jewish women followed by individual introductory statements that demonstrated the commitment to dialogue and the urgent need to resolve the conflict. Presentations on the peace process from the perspective of each community were followed by joint discussion that led into the development of action plans by the two caucuses. The sharing of action plans resulted in the formation of a joint coordinating committee to carry forward the dialogue agenda through various activities to educate both communities about the peace process. Mixed working groups then discussed how to implement different elements of the overall action plan. Participants indicated that the sharing process had led to a feeling of total-group cohesion and that the emphasis on action had created a sense of momentum.

The energy and goodwill created in the two workshops flowed into a third workshop and beyond into various joint activities designed to support the ongoing peace process. Public education initiatives have involved teams of Palestinian and Jewish women speaking in synagogues, churches, universities, and conferences of Jews and Arabs. In addition, two joint trips to Israel, the West Bank, and Gaza were carried out in 1993 and 1994. Meetings were held with formal and informal groupings on both sides and support and training services were provided to women's organizations involved in peace and development activities. In addition, the project has provided training to other dialogue groups in North America who are interested in fostering similar exchanges (Bernards 1994). The project continues to be well organized and balanced with a joint steering committee and cocoordination provided by Reena Bernards and Najat Arafat Khelil.

This illustration is noteworthy for its careful and collaborative planning and implementation. Immediately after the idea for the initiative arose, a move was made to assess mutual interest and to form a joint committee to oversee the work. A professional team of facilitators was engaged to help design the sessions and to inject ideas from the field of conflict resolution as appropriate, for example on the difference between win-lose and win-win approaches in the first workshop. In addition, the workshops evidenced a creative blending of experiential, emotionally focused activities to build relationships along with conceptual, task-orientated ones to address the substance of the conflict and its resolution. The conferences were thus able to create cohesion and trust between the groups of participants, and to harness the resulting positive energy toward concrete peacebuilding activities. Sensitivity to a balanced involvement of the two groups and commitment to the common goal of empowering women leaders are also highlights of the project.

Another useful illustration of dialogue work in the U.S.A. on the Middle East conflict is provided by a project undertaken by members of the Program on International Conflict Analysis and Resolution at Harvard University (Hicks, O'Doherty, Steiner, Taylor, Hadjipavlou-Trigeorgis & Weisberg 1994). PICAR was approached by an organization representing various nationalities to help the group go beyond superficialities to a deeper level of interaction to further their cooperative political mission. Hicks et al. (1994) formed a team of three facilitators and three observer-advisers to design and manage a series of eight two-hour dialogue sessions.

The facilitation team assumed that group identities are an essential aspect of intractable intergroup conflict and that these raise powerful emotions for individuals when they interact with the other group. Each group tends to hold a dichotomous conception of the relationship in that to recognize the legitimate needs of the other's identity is tantamount to denying the needs of one's own group. Thus, following Kelman's model of interactive problem solving, the team worked to move the participants through three stages of development necessary to achieve deeper mutual understanding. The first involves establishing a safe environment for developing a working trust that enables the challenging of perspectives without escalation and entrenchment. The second involves developing understanding and empathy of each other's hopes, fears, constraints, and needs, so that each can consider and incorporate the other's perspectives into their conception of the conflict. The third involves the differentiation and then the integration of the self, other, and national identities. In particular, this means acquiring a more complex view of the variations in the other party and coming to accept that both groups share responsibility for the conflict.

The group of fifteen participants included several Israelis, two Palestinians, and several persons from various Arab countries, all of whom were generally supportive of some form of self-determination for Palestinians in the West Bank and Gaza. The dialogue was initiated at about the same time as the formal peace negotiations got under way in Madrid, thus providing a context of political reality and possibility. To help establish a working trust, the facilitators laid out a number of ground rules, a central one for dialogue being a request for participants to speak to inform rather than convince and to listen to understand rather than to refute.

To initiate the discussions, the facilitators ask what a multiparty group could accomplish in the current context. This approach allowed important issues to crystallize out of the group's response. In ensuing sessions, a number of important and difficult issues were discussed, with the facilitation team providing observations and conceptual inputs where relevant. For example, at one point a facilitator noted how each party was demanding that the other make the first reconciliatory move, thus locking themselves into a state of immobility. As the dialogue progressed, the participants were able to articulate and understand the basic hope for recognized nationhood and the ultimate fear of never being legitimated, which both Israelis and Palestinians shared. These kinds of realizations were instrumental in assisting the participants in reaching their objective of deeper mutual understanding so that their political work together could be strengthened.

The facilitators' description of the dialogue (Hicks et al. 1994) is also notable for the self-awareness and candor in discussing their role and the conflicts they experienced and managed within the team. This form of analysis is extremely useful for educating facilitators in training and others who might presume to take on this challenging role. The development of ICR would clearly benefit from more such expositions.

An example of a long-term dialogue effort between Jews and Palestinians in the U.S.A. comes from the Syracuse Area Middle East Dialogue (SAMED), organized by Louis Kriesberg and Richard Schwartz of Syracuse University along with members of the local community (Schwartz 1989; Kriesberg 1994). This initiative is grounded in the assumption that grass roots, conciliatory dialogue can enhance mutual understanding and ultimately influence public opinion and policymaking toward reducing the damaging effects of apparently intractable conflict and engaging in de-escalatory activities. According to Schwartz (1989), dialogue can demonstrate that adversaries can learn from each other, generate creative ideas toward resolution, and gain access to influentials who can facilitate negotiations between the parties.

SAMED began in 1981 with a core group of twenty-one individuals evenly divided among Jews, Palestinians, and other Americans concerned about the Middle East conflict (Kriesberg & Shomar 1991). The participants were not personally involved in the conflict, but were loyal to their respective sides and relatively equal in social status (Schwartz 1989). They also had to accept the legitimacy of Israel and the right of self-determination for the Palestinians (Kriesberg 1994). Ground rules were laid out based on Kriesberg's understanding of conflict resolution and problem-solving workshops. These conditions enabled interaction that after three years had created a detailed and comprehensive statement of procedures for effective dialogue, covering the selection of participants, the process and content of the meetings, and the structure of the dialogue. For example, in the meetings, presentations on topics are balanced between the different sides and equal air time in discussions is ensured, while at the same time freedom of expression is encouraged by an agreement not to quote members outside the group. An attempt is made to formulate mutually agreeable positions on issues that focus on what the U.S. government and other groups can do to improve Palestinian-Israeli relations.

Along these lines, the dialogue discussed many difficult issues and though not reaching agreement or accommodation on all of them, was eventually able to produce a consensus statement calling for the mutual recognition of the PLO and Israel and for direct negotiations between them based on the legitimacy of both parties. This level of consensus did not come easily and the process was threatened at many points by tragic events occurring in the real world. However, conciliatory and symbolic acts of understanding and support helped keep the group together through difficult periods.

Subsequent to its own successful efforts, SAMED initiated contacts with other Middle East dialogue groups in the U.S. leading to the formation of a national coalition. These contacts indicated that although many efforts had been made to form dialogue groups, only about a half dozen were able to sustain themselves. The sharing of experiences among these coalition members produced a manual for dialogue initiatives (Breslow 1987). Concurrently members of SAMED organized a conference of influential Arab and Jewish scholars focusing on human rights and peace in the Middle East, which exhibited some of the characteristics of a problem-solving workshop (Schwartz 1987). The identity of the participants, who were from both the region and the United States, ensured that the ideas that emerged were passed on to their respective governments and other organizations (Kriesberg & Shomar 1991). In addition, SAMED members have met with members of Congress, State Department officials, and others who have influence in policymaking.

Schwartz (1989) concludes that although the relationship between grass roots dialogue and official policy is uncertain, the positive effects can counteract the negative influence of adversarial pressure groups and thus encourage decision makers toward reconciliatory policies. Along this line, SAMED stands as a unique and laudable example of systematic and sustained dialogue at the local level, which could be replicated in numerous settings to help move seemingly intractable conflicts off dead center.

Additional Illustrations

Different forms of dialogue meetings have been held between antagonists in a range of conflicts at various stages of escalation and de-escalation. Again, much of this work is not documented because the third party organizers do not publish their work for either pragmatic or ethical reasons. For example, over the years the Society of Friends (Quakers) has organized dialogue sessions between informal representatives of parties engaged in destructive conflict, but choose not to publicize these meetings apparently to protect both the process and the participants. For example, Hare (1989) mentions a Quaker-sponsored meeting that brought together American and Soviet social scientists during the height of the cold war for a week-long interchange. Many such dialogues take place under the umbrella of an academic or scientific enterprise to distinguish them from formal policymaking, and yet it is likely that many of them serve an important prenegotiation or paranegotiation function. The dialogues to be described here evidence much variation on numerous dimensions.

Paul Hare has taken part in a number of different dialogue interventions over the past two decades, and has characterized this work as consensus building and more recently as prenegotiation (Hare 1982, 1989). One illustration comes from a private intervention in escalating political conflict on the small island nation of Curaçao in the Caribbean Sea, in which a newly formed and radical party was pitted against conservative business interests (Hare, Carney & Ovsiew 1977). In 1969, the conflict erupted into a riot in the major city, which brought about the downfall of the government and led inhabitants to seek outside assistance on a number of fronts. Hare was invited to conduct a study of attitudes that might help shed light on the situation, but he proposed action research in which he would interview persons from the various factions to understand their basic concerns. The interviews led to some immediate actions to alleviate the situation, but more important to a series of dialogue seminars organized by a social science institute the following summer. These meetings focused on the economic and political concerns that had surfaced in the interviews, and brought together both radical and conservative elements to discuss common problems and consider solutions. The sessions culminated in a participative teach-in broadcast over national radio. Plans for additional meetings were eventually canceled, for the parties were now in direct communication and the normal political processes had been reinstituted. This intervention serves as an example of dialogue playing an important role in arresting escalation at a critical point in a serious political conflict.

A similar intervention in the Cambodian conflict, but at a different point in escalation, involved a week-long workshop on potential reconstruction chaired by Peter Wallensteen of Uppsala University (Wallensteen 1991). This session brought together Cambodian influentials and experts on various areas of development with outside experts to discuss all aspects of reconstruction during the time of the formal peace process. Cambodian participants came both from outside and inside the country, including government officials, and represented a wide spectrum of political opinion. The workshop was organized by two American NGOs (the U.S.-Indochina Reconciliation Project and Organizing for Development, an International Institute) and was hosted by the University Science Malaysia in Penang. Conflict resolution expertise and workshop facilitation was provided by Wallensteen and staff from the two NGOs.

The objectives were to provide a nonpolitical forum in which knowledge and experience from various perspectives could be pooled to develop a broadly accepted strategy for reconstruction. To build trust and confidence, the workshop was designed in three phases. After the exploration of different aspirations and images for the future of Cambodia, participants dialogued on strategic factors essential to an integrated approach for moving from the present reality to the desired future, and then worked cooperatively in teams on proposals for development in several key sectors including agriculture, health, and education.

Wallensteen (1991) concludes that the workshop succeeded in replacing prior fears and suspicion with a sense of trust in ways that initiated a constructive dialogue within the wider Cambodian community. What is also apparent about this intervention is the high level of professional expertise that went into the design and implementation processes, thus assuring a positive experience and useful outcomes for the participants and hopefully for the wider conflict.

Another example of dialogue comes from the work of the International Peace Research Institute in Oslo (PRIO), which houses a multinational staff of social scientists working on various projects in peace research and conflict resolution. Within its program on ethnic conflicts, PRIO has organized and facilitated meetings that informally bring together influential members of antagonistic groups. The clearest examples of ICR are two "consultations" focusing on the bitter sectarian conflict in Sri Lanka (PRIO 1988, 1989).

The first of these two-day sessions brought together a diverse group of participants from Sri Lanka, Europe, Latin America, and the United States to discuss the conditions necessary for a cessation of hostilities and the long-term prospects for peace and reconstruction. Sinhalese and Tamil participants were able to engage in rare and constructive dialogue and confrontation on the major issues in the conflict and their concerns and vision for the future of Sri Lanka. A considerable degree of consensus was reached in the session on the requirements and processes for moving toward resolution.

The second consultation involved Sri Lankans from the different ethnic groups and various political persuasions in an analysis of the conflict, a consideration of the necessary conditions for resolution, and an examination of the problems and prospects for establishing a multi-ethnic, democratic state. The first day of the consultation discussed five different future political scenarios for Sri Lanka and produced a list of more than forty recommendations to various actors who are involved or have influence in the conflict. On the second day, these recommendations were presented and discussed in a wider public forum attended by other Sri Lankans, Norwegians, and various diplomats concerned with the conflict. The first day developed some degree of consensus on directions toward resolution, while the second day addressed the question of transferring these products to the wider political process. The PRIO consultations thus stand as a small but valuable example of how a respected institutional base can be used to mount dialogue initiatives.

A moderately structured example of dialogue intervention comes from an application of the decision seminar to the question of postwar governance in Afghanistan, carried out by two American facilitators in 1990 (Willard & Norchi 1993). The *decision seminar* is a structured and integrated problem-solving technique developed by Harold Lasswell, one of the founders of the policy sciences, to be applicable to instruction, decision making, and policy clarification. The approach provides the participants with an opportunity to mutually identify, analyze, and propose strategies for dealing with shared problems.

The seminar brought together a diverse group of influential, largely academic, Afghan refugees living in Pakistan who represented a wide range of political and other affiliations. The seminar leaders provided input at various points on a number of topics, including the tasks of decision making, basic values and human rights, the functions and drafting of a constitution, and an interactive approach to problem solving. The Afghans then applied these concepts and intellectual tools to their own situation through discussion in small groups as well as in the total seminar. The facilitators reviewed each morning session that afternoon and modified the next day's session to maximize mutual inquiry into common interests. Security concerns made it difficult to assess participant reactions outside the workshop, but a high degree of involvement was observed during the sessions and participants expressed disappointment at the ending. Thus the seminar provided a unique opportunity for a varied and divided group of Afghan influentials to discuss in an interactive, consensual manner the postwar governance of their country, and as such demonstrates a useful prototype both scholarly and political (Willard & Norchi 1993).

Various dialogue interventions in situations of intergroup and international conflict have been organized through the Center for Psychology and Social Change affiliated with the Harvard Medical School. The center's project on facilitating dialogue across ideologies has developed a structured process, based at first on family systems therapy, to promote understanding between groups whose intergroup perceptions are distorted by hostility, and to encourage cooperation across ideological or cultural divides.

An initial example of this approach was an experiential workshop held in 1987 at the Congress of the International Physicians for the Prevention of Nuclear War (Chasin & Herzig 1988). The objective was to create an atmosphere in which some forty participants from fifteen countries, particularly the Americans and the Soviets, could openly and respectfully discuss the common assumptions that they held of one another. Using a technique known as circular questioning, the facilitators asked five separate groups (Soviets, Soviet allies, Americans, American allies, and nonaligned) to generate the assumptions they believed others held of their group, and then to indicate which of these were least widely held in their own group. Also, each of the participants constructed a one-sentence refutation of the erroneous assumption that aroused the most negative emotional response in them. The groups then shared these two pieces of information in a structured exchange, with a wide range of useful confrontations and realizations on all sides. Chasin and Herzig (1988) conclude that these techniques produced dialogue at a much deeper level than in most other exchanges, so that dangerous modes of thinking could be challenged and differences in values could be better understood.

Further workshops on Soviet and American perceptions were held at the next three IPPNW congresses, and similar dialogue interventions have been carried out between whites and Asians in Australia, between American and Soviet film makers, and between peace activists and defense analysts in the United States (Chasin and Herzig 1993). More recently, through the Public Conversations Project of the Family Institute of Cambridge, a team of dialogue facilitators has developed a systematic model to address the schism between pro-life and pro-choice advocates (Becker, Chasin, Chasin, Herzig & Roth 1992). About twenty evening workshops have been held, which bring together a small group of people evenly split on the abortion issue in a structured process that promotes respectful exchange and enhances safety. Clear communication of expectations, a dinner together to build familiarity, and the laying out of ground rules are followed by the careful posing of a series of questions designed to encourage openness and authenticity among participants and to explore any "grey areas" or uncertainties in their beliefs. Participants then ask one another questions arising from curiosity rather than rhetorical questions, which are usually disguised statements. The final phase involves identifying useful themes for further discussion and inviting reflections on the process and closing comments from participants. The closing comments generally contrast the productivity of the dialogue sessions with the futility of adversarial debate, and follow-up contacts with participants generally indicate the experience to be personally enriching and eye-opening in regard to the genuine concerns of the other side. Although the project's focus on the abortion issue may seem removed from intercommunal conflict, the highly professional delivery of a carefully crafted dialogue process has applicability not only to other divisive public issues but also to more complex intergroup conflicts.

The final illustration of dialogue is unique in two respects. First, it focused on a nonviolent rather than a destructive protracted conflict, and second, it was sponsored by a national newsmagazine. The focus was the long-standing conflict between separatists in the province of Quebec and federalists from all parts of Canada who wish to keep the confederation together. Since the 1960s, when there was a brief period of violent activity by some elements of the separatist movement, the conflict has taken a largely political turn, with both provincial and federal separatist parties enjoying much support in the province. The Canadian confederation of ten provinces and two territories is thus at the most serious point of potential dissolution in its 125-year history. A number of constitutional conferences and proposals in the early 1990s failed to garner the required governmental or public support, and the issue of addressing the aspirations of the largely French-speaking province of Quebec remains unresolved. In this context, *Maclean's* magazine engaged Roger Fisher and colleagues from the Conflict Management Group to lead a weekend workshop focusing on the future of Canada (Maclean's 1991).

The twelve participants were selected by a national polling firm as representative of important clusters of conflicting opinions on national issues—the primary one being whether Quebec should remain in Canada or become an independent country. The facilitators invited a sharing of concerns that identified three major topics for discussion—the constitutional issue centering on Quebec separation, economic problems in the confederation, and a need for mutual understanding to overcome the current crisis. This led into the development of strategies for action on major problems, which were expressed through the use of the single text procedure to produce a mutually acceptable set of suggestions for the future of the country. According to the report, the most unique aspect of the workshop in contrast to other meetings was real dialogue—an opportunity through both task and social interaction for the participants to engage in searching, challenging, and frequently touching interaction in pursuit of a shared vision for their country. This intense form of exchange took the participants beyond the usual sterile debate to a vision of a renewed Canada in which all citizens would feel accepted and fairly treated. This vision provided for both general strategies and specific proposals in the three major topic areas to serve as a basis for further discussion.

A follow-up workshop six months later brought together the same twelve participants and facilitators to discuss and provide suggestions on the future of the country in the light of the ongoing constitutional proposals (Maclean's 1992). Five politicians were also invited to act as observers and advisers on the complexities and difficulties of constitutional reform. The discussions evaluated the federal government's current constitutional proposal and developed a formula for renewed federalism and shared Canadian values, which all participants, including Quebec separatists, found acceptable. The consensus produced an action plan that warmly endorsed the recognition of Quebec as a distinct society, argued for self-government for native peoples, and dealt with several matters of constitutional reform. These results were communicated to politicians involved in constitutional discussions, and the process and outcomes of the session were reported in *Maclean's* and also in a nationally televised documentary. Unfortunately the constitutional package later agreed to by the federal and provincial governments was rejected in a national referendum, and Quebec separation now looms as an even stronger possibility.

The Methodology of Dialogue

Although the different interventions evidence variation on several dimensions, they also exhibit common elements. In general, these interventions are directed toward open and respectful communication between antagonists with a focus on underlying concerns and the emotional as well as the cognitive aspects of contentious issues. Dialogues thus usually provide for ventilation or catharsis between the parties that is often conducive to the subsequent steps of problem solving and reconciliation. An important emphasis is on simply understanding the other party and the conflict as a mutual problem, rather than attempting to change the other or to resolve the conflict. These elements are often seen as prerequisites to other processes, such as negotiation or problem solving, at least within the context of a conflict resolution approach.

A final essential element of dialogue is the involvement of the third party facilitator, often as a team of professionals from relevant disciplines. The facilitation team acts as an initial repository of trust for the participants, sets appropriate expectations, provides a design for the sessions, serves to open up and improve communication, and confronts adversarial and destructive behavior when necessary. Thus the facilitator requires a particular identity and role and carries out essential functions in the form of behavioral tactics, very much like the third party consultant described in chapter 7. These commonalities underscore the appropriateness of considering dialogue a form of ICR.

Dialogue practitioners have drawn on various sources for their methodology, and have also developed procedures through their own experience. Some intervenors find a source in cultures, societies, or organizations that take a consensus approach to decision making and problem solving. Paul Hare, for example, notes how both the Society of Friends and the followers of Gandhi use a consensus method in reaching decisions (Hare 1982, 1989). A well-known Quaker peacemaker, Adam Curle (1990), notes how the Quaker business meeting promotes the expression of diverse opinions and seeks the sense of the meeting without the casting of votes. Hare (1989) elaborates that members are encouraged to come to meetings with an open mind, to be ready to listen to one another to gain new facts and insights. Members are asked to interact without antagonism, but not to give up strong convictions or to remain silent simply to reach superficial agreement. The goal is to discover new ways out of difficult problems through a deeper search for unity in which integrative solutions emerge that were not at first perceived by anyone. This plan can lead either to consensus, in which the chosen solution is acceptable to everyone although it is not everyone's first choice, or possibly to unanimity, wherein it is the first choice of all members.

Hare (1982) has produced a summary set of guidelines for the consensus method, based on Quaker and Ghandhian principles as well as results from social science laboratory experiments that have demonstrated the advantages of consensus over majority vote. First, participants are urged to seek a solution that incorporates all points of view, rather than using majority vote, averaging, or bargaining procedures. Second, participants must approach the task on a logical basis, giving their own opinions while seeking out differences, rather than arguing to gain more information. Third, participants are asked to address the group as a whole while showing concern for each individual opinion, rather than confronting and criticizing individuals. Fourth, a group coordinator is useful to help formulate consensus and to ensure agreement is at a fundamental rather than a superficial level. Fifth, it is essential not to press for agreement primarily for time's sake, but to hold more meetings if necessary and to share responsibility in the group for the continuing use of consensus. These guidelines not only spell out some of the behaviors that are essential to dialogue but also underscore why consensus decision making is an integral part of interactive methods directed toward mutually acceptable solutions in situations of intense conflict.

The Syracuse Area Middle East Dialogue (SAMED) has articulated procedures out of its own experience over a lengthy period and with considerable self-insight. The SAMED model of reconciliatory dialogue began with the assumptions that the parties need to be relatively equal and need to maintain acceptance in their own group at the same time they develop loyalty toward each other as individuals and work to understand each other's positions (Schwartz 1989). After three years of monthly meetings, the members crafted a set of detailed procedures covering the dialogue process and structure.

With regard to the selection of SAMED members, although all are U.S. citizens, Jewish and Palestinian participants must have a significant identification with their respective parties in the conflict, that is, Israel and the Palestinian people. Members should evidence diversity in various social characteristics including gender, and must be regarded as respectable, mainstream members of their communities. In structure, SAMED formed a steering committee composed of two persons from each community (on a rotating basis) to plan agendas and draft statements for discussion and possible release.

The procedures covering the process and content of the discussions constitute the essence of dialogue from the point of view of ICR. At initial meetings (and one assumes when new members join the group), much attention is given to getting acquainted by having each member talk about his or her history and involvement in the Middle East without interruption or discussion, and by socializing after the formal meeting. Ongoing meetings are governed by careful ground rules involving balanced presentations, equal air time in discussions, and no attribution of statements outside the group to encourage free discussion.

In content, the emphasis has been on sharing information from the participants' different backgrounds and networks, both personal as well as articles or other material. Besides the initial consensus statement, SAMED has worked to develop agreed-upon positions on various aspects of Israeli-Palestinian relations, particularly as affected by

U.S. policy. Finally, the dialogue has tried to gain attention for its statements and recommendations with an emphasis on what the government and other groups in the U.S. can do to help de-escalate and resolve the conflict. In this way, SAMED demonstrates how an initial dialogue can be systematically implemented to build a strong base from which additional conflict resolution activities can flow.

The dialogue work of Richard Chasin and his colleagues illustrates how theoretically based principles and procedures from one domain of professional practice can be adapted to another—in this case from family therapy to polarized public controversies and protracted sociopolitical conflicts. These family therapists make the point that adversaries in intense conflicts behave very much like family members locked in unending games or engaged in acrimonious divorce litigation (Chasin & Herzig 1993). Each side perceives itself as morally right and as the victim of unwarranted attacks from a self-centered and destructive enemy. Each side works to enlist allies to support its interpretations and actions as the stakes in the conflict become greater and greater. Patterns of interaction between the antagonists become ritualized, increasingly costly and highly resistant to change. In particular, the parties constantly engage in polarized debate and appear unable to enter into constructive interaction.

The general objective of the family therapy approach is therefore to lead participants away from deadlock and toward authentic dialogue (Chasin & Herzig, 1993). This is accomplished by drawing on systemic interventions taken from different schools of family therapy. Examples include giving instructions that obstruct unproductive interaction cycles and promote problem solving, and asking questions that challenge participants to increase the number and variety of connections and distinctions that they are making. Through such techniques, adversaries are stimulated to think and act in new ways that are like family members engaged in therapy sessions. The role of the third party professional is to provide an appropriate structure for the dialogue and to facilitate interaction for optimal usefulness.

Based on their experience applying a family systems approach in a number of different contexts and conflicts, Chasin and his colleagues have developed principles and guidelines for planning and conducting systemic dialogue interventions (Chasin & Herzig 1993). These cover the planning and preparation for the dialogue, the structure and facilitation of the meeting, and follow-up activities. Preparation requires forming a team of experienced facilitators who also collectively have a well-informed grasp of the conflict, so that they understand the key players and the chronic patterns of destructive interaction. Participants are chosen as influentials, grass roots individuals, or members of common professions or interest groups depending on the nature of the intervention. In all cases, it is essential to build trust with the participants and to clearly communicate goals and set expectations for the intervention.

To structure the meeting itself, Chasin and Herzig (1993) propose five stages that assist the participants in becoming acquainted, agreeing on ground rules, sharing information through opening questions, engaging in further discussion tailored to the specific dialogue, and experiencing a sense of closure. To manage the dialogue effectively, it is essential that the facilitators maintain their role clarity, avoid bias, be clear on process expectations, and consistently enforce the ground rules. In addition, the facilitators encourage participants to speak from personal experience, to avoid attributions to others, and to note exceptions to old patterns when they occur. They also constantly monitor and redesign the agenda as necessary.

With regard to follow-up, Chasin and Herzig (1993) emphasize how evaluations of the dialogue and later calls to participants communicate continuing concern about their well-being and also provide valuable feedback for program improvement. Information gleaned from these sources has reinforced their belief that effective dialogue is much more than a pleasant conversation to be contrasted with typical political exchanges. Indeed, these opportunities for authentic and respectful interaction may be crucial for ending the many cycles of hatred and violence that pervade our diverse and divisive world (Chasin & Herzig 1993). This proposition underscores the centrality of dialogue processes in ICR.

7

Third Party Consultation
A Core Model of Interactive Conflict Resolution

Interactive Conflict Resolution was defined in a focused manner as involving small-group, problem-solving discussions between unofficial representatives of parties (groups, communities, states) engaged in protracted social conflict (see the Introduction). However, depending on the exact identity of the participants and the approach used, there are different variants of ICR (see especially chapters 5 and 6). The broader definition of ICR as facilitated activities in communication, education, training, and consultation provides for even greater variety and complexity in the field.

To gain some sense of order and understanding amid this variety, it is useful to posit a generic and yet focused model of practice that captures and elucidates the core of the methodology. The model of *third party consultation* (TPC) that I developed in the early seventies is an attempt to do this (Fisher 1972, 1976). This model emphasizes the central if not essential role of the third party in conflict analysis and resolution, and also makes clear that ICR is a form of consultation. These emphases carry important implications that need to be explicated.

The chapter begins with a description of the development of the generic model of TPC, based primarily on the pioneering work of Walton (1969), Blake, Shepard and Mouton (1964), and Burton (1969). Applications and evaluations of the model are then presented to assess its validity and utility as a descriptive and prescriptive model of practice. Finally, the ethics of ICR will be addressed by considering the field as a variant of professional consultation.

A Model of Third Party Consultation

My initial interest in undertaking doctoral study at the University of Michigan (in social psychology with a minor in international relations) was to explore ways of understanding and improving international negotiation. However, an initial foray through the literature indicated that there already was considerable wisdom about effective negotiation, and that often it was attitudinal and relationship problems rather than faulty negotiation practice that made agreement difficult. This led to a search for innovative methodologies designed to clarify misperceptions, broaden attitudes, and improve relationships so that conflict could be effectively addressed by the parties themselves.

The term "third party consultation" was coined by Richard Walton (1969) in his seminal work on interpersonal peacemaking between corporate executives. Based on his professional expertise as a sensitivity group trainer and organization development consultant, Walton intervened successfully in a number of dysfunctional interpersonal conflicts between role-related individuals in organizational settings. These case studies provided the empirical basis for constructing what Walton termed "a middle range theory of a form of sociotherapy," that is, the science and art of treating dysfunctions in social relationships.

Walton (1969, 1987) emphasizes the critical role of the third party in arranging and facilitating productive confrontations, that is, dialogue meetings, in which the parties engage each other and directly discuss the difficult issues between them. His approach is rooted in a diagnostic model of interpersonal conflict that acknowledges both substantive and emotional issues and serves as a conceptual basis for intervention. The third party role is implemented through a number of strategic functions that capture the core of the methodology— encouraging mutual positive motivation to reduce the conflict, balancing the situational power of the parties, synchronizing confrontation efforts, pacing the phases of the dialogue, promoting openness, enhancing communication, and maintaining an optimum level of tension. The functions are enacted through a range of tactical choices and behavioral interventions within an overall consultation effort, which includes preliminary interviewing of the principals, influencing the physical and social context for the confrontation, intervening in the dialogue, and planning for future dialogue.

Walton also considers the necessary attributes of the third party, including professional expertise, high control over the process, moderate knowledge of the conflict, and neutrality regarding outcomes. All in all, Walton contributes a systematic, theoretically based, empirically derived conceptualization that captures many of the essentials of facilitative third party intervention in a conflict system. His approach to interpersonal peacemaking is widely considered a form of "process consultation" and has taken its place as a standard offering in the practice of organization development (e.g., French & Bell 1995).

Also in the organizational domain, the ground-breaking work of Robert Blake, Jane Mouton, and colleagues stands as a central contribution to the social technology of intergroup conflict resolution. Based on management training studies by Blake and Mouton (1961), which documented insidious intergroup conflict, Blake, Shepard, and Mouton (1964) present a number of consulting interventions that address dysfunctional relationships between organizational groups, such as management and union, headquarters and field offices, and companies brought together in a merger. These interventions generally follow the design of structured human-relations training laboratories, wherein the members of the conflicting groups focus on the conflict between them with third party regulation. Different procedures can be used to facilitate the mutual diagnosis of the conflict (e.g., the development and exchange of group images) and to initiate joint problem solving (e.g., searching together for alternative solutions). The overall goal of the interventions is to transform a mutually hostile "win-lose" orientation into a collaborative "win-win" relationship.

The type of intergroup interventions pioneered by Blake and Mouton have also taken their place in organization development (e.g., Burke 1974; French & Bell 1995). Blake and Mouton (1984) redesign the intergroup problem-solving technology into a format that can be used by the groups in conflict themselves to diagnose causes and restore trust and respect. The potential utility of this line of work for developing interventions at the intercommunal and international levels is considerable, although the greater complexity, cultural variability, and other unique elements at these levels need to be taken into account.

The contributions of John Burton to ICR were described in chapter 1. Burton's theory of practice, first expressed as controlled communication and later as problem-solving conflict resolution, has many elements that are compatible with a generic TPC model. In particular, Burton (1969, 1987) emphasizes the essential role of the third party panel in creating a nonthreatening atmosphere and in establishing effective communication. Moreover, the identity of the panel as social scientists allows them to inject knowledge about conflict processes into the discussions for the use of the participants. Burton also clearly sets this innovative methodology apart from traditional third party interventions such as arbitration, conciliation, and mediation.

The development of the TPC model (Fisher 1972) was largely based on the theorizing of Walton, Blake, Shepard, Mouton, and Burton, but was also informed by the work of Satir (1967) on family therapy, Lakin's (1969) intercommunal interventions (see chapter 6), and Doob's workshop approach (see chapter 2). In addition, it soon became clear that the basic tenets of the model were compatible with the conceptualizations of Herbert Kelman and his colleagues on problem-solving workshops (Kelman 1972; Kelman & Cohen 1976) as well as other leading scholar-practitioners in the field (e.g., de Reuck 1974; Mitchell 1981).

A revised version of the model is presented in fig. 7.1, each circle denoting a major component of the method (Fisher 1976). The model was developed to emphasize the unique and essential role, identity, and strategies of the impartial and skilled third party who enters directly into the arena of conflict to aid the antagonists in analyzing and dealing with the underlying attitudes and issues in their relationship. The third party *identity* requires the consultant to be an impartial, knowledgeable, and skilled scholar-practitioner with the expertise to facilitate productive *confrontation* between the parties, that is, the direct discussion of contentious issues. This requires skills in human relations, professional consultation, and systematic group problem solving. Knowledge of conflict and its resolution in a range of systems is essential as is moderate understanding of the conflict being analyzed.

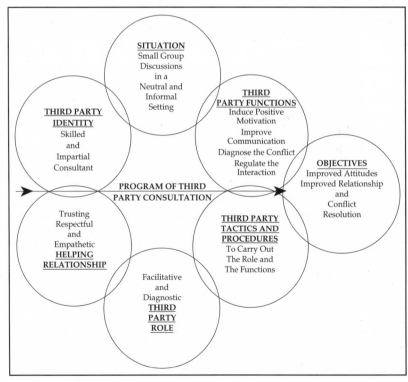

Source: Fisher 1976.

Fig. 7.1. A Model of Third Party Consultation

The initial TPC model (Fisher 1972) also included the identity and the role of the participants, who may vary from being simply loyal and representative members of their respective groups, to being appointed representatives, who while unofficial, are influential with their respective decision-making elites. The role of participants is expected to shift during the discussions from adversarial defenders of their groups' positions and behavior to collaborating analysts and problem solvers who work jointly to understand the conflict and search for mutually acceptable avenues to resolve it.

An adequate third party identity lays the basis for a *helping or consulting relationship* with the parties characterized by trust, respect, and understanding, which is essential to constructive confrontation and problem solving. The third party arranges a setting, or *situation,* for the discussions, often away from the usual environments of the participants, to allow for informal and flexible interaction like to that of an academic seminar. The *role,* or appropriate pattern of behavior, for the third party is basically facilitative and diagnostic, but is also noncoercive, nonevaluative, and nondirective over outcomes—in contrast to other third party roles including arbitration and most forms of mediation (see Fisher & Keashly 1988, 1990).

The third party *functions* capture the core strategies of the method that are necessary to institute productive confrontation and effective problem solving. The consultant works to induce mutual positive motivation for problem solving, improves both the openness and accuracy of communication through interpersonal and small-group facilitation skills, assists in the analysis or diagnosis of the conflict by applying concepts from social science, and regulates the interaction by confronting adversarial and disruptive behavior and by moving the discussions through the phases of group problem solving. The functions are brought to life through specific behavioral *tactics* (e.g., summarizing, stopping repetitive interactions) and more general *procedures,* or exercises (e.g., the exchange of intergroup images).

Supportive activities by the third party, such as preliminary interviews and follow-up activities, are also required to build an overall *program of consultation* directed toward a set of *objectives.* Although these will vary from program to program, they usually include improved, that is, more veridical, complex, and positive attitudes, an improved relationship involving greater appreciation and trust, and resolution of the conflict in the sense of mutual, self-sustaining solutions. Furthermore, the study of conflict was identified as an objective in the initial model to underscore the unique learning opportunity that the method provides for the consultants themselves and their disciplines (Fisher 1972).

Evaluation of the Model

The TPC model has been used as a guide in planning programs of intergroup problem solving in organizational, community, and international settings (see Fisher 1990). These programs have taken a demonstration research approach, which assesses the process and the outcomes of the intervention to gauge the utility and effectiveness of the model. Selected interventions at the intergroup and international levels will illustrate how the model has been evaluated as a theory of practice.

One initial applications involved a community intervention in a recently built neighborhood in a small Canadian city that was experiencing the insidious and deleterious effects of intergroup conflict (Fisher & White 1976b). Through a questionable decision in community planning, five streets in the neighborhood of about a thousand dwelling units were physically split down the middle, with attractive and varied private homes on one side, and drab, uniform public-housing units down the other. Over several years, the physical split, which was paralleled by differences in economic well-being, had escalated into a social-psychological schism between private home owners and public-housing tenants that evidenced many of the classic symptoms of intergroup conflict. Members of the two groups spoke openly about the other in ways that demonstrated stereotyping, discrimination, antagonism, ineffective communication, and low motivation to deal constructively with the conflict. A number of efforts at improvement, for example, the acquisition of a community center, not only were thwarted but became issues in the escalation of the conflict (see Fisher & White 1976a).

A colleague, James White, and I had been involved in community research and development activities in the neighborhood. In consultation with community members, we decided to initiate a pilot program of third party consultation designed to induce positive attitude change with a view to improving the wider relationship and de-escalating the conflict. The project was designed along the lines of experimental action research, with an emphasis on rigorously evaluating the outcomes in attitude change. Participants were recruited from influential members of the two groups who were involved in community activities. An experimental design was implemented with two consultation groups and two parallel, nondiscussion control groups, all of whom took part in extensive interviews before and after the intervention. The consultation groups consisted of eight participants each (four private home owners and four public housing tenants), who engaged in four discussion meetings of three hours each over a two-week period. The agendas were modeled on the work of Blake, Shepard, and Mouton (1964) and involved the development and exchange of intergroup images and perceptions of an ideal relationship as well as a discussion of joint activities that would improve the neighborhood.

The implementation of the TPC model was comprehensively evaluated using a combination of qualitative and quantitative methods. The meetings were tape recorded for later process analysis, and the substance of the discussions was captured on a large sketch pad. The pre- and post-interviews of about one hour each were conducted by a research assistant who was blind to the group identity of the interviewees, and covered the respondent's perceptions of the neighborhood, the other group, the intergroup relationship, an ideal relationship, and the future of the neighborhood. Transcriptions of the recorded interviews were subjected to content analysis using rating scales and coding categories that reliably assessed the complexity, positiveness, and behavioral orientations of each respondent's attitudes (Fisher 1977). Four weeks after the consultation groups ended, participants completed an evaluation questionnaire, which assessed their reactions to the program.

The most important results of the project are the attitudinal changes induced by the consultation program, for very few applications of TPC have undertaken a detailed and rigorous evaluation of such effects, even though many claim them based on case study impressions (see Fisher 1983 and chapter 9). The ratings and codings in each attitudinal area were combined into three composite scores, and the differences between pre- and post-scores were tested statistically. Table 7.1 presents the outcomes on attitude change in complexity, positiveness, and behavioral orientations.

In comparison to the control groups, members of the consultation groups demonstrated increased complexity and increased positiveness of attitudes, but not increased behavioral orientations to improve the situation. The differences are partly due to decreases in the scores for the control groups, which are likely attributable to a decrease in task motivation in the second interview, as well as a sense of increasing pessimism in the neighborhood during the time of the consultation program. This latter factor also may explain the lack of change in behavioral orientations, with respondents feeling little could be accomplished without changes in public-housing policy and other structural elements of the situation. This feeling led the consultants to initiate other programs of consultation that brought together a number of organized groups in the neighborhood to address the issues (Fisher 1976; Fisher & White 1976a).

Theoretically, the project demonstrated the utility of the TPC

Table 7.1.
Analysis of Attitude Change in the Housing Groups Study

| | Composite Rating Scores | | | | | | |
| | Consultation Group | | Comparison Group | | | | |
Score	M	σ	M	σ	t	df	p
	1. Complexity						
Pretest	16.62	3.38	16.21	4.17			
Posttest	18.00	4.34	14.50	4.99			
Change	1.38	3.57	−1.71	4.14	2.07	25	<.05
	2. Positiveness						
Pretest	19.62	4.61	21.14	6.44			
Posttest	22.62	7.58	17.28	6.02			
Change	3.00	8.26	−3.86	7.38	2.28	25	<.05
	3. Orientations						
Pretest	19.23	7.01	15.64	5.68			
Posttest	18.77	4.99	15.93	5.18			
Change	−0.46	5.80	0.29	5.28	0.35	25	n.s.

Source: Fisher and White 1976a.

model as a useful guide for the design of the program, including the behavior of the consultants. The discussions demonstrated constructive dialogue on issues of mutual concern and pointed the way toward an ideal relationship involving trust, respect, and cooperation. Participants' responses on the evaluation questionnaire affirmed that an honest, informal atmosphere for productive confrontation had been established, and that the third party team was seen as impartial and effective. Participants reported increased awareness and understanding of the other group, thus paralleling the changes in attitudinal complexity and positiveness. In short, the model appears to have been successfully implemented and to have produced the predicted changes, thus providing an initial indication of its validity.

The TPC model was also implemented and evaluated at the international level through a pilot workshop on the India-Pakistan conflict (Fisher 1980). With the assistance of William Feader, the International Student Advisor at the University of Saskatchewan, I was able to organize a series of problem-solving discussions involving Indian and Pakistani nationals living in Canada. The design of the sessions followed procedures created by Blake, Shepard, and Mouton (1964) for the development and exchange of intergroup perceptions. Specifically, each week for four weeks, the two national groups first met separately to develop their perceptions and then met jointly to share and clarify these. The topics included the present relationship, the self and other national images, an ideal relationship, and the major issues and potential solutions to the conflict.

The workshop sessions were tape recorded and pre- and post-interviews were held with the participants. Given the small n, the interview protocols were not subjected to content and statistical analyses, but the responses generally showed increased understanding and more positive attitudes. More important in assessing the implementation of the model, this project is the only one in the literature that provides a detailed and systematic analysis of workshop discussions.

The recordings of the joint sessions were subjected to two forms of process analysis. The first used interaction process analysis, as developed by Bales (1950), to monitor behaviors that are common to small-group, problem-solving discussions. This analysis indicated that the sessions followed a pattern of interaction like other types of interactive groups, thus supporting the validity of the model. That is, the observed percentages for various behavioral categories (e.g, agrees, asks for opinion, shows tension) were within the ranges suggested by Bales as characteristic of problem-solving discussions.

The second process analysis used coding categories developed to capture the third party functions and tactics. The coding of each of the four functions was operationalized by three or four coding categories that the model depicts as the predominant tactics used to implement that function. Table 7.2 presents the percentage of total third party behaviors that each tactic and function accounted for in each of the four joint meetings and overall. In overall percentages, two functions stand out—inducing motivation and improving communication. Given the short duration of the workshop, it is not surprising that encouraging and supporting the participants to engage in problem solving and assisting them in communicating with each other are the most frequent functions. In a longer workshop, one would expect greater diagnosis of the conflict as more time would be available for injecting concepts and stimulating self-diagnosis by the parties. The low amount of regulation was likely due to the use of structured procedures for the sharing of perceptions, and also perhaps to the existence of single meetings before the joint meetings, in which the norms for constructive discussion were first set.

The relative contribution of the different functions over the course of the workshop is a useful indicator of the overall flow of the model. Inducing motivation was very high in the first meeting, and though it remained prominent throughout the workshop, was lower in the three subsequent meetings. Improving communication was also prominent

able 7.2.
hird Party Functions and Tactics in the India-Pakistan Workshop

	Observed percentage of total acts				
'unction and tactic	*Meeting one*	*Meeting two*	*Meeting three*	*Meeting four*	*All meetings*
. Inducing positive motivation					
a. Encouraging problem solving	5.7	6.7	3.6	1.1	4.5
b. Supporting participants	40.3	19.2	37.8	28.6	30.8
c. Maintaining optimum tension	2.2	3.0	1.0	8.2	3.5
d. Balancing situational power	1.5	3.7	1.3	.0	1.8
Total	49.7	32.6	43.7	37.9	40.6
. Improving communication					
a. Eliciting information	9.5	16.6	12.0	6.0	11.4
b. Paraphrasing, empathizing	3.2	1.0	3.3	.5	2.0
c. Translating, clarifying	8.5	18.6	23.0	14.2	16.2
d. Summarizing	2.7	3.4	6.5	1.9	3.6
Total	23.9	39.6	44.8	22.6	33.2
3. Diagnosing the conflict					
a. Injecting information	5.5	11.5	4.6	34.9	13.6
b. Processing and feedback	.2	.4	.3	.8	.4
c. Stimulating self-diagnosis	2.5	1.8	1.8	.5	1.7
Total	8.2	13.7	6.7	36.2	15.7
4. Regulating the interaction					
a. Pacing the phases	4.5	1.6	1.0	.0	1.8
b. Initiating-monitoring agenda	12.7	8.9	2.8	3.3	7.1
c. Controlling disruptive interaction	1.0	3.6	1.0	.0	1.6
Total	18.2	14.1	4.8	3.3	10.5

Source: Fisher 1980.

through all four meetings, but was lower at the beginning and end, and higher in the middle. These findings make sense in that facilitating motivation for problem solving is essential in the early going, whereas controlling and improving communication takes on more importance after the necessary climate has been established. In addition, once the participants come to share the approach and norms of the discussions, there is less need for third party intervention in the communication process. Also congruent with the model, regulating the interaction was high in the initial meeting and declined throughout, ostensibly as the participants became used to the agenda and procedures. Similarly, diagnosing the conflict, while a less prominent function overall, was more frequent in the fourth meeting, at which point motivation, communication, and regulation have all been established. Also, the agenda for the fourth meeting (issues and potential solutions) called for more diagnosis than previous meetings.

Thus the process analyses of workshop sessions generally support the validity of the TPC model in participant and third party behaviors. The discussions appear like other forms of small-group problem solving. The third party interventions are largely captured by the strategic functions as operationalized by the behavioral tactics, and the dynamic flow of interventions over time makes sense in relation to the model. The model is thereby supported as a useful guide for practice and as a conceptual framework for articulating and understanding the approach and behavior of third party consultants.

The TPC model has also served as a useful touchstone in planning and implementing more recent work on the Cyprus conflict (Fisher 1991, 1992). Through the auspices of the now-defunct Canadian Institute for International Peace and Security (CIIPS) two conflict analysis workshops were held on the Cyprus conflict (see chapter 2). Given the sensitivity and intractability of the conflict, considerable attention was given the initial components of the model, that is, the third party identity and the building of a respectful consulting relationship with the two parties. This emphasis was even more salient because there have been several informal third party interventions, both attempted and completed, during the conflict that have been judged inappropriate and at times unacceptable by some of the Cypriots themselves. Thus it has become particularly demanding, as perhaps it should be, for an interested third party consultant to initiate a program of interaction.

CIIPS was established by an act of Parliament in 1984, and abolished through a similar process in 1992, after an unfortunate and shortsighted budget cut by the government. Its mandate was to increase knowledge and understanding of peace and security issues from a Canadian perspective in arms control, disarmament, defense, and conflict resolution. Within conflict resolution, CIIPS sponsored conferences and seminars on regional conflicts in which there is a Canadian interest. I participated in most of these events, and during 1989–91 served as a senior research fellow at CIIPS. There was an interest in the Cyprus conflict, because of the role that the Canadian forces played in the establishment and maintenance of the U.N. peacekeeping force on the island from 1964 to 1993. In addition, Canadians of Greek and Turkish Cypriot origin encouraged the government and CIIPS to undertake studies of the conflict and its possible resolution.

During 1988–89, CIIPS held a series of four seminars on the Cyprus conflict, bringing together academics, analysts, diplomats, policymakers, peacekeepers, and concerned Canadians of Cypriot origin to discuss the various elements of the conflict in historical, political, economic and constitutional terms. Papers and presentations were discussed by the multidisciplinary and multinational participants and a summary report and a collected volume of selected papers were published (Lafreniere & Mitchell 1990; Salem 1992). The last seminar, in June 1989, included ten Cypriots from the island, five from each community, who held influential positions in their respective administrations. The reaction to the seminars was highly positive, and the series established CIIPS as a credible, impartial, and legitimate third party institution in the eyes of the two parties.

In 1990, CIIPS instituted a follow-up project on Cyprus, under my direction, to assess the usefulness of TPC for examining the difficult transition from peacekeeping to peacemaking, and to see if conflict analysis workshops could serve as a means of dialogue and peacebuilding between the two sides. Over the next year, two workshops were held, one in Canada with Canadians of Turkish and Greek Cypriot origin, and the second in England bringing together influential individuals from the two communities on Cyprus (Fisher 1991, 1992).

To implement the project, emphasis had to be on continuing to establish an adequate third party identity and building a solid consulting relationship with the two parties involving respect, understanding, and trust. This approach was at first accomplished through a series of three site visits to the island, many ongoing contacts by mail and by telephone, and by holding a first workshop of lower risk. Coming from a Canadian base and building on the success of the seminar series, the project was perceived in the first instance as an impartial and credible enterprise. However, many questions about the approach and utility of any such intervention, especially a nontraditional one, abounded in the minds of the official decision makers, who must give informal if not formal approval, as well as potential participants, who must decide whether to invest considerable time and energy.

Besides the institutional base, the personal identity of each member of the third party team must be considered carefully. As noted in the model, the third party needs to possess professional expertise and knowledge, moderate knowledge about the conflict, and be perceived as impartial. The first task was to build a team that in total possessed these qualities. My role as director was congruent with my identity as a Canadian social psychologist with expertise in intergroup and international conflict analysis and resolution and my involvement in the seminar series. The team also included Brian Mandell from the Norman Paterson School of International Affairs at Carleton University in Ottawa, Herbert Kelman from the Department of Psychology at Harvard University, Christopher Mitchell from the Institute for Conflict Analysis and Resolution at George Mason University, and A. J. R. (John) Groom from the Centre for the Analysis of Conflict at Kent University. Together the team possessed a high degree of expertise in workshop processes and a wide range of knowledge about international conflict resolution. In addition, all members possessed moderate to substantial knowledge about the Cyprus conflict based on academic study, personal contacts, and previous workshop experiences. Finally, the national identities of the members (Canadian, British, American) are regarded as impartial, although not necessarily completely neutral in preferred outcomes.

The first site visit to the island by Mandell and myself was carried out with the support of the Canadian Department of Defence and the United Nations Force in Cyprus (UNFICYP), including the Canadian Contingent, which at that time patrolled the "Green Line" through the divided capital city of Nicosia. Accommodation was provided at the Canadian Barracks in the old Ledra Palace Hotel in the buffer zone between the Greek and Turkish Cypriot sections. This manner of entry and accommodation strongly reinforced the perception of impartiality. Informal interviews were held with a wide array of Turkish and Greek Cypriots in both official and unofficial roles to assess initial interest in the project. We found moderate to substantial support mixed with a healthy scepticism and useful questions.

Five months later, I went on a second site visit to further gauge and elicit support and seek guidance on workshop design. Key associates were identified in each community, who served as consultants to the third party team on many questions, including the selection of participants. Based on numerous official and unofficial contacts, it was concluded that there was sufficient interest in a workshop and that tacit official approval had been obtained. In short, an initially adequate consulting relationship had been established from which to plan and implement a workshop intervention. Four months later, I carried out a final visit to invite participants for the workshop and to seek guidance on timing and location. Invited participants were informed verbally and in writing about the nature of the workshop, particularly its research aspects, and the date was set for four months down the road in England.

Between the second and third site visits, a weekend, "pilot" workshop was held at CIIPS in Ottawa with Mandell, Kelman, Mitchell, and I serving on the third party panel (Fisher 1991). The participants were composed primarily of Canadians of Greek and Turkish Cypriot origin who maintained an active interest in the conflict and had influential connections with the two parties. The purpose was to provide an unofficial forum for dialogue, an analysis of the current situation, and the creation of ideas for de-escalation and resolution. The flexible agenda followed most closely the work of Kelman (1986) and covered individual perspectives on the conflict, the underlying concerns (i.e., needs and fears) of the two communities, the ways of meeting these within a mutually acceptable solution, the resistances and constraints impeding de-escalation, and possible mechanisms for providing mutual reassurance.

The discussions involved a useful exchange of perceptions with some new realizations and some consensus on a renewed understanding necessary to resolve the conflict. Participant evaluations were high on satisfaction and usefulness, and also provided the third party panel with some constructive advice on controlling argumentative interchanges that occurred in the earlier stages of the workshop. The workshop was a useful event in its own right and provided essential preparation for the third party to move forward to the next workshop. The successful implementation of the TPC model in this instance also added to the perceived credibility and expertise of the third party and further developed the consulting relationship.

The main workshop of the project was held in early summer at a secluded yet accessible conference center in the English countryside close to London, an ideal setting in the requirements of the model (Fisher 1972, 1992). Participants were influential individuals who represented a broad political spectrum in their communities and were professionals in social research, education, journalism, and business. As leaders in their respective professions, they had varying degrees of connection and influence with the decision-making elites of the two communities. However, their role was seen as entirely unofficial and informal, and they were invited by the third party rather than appointed by their leaderships.

The workshop ran over four days and five nights and involved a rich combination of structured and informal interaction. Besides the discussions, participants took their meals together and spent the evenings socializing. A flexible yet sequenced agenda covered individual perspectives on the major issues, the needs and fears of the two communities and the acknowledgements and assurances necessary to address these, the principles and qualities of a renewed relationship, and potential peacebuilding activities to de-escalate the conflict. The discussions provided for an intensive, mutual analysis of the conflict with a number of third party contributions. Most importantly, the two panels came close to achieving complete consensus on the form of the desired future relationship between the communities. An extended discussion of peacebuilding activities included cooperative social research on the Cyprus problem, the holding of joint art exhibits, and the encouragement of intercommunal contacts. After the workshop, initiatives in social research soon succumbed to political resistances, but a number of cross-line visits by business people were carried out, and a series of joint art exhibits was instituted. Also, some participants were eventually able to help form a bicommunal steering committee to foster intercommunal interactions with initiative and assistance provided by an American-based training project in conflict resolution (see Diamond & Fisher 1995).

Workshop evaluations were highly positive, indicating that it was a rare opportunity for dialogue resulting in increased understanding and mutual learning. There was a call for more workshops involving an ever-widening network of influentials. Indirectly the workshop established the third party team as a viable actor in facilitating intercommunal dialogue in an effective and respectful manner. Thus the project paved the way for further TPC initiatives on the Cyprus conflict, and after a delay in funding caused by the demise of CIIPS, two further workshops were held in 1993 (Fisher 1994a). These workshops are described in chapter 11 as an illustration of demonstration research in ICR.

Each of the three projects highlights the importance of different components of the TPC model. The Cyprus project demonstrates the challenge of establishing an adequate third party identity and an effective consulting relationship in the sensitive and cynical environment of a protracted social conflict. The ethical and professional requirements placed on a potential third party in this type of situation are also significant (see below). The pilot workshop on the India-Pakistan conflict provides a detailed documentation of the operationalization of the third party functions through the coding of specific behavioral tactics. It appears to be the only study that looks systematically in a fine-grained way at the behaviors of the consultant in implementing a model of practice. Finally, the project involving members of conflicting community housing groups provides for a rigorous evaluation of the objectives of the model in attitude change. Few studies of intergroup conflict resolution have used complex pre- and post-measures within a control group design.

In all three projects the utility and validity of the TPC model have been partly affirmed. The overall planning, implementation, and evaluation of each project had to consider all components of the model to be successful. The model therefore continues to be proposed as a comprehensive framework that captures the essential elements of third party consultation as the primary form of ICR.

The Ethics of Consultation

Third party consultation is a professional practice that deals with sensitive and highly charged situations of human social conflict. It is therefore a practice that must not be entered into lightly, naively, or incompetently, for the potential risks to participants and consultants can be great. All of the ethical admonitions and guidelines that bear upon applied social scientists as both researchers and consultants are relevant (see Fisher 1982a and 1982b; chapters 3 and 4 for an overview). In short, ICR entails all of the ethical requirements that attend professional practice in social relations.

Seeing ICR as a professional endeavor requires sensitivity to the basic characteristics of a profession. According to Lippitt and Lippitt (1986), in their treatment of professional consulting, most definitions of professions include:

1. a knowledge base gained through extensive training
2. a continuing responsibility to advance the knowledge of the profession
3. a dedication to the welfare of society
4. ethical standards of conduct and a sense of integrity which govern relationships with others
5. a pride in the worth of the profession and in applying one's knowledge and skills.

These characteristics imply and support a posture for professional consultants that includes sensitivity to ethical issues and adherence to an explicit set of ethical guidelines.

Consultation is generally defined as a help-giving process in which the consultant uses his or her expertise to facilitate the problem solving of the client (Fisher 1982b). It typically flows from, and indeed *should* flow from, a professional base that allows for the full implementation of ethical standards. Thus the general requirements for those who wish to be involved in third party consultation as a form of ICR are relatively clear. They should acquire professional competence in a relevant base of knowledge and practice, should tailor this competence to addressing protracted social conflicts, and should operate at all times with the highest ethical regard for the welfare of their clients, that is, the parties in the conflict and the participants involved in their interventions.

Many involved in ICR come from professional disciplines—they are psychiatrists, lawyers, psychologists, diplomats, political scientists, educators, sociologists, social workers, and so on. As such, they are typically trained to varying degrees and in varying combinations in the ethics of social research and practice. Thus numerous codes of ethics have relevance to ICR practice, and it is beyond the scope of this work to produce a distilled core of specific guidelines that are uniquely relevant. However, two examples will help illustrate the kinds of principles and standards that are generally appropriate.

The first example is drawn from the ethical principles and code of conduct produced by the American Psychological Association, a professional organization that has consistently been at the forefront of articulating ethical concerns about social research and practice. The recently revised code of the association (APA 1992) presents a wide range of detailed ethical standards relevant to the particular activities of psychologists, but more important here, predicates these on a set of five basic principles, which in précis form include the following.

1. Competence—the maintenance of high standards of expertise, the recognition of the limitations and boundaries of competence, and the continued acquisition of relevant scientific and professional knowledge.

2. Integrity—the promotion of honesty, fairness and respect for others, an avoidance of false, misleading or deceptive statements, and an awareness of one's own values, beliefs and needs, including the effects of these on one's work.

3. Professional and Scientific Responsibility—the upholding of professional standards, clarification of professional roles and obligations, the acceptance of responsibility for one's behavior, and the adaptation of methods to the needs of different populations.

4. Respect for People's Rights and Dignity—respecting the rights of individuals to privacy, confidentiality, self-determination and autonomy, the awareness of individual, role and cultural differences, and the elimination of biases and discrimination related to these differences.

5. Concern for Other's Welfare—seeking to contribute to the welfare of clients, performing roles in ways that avoids or minimizes harm, and being sensitive to differences in power between oneself and others.

6. Social Responsibility—awareness of professional and scientific responsibilities to society, application and dissemination of knowledge to contribute to human welfare, and avoidance of the misuse of one's work.

These six principles cover the major areas of concern regarding ethical practice in providing professional services to others. They also underlie the ethical standards essential to high quality research. As action research that involves both intervention and data collection, ICR is obligated to protect the welfare of participants on both dimensions.

The second example comes from a generic code of ethics developed for professional consultants by Lippitt and Lippitt (1986). These authors note that consultants often find themselves in difficult situations in which value conflicts force them to choose or to find a balance among competing interests of the parties. Thus a situational rather than a legalistic approach to ethical decision making is most appropriate in which principles are applied to each unique situation as maxims rather than as laws. From this basis, Lippitt and Lippitt (1986) develop a code of ethics for consultants by drawing on a number of codes prepared by professional consulting associations (fig. 7.2). In combination with a code of ethics for social research, covering such concerns as informed consent, privacy and confidentiality, and respect for and obligations to participants, this generic statement could help lay the foundation for a code of ethics for ICR. Such a code would include principles and guidelines tailored to this particular professional endeavor, with a special focus on the types of ethical dilemmas that arise through intervention in protracted social conflicts. Such a statement would be inclusive of existing initial statements regarding ethics, such as those presented by Burton (1987) and McDonald (1991).

To illustrate the types of ethical issues that arise in ICR, two concerns and related examples that surfaced in the interviews with senior scholar-practitioners will be briefly described. The first has to do with the existence of would-be consultants who purport to have the knowledge and the skills to design effective programs for intergroup dialogue or conflict analysis in situations of protracted social conflict. In some cases, these individuals are well meaning but naive. One example is the consultant who emphasizes a process approach to conflict resolution, but who lacks substantive knowledge about the nature and depth of the problem they are addressing. Thus they bring to bear workshop techniques or exercises that miss the heart of the issues and may leave participants more confused and disheartened than before. A second type of inappropriate consultant is one who is enterprising and possibly unscrupulous. These individuals have consulting careers in community or organizational settings with some commercial success and see the international sphere as a new market for their services. However, they may be woefully underequipped to deal with the demands and risks attendant to protracted social conflicts. In each case, incompetent individuals may organize programs of interaction that have limited or negative effects, thus feeding the misperception that ICR methods are ineffective or dangerous. Hopefully, political gatekeepers and funders weed out these types of consultants, but their

Responsibility: The Consultant:
- Places high value on objectivity and integrity and maintains the highest standards of service; and
- Plans work in a way that minimizes the possibility that findings will be misleading.

Competence: The Consultant:
- Maintains high standards of professional competence as a responsibility to the public and to the profession;
- Recognizes the boundaries of his or her competence and does not offer services that fail to meet professional standards;
- Assists clients in obtaining professional help for aspects of the projects that fall outside the boundaries of his or her own competence; and
- Refrains from undertaking any activity in which his or her personal problems are likely to result in inferior professional service or harm to the client.

Moral and Legal Standards: The Consultant:
- Shows sensible regard for the social codes and moral expectations of the community in which he or she works.

Misrepresentation: The Consultant:
- Avoids misrepresentations of his or her professional qualifications, affiliations, and purposes and those of the organization with which he or she is associated.

Confidentiality: The Consultant:
- Reveals information received in confidence only to the appropriate authorities;
- Maintains confidentiality of professional communications about individuals;
- Informs the client of the limits of confidentiality; and
- Maintains confidentiality in preservation and disposition of records.

Client Welfare: The Consultant:
- Defines the nature of his or her loyalties and responsibilities in possible conflicts of interest, such as between the client and the consultant's employer, and keeps all concerned parties informed of these commitments;
- Attempts to terminate a consulting relationship when it is reasonably clear that the client is not benefiting from it; and
- Continues being responsible for the welfare of the client, in cases involving referral, until the responsibility is assumed by the pro-
continued

fessional to whom the client is referred or until the relationship with the client has been terminated by mutual agreement.

Announcement of Services: The Consultant:
- Adheres to professional standards rather than solely economic rewards in making known his or her availability for professional services.

Intraprofessional and Interprofessional Relations: The Consultant:
- Acts with integrity toward colleagues in consultation and in other professions.

Remuneration: The Consultant:
- Ensures that the financial arrangements for his or her professional services are in accordance with professional standards that safeguard the best interests of the client and the profession.

Responsibility Toward Organization: The Consultant:
- Respects the rights and reputation of the organization with which he or she is associated.

Promotional Activities: The Consultant:
- When associated with the development or promotion of products offered for commercial sale, ensures that the products are presented in a factual way.

Source: Lippitt, G., and R. Lippitt. 1986.

Fig. 7.2. A Code of Ethics for Consultants

existence points to the need for long-term professionalization of the field (see chapter 11).

The second ethical concern relates to potential risks for participants in programs focusing on protracted social conflicts. Typically the parties are locked into a destructive, hostile relationship in which in-group solidarity is accentuated. Any form of contact with the enemy can be labeled from inappropriate to treason, and can carry punishments on an increasing scale of severity. A member who interacts with the other side can be discredited as soft, ostracized as a traitor, removed from a position of influence, suffer social or economic persecution, and ultimately be injured or killed. A number of such incidents were mentioned by some of the interviewees, either from their own experience or their secondhand knowledge of other consultants' experience. It must be stressed that these comments are anecdotal and also refer to events that are likely related to various causal factors other than the consultation program. Nonetheless, ethical responsibility requires that such events be taken seriously even if the causes cannot be fully identified.

1. After one program of consultation on a protracted sectarian conflict, participants who tried to maintain contact with the other side were threatened with physical violence by members of their group. Some time after this same program, which involved very intense interaction, one participant committed suicide and some observers attributed this at least in part to the workshop experience.

2. Before a workshop focusing on a hostile and violent intercommunal conflict, a close relative of one participant was murdered and the body was buried in a shallow grave in the participant's front yard, possibly as an atrocious attempt to dissuade participation.

3. After a secret meeting of representatives of one of the sides engaged in a bitter sectarian conflict to develop proposals to take to the other side, a leading participant was murdered in his own community, possibly by his fellows as a traitor, but possibly by agents of a regional power that did not want to see a settlement.

4. In working to arrange a program of consultation, a third party sought out an influential member of an underground organization and in so doing may have revealed his identity and location to authorities. A week later the person was jailed without trial for two years.

These events cannot be clearly attributed to the consultation activities, but their occurrence within the same time frame and sequence raises the possibility of association. It is therefore incumbent upon consultants to make every possible effort to safeguard the welfare of participants and to inform them of all potential risks. Although participants will make their own choices in this regard, there may likely be situations of conflict that are so fragile or dangerous that consultants should not even attempt to carry out an intervention. Nonintervention may result in greater human costs in the long run (assuming consultation has long-term beneficial effects—which at this stage *is* an assumption), but the first responsibility of the consultant is to participants in the here and now. Thus the adherence to a comprehensive and demanding set of ethical principles is paramount, and is worthy of greater discussion and determination in ICR than exists at present.

8

A Contingency Approach to
Third Party Intervention

The potential utility of ICR does not lie simply in its application as a solitary method, but in its complementarity with existing methods of conflict management, especially in de-escalating apparently intractable conflicts toward some degree of malleability. ICR may thus provide a valuable supplementary service to traditional diplomatic activities. However, it may also be that this service is essential, if there is to be movement toward resolution, at least within the near term future of a conflict. At the same time, it is important not to overestimate the influence of any third party interventions on conflict de-escalation— a complex, difficult, and only partially understood phenomenon that is determined by a host of variables (Kriesberg 1992; Kriesberg & Thorson 1991).

The rationale for ICR and its complementarity with other methods lies in the assumptions that one makes about conflict and its escalation and de-escalation. Proponents of ICR generally assume that conflict at all levels is a combination of objective and subjective factors (e.g., Fisher 1990; Mitchell 1981). Sources are to be found in both realistic differences in interests over resources that generate goal incompatibilities, as well as in differing perceptions of motivations and behaviors. Conflicts based in value differences or that threaten basic needs are not expressed in substantive issues amenable to negotiation, but involve preferences and requirements of living that will not be compromised, and must be given expression in some satisfactory fashion. Escalation does not simply involve the realistic application of threats, sanctions, and actions of increasing magnitude, but elicits subjective elements that come to drive the conflict more than the substantive issues. Hatred between two ethnic groups coveting the same land, which escalates to reciprocal massacres, cannot be understood or managed by simply dealing with tangible issues. In short, ICR assumes that the phenomenological side of conflict must be considered as it is expressed in the perceptions, emotions, interactions, and social institutions of the parties.

These assumptions provide the rationale for a contingency approach to conflict resolution, in which third party interventions are coordinated and sequenced to deal effectively with the complex interplay of objective and subjective factors (Fisher & Keashly 1990; Keashly & Fisher 1990). Such coordination requires that key elements of a conflict are identified and that interventions are then matched to these elements. In basic terms, ICR is seen as more effective in dealing with subjective aspects of conflict, while traditional interventions, such as mediation, are more useful in addressing objective interests. Unfortunately the subjective side of conflict is seldom addressed directly at the international level, and interventions are seldom coordinated, thus indicating the need for much development. At the same time, contingency thinking is in its infancy, consisting primarily of conceptual creations which, though appealing in logical terms, have very few empirical referents let alone practical applications.

The Contingency Model

To match third party methods to selected aspects of conflict, one first needs a classification and definitions of the interventions themselves, that is, a taxonomy. Unfortunately a clearly articulated and accepted one does not exist. The UN once produced a handbook on methods of dispute resolution, but it tends to follow legal definitions relevant to international treaties, and appears not to be generally well known. The academic literature does not evidence consistency in its use of intervention labels, with, for example, conciliation and mediation often connoting the same activities, and also often subsumes different procedures under the same term, for example, varying forms of arbitration. Given this situation, Fisher and Keashly (1990, 1991) took the approach of laying out a simple, initial taxonomy of third party interventions consisting of the following labels and definitions.

> *Conciliation:* A trusted third party provides a communication link between the antagonists to assist in identifying major issues, lowering tension, and moving them toward direct interaction, typically negotiation.
> *Consultation:* A knowledgeable and skilled third party attempts to facilitate creative problem solving through communication and analysis using social-scientific understanding of conflict processes.
> *Pure Mediation:* A skilled intermediary attempts to facilitate a negotiated settlement on a set of specific substantive issues through the

use of reasoning, persuasion, control of information and suggestion of alternatives.

Power Mediation: The intermediary provides the functions of pure mediation and adds the use of leverage in the form of promised rewards or threatened punishments to move the parties toward a settlement.

Arbitration: A legitimate and authoritative third party provides a binding judgement through considering the merits of the opposing positions and imposing a settlement deemed to be fair and just.

Peacekeeping: An outside third party (typically the UN) provides military personnel to supervise and monitor a ceasefire between antagonists.

The different interventions can be distinguished in assumptions, with consultation, and to some degree conciliation, taking a subjective approach, while mediation and arbitration tend toward an objective one. Mediation and arbitration attempt to work around subjective elements and accept a competitive and distributive orientation to conflict, which is compatible with eliciting concessions resulting in a compromise settlement. In contrast, consultation or ICR assumes that the subjective elements, such as perceptions, attitudes, and relationships, must be jointly considered to induce de-escalation and movement toward settlement on substantive issues.

The power or control of the third party is seen as the primary distinguishing feature of the different methods. Fisher and Keashly (1990) assessed control over process and over content in relation to the stages of problem solving, which are common to all methods, although implemented differently by each one. This analysis generally revealed that conciliation and consultation show low to moderate levels of control, mediation moderate to high, and arbitration a high degree. This range is also true with regard to control over outcomes. Not surprisingly, the sources of power (following the Raven typology) also increase as one moves through the taxonomy, with conciliation having very few and arbitration having very many bases of influence. Thus the taxonomy seems to offer a useful classification of third party interventions, which relates to some important elements of social reality relevant to conflict resolution.

In developing a contingency model, a critical question is what aspects of conflict might serve as cues for the application of the different interventions. Conflict has an inherent tendency to escalate, and the degree of intensity or stage of escalation has been identified as a potential cue for method selection. Glasl (1982) constructed an escalation model drawn mainly from work on organizational conflict that identifies nine stages, which are then combined into three phases of escalation. Six forms of intervention are then connected to the stages of escalation in a slightly overlapping fashion to indicate where each approach is most appropriate. Glasl concludes that a long-term strategy of handling conflict should involve starting with the most appropriate method and moving to others in a conscious and open fashion. Other contributions to contingency approaches in organizations are found in Prein (1984) and Sheppard (1984).

Building on the work of Glasl (1982) and others (e.g., Deutsch 1973; Wright 1965), Fisher and Keashly (1990) developed a *model of escalation* with four stages of increasing intensity (fig. 8.1). The stages of discussion, polarization, segregation and destruction are characterized by increasing negative intensity in interparty communication, the parties' perceptions of each other and their relationship, the prominent issues, the perceived likely outcomes, and the approach to managing the conflict. The escalation of a conflict is not simply characterized by heightened emotionality, greater distortion of perceptions, and the use of more contentious tactics, but also by the nature of what is seen to be at stake, that is, the issues. It follows that different interventions will be more effective at different levels of escalation.

The initial *contingency model*, matching the taxonomy of interventions to the stages of escalation is given in fig. 8.2 (Fisher & Keashly 1990). At each stage, a lead intervention is specified, followed by a sequence of interventions designed to de-escalate the conflict back down

	Dimensions of the Conflict			
Stage	*Communication/ interaction*	*Perceptions/ relationship*	*Issues*	*Outcome/ management*
I	Discussion/ debate	Accurate/trust, respect	Interests	Joint gain/ mutual decision
II	Less direct/ deeds, not words	Stereotypes/ other still important	Relationship	Compromise/ negotiation
III	Little direct/ threats	Good vs. evil/ distrust, lack of respect	Basic needs	Win–lose/ defensive competition
IV	Nonexistent/ direct attacks	Other nonhuman/ hopeless	Survival	Lose–lose/ destruction

Source: Fisher, R. J., and L. Keashly 1990.

Fig. 8.1. Stages of Conflict Escalation

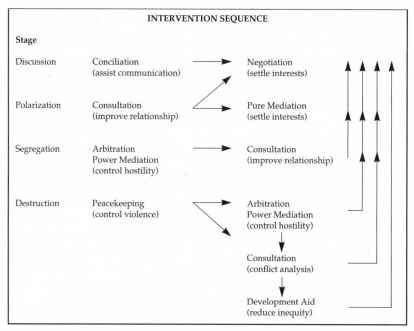

Fig. 8.2. A Contingency Model of Third Party Intervention

to stage one, where the parties can handle their differences through negotiations. The rationale for each of these matches and sequences is given in Fisher and Keashly (1990). The model also indicates the primary objective of each intervention (in parentheses), which must be achieved for de-escalation to occur.

The model specifies two points where consultation or ICR may be critical in conflict de-escalation by providing a complementary role to mediation (Fisher & Keashly 1991). The first is where consultation provides a prenegotiation, or "premediation," function by improving the relationship between the parties before dealing with substantive issues. Some support for this linkage comes from Prein's (1984) research at the organizational level indicating that consultation was more effective in conflicts characterized by emotional disturbances, misunderstandings, and mutual distrust, whereas mediation was more successful in addressing conflicts of low escalation involving primarily substantive issues. Also in industrial relations, some useful cases of consultation interventions helped pave the way for successful negotiations (Birnbaum 1984; Brett, Goldberg & Ury 1980). Current work on prenegotiation in international relations follows a similar rationale.

The second point of complementarity comes at a higher level of escalation where peacekeeping has controlled the violence and arbitration or power mediation may have controlled some of the hostility through an initial and partial settlement. At this point, consultation may play a valuable role in conflict analysis, bringing the parties together for intense and complex discussions focusing on issues and the escalation that has brought them to the point of apparent intractability. The rationale is that only this form of analysis can prepare the parties to work toward a comprehensive and lasting agreement, including mutually acceptable procedures for dealing with future differences. This use of consultation is supported by the work of scholar-practitioners in ICR, such as Burton and Azar, who see analysis as the most effective initial response to protracted conflicts.

A revised, alternate model of the contingency approach is developed in Fisher (1993b) through combining third party interventions into broader approaches to peace, based on Galtung's (1976) tripartite conceptualization of peacemaking, peacebuilding, and peacekeeping, Fisher (1993b) sees conciliation and mediation as forms of *peacemaking*, which attempts to improve communication, suggest alternatives, and use information and persuasion to motivate the parties toward a settlement. *Peacekeeping* involves the interposition of a military force to supervise a cease-fire between antagonists. *Peacebuilding* combines the classic meaning of social development to reduce inequity with a new interactive element designed to improve the relationship and de-escalate the hostility between the parties, that is, ICR. To capture the essence of power mediation and arbitration, Fisher (1993b) coins the label of *peacepushing*, which denotes the higher degrees of control, judgment, and coercion that the third party utilizes to impose a settlement on the parties. This provides four approaches to peace, which are then linked to the four stages of conflict escalation as the lead intervention of choice (fig. 8.3).

The challenge with highly escalated and protracted conflicts is to institute peacekeeping as soon as possible to control the violence and to follow that initial intervention with other ones to facilitate de-escalation before intractability sets in. Peacepushing may be useful to obtain partial agreements that regulate the interaction and settle some immediate issues. However, peacebuilding is essential to induce significant de-escalation, for only it will improve the relationship and address the basic needs whose frustration is at the core of the conflict. Interactive activities that rebuild trust and cooperation, and development activities that begin to reduce inequity should pave the way for peacemaking to negotiate specific interests and develop detailed agreements that will guide future interaction. Thus all four approaches have an essential role to play, but peacebuilding is seen as the most important contributor and yet often the most lacking in de-escalation and

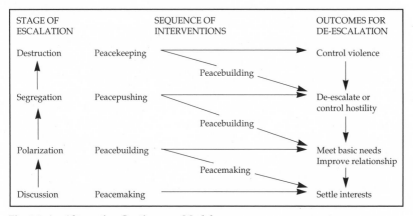

Fig. 8.3. An Alternative Contingency Model

resolution (Fisher 1993b). This conclusion again underscores the potential role that ICR may be able to play in addressing protracted social conflicts.

Consultation as a Prenegotiation Intervention

The prenegotiation phase of international conflict management has been receiving increased attention in recent years following contributions by Saunders (1985), Zartman (1985), and Laue (1989). Saunders (1985) called for a larger theory of negotiation that would acknowledge and illuminate the complex challenge of bringing parties to negotiation. He posited the prenegotiation phases of: (1) defining the problem, (2) producing a commitment to a negotiated settlement, and (3) arranging a negotiation; and he illustrated these through his experience as an American mediator in the Arab-Israeli peace process. Zartman (1985) explicated the diagnostic phase of negotiations and the appropriate conditions that influence the parties toward a turning point of mutual seriousness about a negotiated solution. Laue (1989) highlighted the phrase "getting to the table" and articulated the elements of the forum for negotiations, such as auspices and procedures. He described a number of alternate paths to the table and the value choices to make in constructing it, such as cooperative or adversarial.

The first systematic study of international prenegotiation is offered in a collection by Stein (1989a), who defines it as the process that begins when one or more parties consider negotiation an option and communicate this intention; prenegotiation ends when one party abandons negotiation as an option or when the parties agree to formal negotiations. Following a number of case studies of prenegotiation in both economic and security arenas, Stein (1989b) draws a number of conclusions about the triggers, stages, functions, and consequences of the process. She suggests that a recent or impending crisis, or a perception of threat combined with opportunity, trigger a consideration of prenegotiation as a policy option. Prenegotiation is appealing because it helps decision makers reduce uncertainty and manage complexity in a low risk and low cost manner as compared to formal negotiation. Prenegotiation also functions to structure negotiation by specifying the boundaries, the participants, and potentially the agenda, all in an exploratory, noncommittal manner. Stein concludes that prenegotiation is important whether parties get to the table or not, because it provides opportunities for mutual learning.

The prenegotiation process provides a unique occasion for applications of consultation or ICR. Burton (1969) acknowledged a prime function of controlled communication as establishing the conditions in which negotiation will lead to de-escalation. Kelman and Cohen (1976) proposed that problem-solving workshops could create a conducive atmosphere and establish a framework for negotiation as well as allowing the parties to assess the feasibility of negotiation in a low risk manner. Fisher (1989) makes a broad case for the use of consultation to enhance the potential for successful negotiation, and illustrates it with reference to Kelman's work on the Israeli-Palestinian conflict and the role of the Commonwealth in resolving the Rhodesia-Zimbabwe conflict. Fisher (1989) proposes that consultation can positively affect perceptions, attitudes, and orientations in ways that improve the chances of both prenegotiation and negotiation.

The rationale for ICR as a prenegotiation intervention is found largely in social-psychological theory and its connections to international relations (Fisher 1989). Workshops provide an opportunity for influential representatives of the parties to engage in a mutual analysis of social-psychological aspects of their conflict (images, needs, interaction patterns, escalation processes, ideologies, institutions) and to connect these to policymaking and public opinion. The intense, face-to-face interaction provides authentic information that can shift attitudes in a more realistic and less stereotyped direction. Changed attitudes can lead to less distortion in perception and more complexity in cognition, which support the consideration of a wider set of policy options, including that of negotiation. The empathic sharing of information can result in more accurate assessments of intentions and build trust, both of which may influence the parties toward cooperative rather than unilateral strategies. Group norms in the workshop come to sanction mutuality, reciprocity, and collaboration, all of which support a move toward negotiation. The respectful and equal status interaction within the workshop provides a model for intergroup relations, which the participants can attempt to take back to their ongoing behavior. An examination of nationalism and ethnocentrism as they are expressed in the relationship between the parties can also aid them in understanding their interactions, including that of negotiation. In short, consultation interventions can result in a shared perceptual shift, wherein the adversary is now seen as adequately reasonable and trustworthy and the potential benefits of negotiation are now evaluated as outweighing the risks.

A structured approach to prenegotiation that provides further rationale for ICR's role is provided by Rothman (1990, 1991), who directed a multiyear project at the Hebrew University of Jerusalem. The project focused on the role of prenegotiation in protracted social conflicts through research into concepts and methods and through the development of training programs and materials. An innovative model of prenegotiation laid the basis for various educational events, including an Israeli-Palestinian prenegotiation workshop on the question of Jerusalem and a training seminar for midlevel diplomats on getting to the table. Rothman (1990) defines prenegotiation as "an integrated process in which highly placed representatives of parties in conflict prepare for negotiations by jointly framing the issues of conflict, generating various options for handling them cooperatively, and interactively structuring [the] substance and process of future negotiations" (4). In contrast to Stein's (1989) descriptive definition, Rothman's is a prescriptive one, indicating what should occur in prenegotiation for the parties to get to the table and to negotiate effectively.

Rothman's model amplifies the stages that are implicit in the definition: (1) *framing*, which involves the parties in deriving shared definitions of the parameters of the conflict and in building the will to negotiate; (2) *inventing*, which involves creating cooperative strategies for solving the central aspects of the conflict and building confidence in negotiation; and (3) *structuring*, which involves the parties in making joint decisions about the variables to be considered in setting the formal table and in building a momentum of negotiation. Framing requires moving the parties away from their negative assumptions about conflict and each other through sharing their deeper concerns and providing them with conceptual tools to make distinctions among positions, interests, and needs. Inventing necessitates the parties adopting an integrative approach (rather than a competitive one) in which they work to satisfy their own needs without undermining the other's needs. To facilitate problem solving, Rothman proposes techniques drawn from work on integrative bargaining and categorizes these as resource expansion, exchange, and functional cooperation. Structuring requires the parties to make decisions about the agenda for negotiations, so that the broad agreements in principle and integrative options produced in prenegotiation can be made politically feasible and implemented. Procedural questions, for example, selecting participants, are also addressed in this phase.

Rothman's model puts much more into prenegotiation than most other theories and most diplomatic practice. It represents a highly structured and demanding sequence of procedures that would need to be tailored with considerable flexibility to any given situation. At the same time, it is clearly an ICR model that articulates many of the activities and outcomes of ICR workshops, and incorporates elements of dialogue, conflict analysis, and problem solving. Rothman notes that his model integrates a wide range of theory and experience in conflict management and maintains that each part has been found effective. However, he concedes that the model has not been implemented in its entirety and that parties might be reluctant to use it. Nonetheless, he concludes that the model proved useful as a guide in the project's educational initiatives, and its effectiveness in promoting successful negotiations deserves to be tested. Many in the field of ICR would agree.

The history of ICR documented in previous chapters provides examples where consultation appears to have performed a useful prenegotiation function. Indeed, the very first application of Burton's (1969) innovative methodology to the Malaysia-Indonesia conflict enabled the parties to reassess their objectives and envisage new policy options (de Reuck 1974). More to the point, the parties, who had broken off diplomatic relations, were able to reach a shared understanding on the overall framework of a solution. After the 1966 coup in Indonesia, the new government moved into negotiations and the basic elements of that framework were reflected in the final peace agreement.

Another example comes from the work of Azar (1986, 1990) on the Lebanese conflict. Two problem-solving forums held at Maryland produced a set of principles for a united Lebanon. These principles were used by the informal network of participants and other influentials in producing the "National Covenant Document." This statement outlined the steps required for reunification, which were subsequently integrated into the Taif peace accord. Besides affecting the substance of the agreement, it is likely that the principles affected the negotiations as well.

The most extensive use of ICR as a prenegotiation method comes from Kelman's work on the Israeli-Palestinian conflict over the past twenty-five years. Kelman (1978, 1982, 1987) produced analyses of the psychological prerequisites for mutual acceptance, identified the barriers to negotiation, and proposed a prenegotiation process of successive approximations—largely on the basis of his workshop experiences. Through an expanding network of influentials, Kelman's workshops contributed to a changing and more constructive political dialogue, the humanization of the enemy, and a sense of possibility that the conflict is resolvable. Kelman (1992) identifies learnings from the workshops that have been communicated to political elites, including insights into the other's priorities and areas of flexibility, signs of readiness for negotiation, and ideas on ways of moving to the table. Finally, when formal negotiations began, a number of the advisers and negotiators on both sides were graduates of Kelman workshops (Kelman 1995).

A recent illustration of ICR as prenegotiation comes from the third party role of the Roman Catholic Community of Sant' Egidio in helping de-escalate and resolve the tragic civil war in Mozambique (United States Institute of Peace, 1993). This bitter and costly conflict between the Frelimo government and the Renamo guerrillas showed no signs of abatement in its insidious process of destroying the country. According to Andrea Bartoli, vice president of Sant' Egidio, the church had been able to maintain a good relationship with the Marxist government, and in 1988, the president agreed to permit church leaders to contact Renamo. This initial channel of communication (categorized as conciliation in the contingency model) succeeded where official efforts failed, and convinced both sides that a political settlement was feasible and desirable. After two years of using the church as a go-between, the two sides began meeting in Rome for informal discussions (consultation), which focused on creating common ground, improving communication, and building trust. This dialogue process shifted naturally into negotiations on a political settlement, to which official actors were invited to assure implementation. Thus the work also serves as an example of complementarity between unofficial and official efforts in an overall peace process.

There is also experimental evidence for the potential usefulness of consultation in prenegotiation, on the initial question of whether such interventions lead to the perceptual, attitudinal, and relationship changes that augur well for negotiations. Quantitative results of such effects were found by Keashly, Fisher, and Grant (1993) in their comparison of consultation and mediation within a complex laboratory simulation of intergroup conflict. The simulation engaged small groups of male university undergraduates in both intra- and intergroup interaction over an economic and value conflict involving the division of five tracts of land. The complex and lengthy simulation allowed for sufficient in-group development, followed by the formulation of positions and negotiation with the other group (Fisher et al. 1990; Grant et al.

1990). Midway through negotiations, half of the interacting groups were randomly assigned to a consultation intervention, while the other half received mediation. The consultation groups evidenced significantly more positive attitudes and greater trust toward the competing group, perceived the intergroup relationship as more satisfactory and collaborative, and were more willing to work with the other group in the future. At the same time, there were no differences between the conditions in outcomes, partly because most groups achieved relatively high integrative settlements, but also because the interventions did not appear to differentially affect negotiating behavior (Keashly 1988).

These findings were extended by Forster (1990), who examined the differential effects of consultation and mediation on aspects of group functioning relevant to the intergroup relationship. Her analyses indicated that simulation groups who received consultation evidenced decreased levels of ethnocentrism and competitive norms, that is, they became less derogatory and adversarial toward the other group. Moreover, these changes were related to increased perceptions of trust and collaboration in the intergroup relationship. Thus the consultation intervention operated in part through the medium of the group, rather than simply affecting individual perceptions and attitudes.

A direct linkage between an ICR intervention and negotiation processes and outcomes is provided by Druckman, Broome, and Korper (1988). This experiment used a simulation resembling the Cyprus conflict to assess the effects of a prenegotiation "facilitation" condition in which information about a consultation workshop on understanding value differences was provided to negotiating dyads. In subsequent negotiations, participants in this condition were more cooperative, more willing to move from their initial position, resolved more issues, and achieved more symmetrical outcomes than negotiators who received information that justified positions by using values. Druckman and Broome (1991) elucidated these results by demonstrating in two further experiments that increased familiarity and liking, produced through prenegotiation conditions, had positive effects on both negotiator expectations and behavior. Using the same simulation, they found that induced liking was related to more positive perceptions of the opponent and expectations of greater movement from initial position. Higher familiarity was related to a number of positive aspects, including greater willingness to compromise and a view of the situation as being collaborative. In processes and outcomes, liking and familiarity led to more movement from initial positions, produced more compromise (as opposed to one-sided) agreements, and led to more positive postevaluations of the negotiations.

In conclusion, the social-psychological rationale for ICR as a pre-negotiation methodology is supported by cases of international conflict resolution. Many other factors influence the course of events in a complex world, and much more rigorous evaluation research is necessary to better document the contributing effects of ICR interventions. At the same time, the experimental evidence, although limited in many ways, helps further substantiate the potential utility of ICR as an effective prenegotiation intervention.

De-escalation, Timing, and Interactive Conflict Resolution

The prescriptive stance of the contingency model proposes that when third party activities are matched to escalation level, they can induce or contribute to de-escalation. This does not deny that many de-escalation initiatives are taken by the parties themselves out of their self-interests. In either case, it does appear that de-escalation, as compared to escalation, has been a neglected study in social science (Kriesberg 1982; Pruitt & Rubin 1986). Fortunately this deficit is now being addressed (e.g., Kriesberg 1992; Kriesberg & Thorson 1991).

In part, *de-escalation* is the reverse process of escalation, that is, simply walking back down the staircase of *intensity*—defined as both the difference between winning and losing and the subjective investment in the conflict (Deutsch 1973; Fisher 1990). In addition, de-escalation involves the application of sanctions of decreasing magnitude; again the reverse of escalation, which is the application of sanctions of increasing magnitude (Bonoma 1975). However, de-escalation is more than reverse escalation, for escalation creates "residues" that must be removed for de-escalation to succeed (Pruitt & Rubin 1986). These authors contend that "in the process of waging a contentious struggle, relationships often change in ways that make it exceedingly difficult to reverse course" (111). They identify factors that induce intractability—at the level of individuals as negative attitudes and their attributional effects, and at the level of collectivities as aggressive norms and vested interests that support the conflict. Furthermore, the phenomena of over-commitment and entrapment lead the parties to continue expending resources in the conflict to justify past actions and investments (Brockner & Rubin 1985).

Thus the de-escalation staircase is one littered with debris, which must be cleared away for each step down to be taken. This debris is largely psychological and social, built into the minds, norms, institutions, and even cultures of the societies involved, and needs to be addressed through social-psychological as well as political and economic measures. An even more daunting metaphor is to see escalation not as a retreat down a staircase of hostilities, but a climb up a war-to-peace staircase with turnings that change the nature of the relationship between the parties (Hurwitz 1991). That is, de-escalation comprises a series of efforts by the parties to redefine their relationship according to different principles—ones supporting restraint, reciprocity, and ultimately cooperation. Moreover, Hurwitz (1991) cites data from Sherman's (1987) analysis of international disputes to emphasize that de-escalation is typically not a smooth, linear process, but often involves relapses into violence.

Kriesberg (1992) has recently offered a descriptive model of de-escalation in international conflict resolution (fig. 8.4), which has four phases: (1) initiating de-escalation which involves questions about why hostility begins to decrease and what actions can reduce it, including prenegotiation; (2) undertaking negotiations, which represents a major shift in the parties' approach to the conflict from unilateral to bilateral efforts; (3) reaching agreement, which raises the question why some negotiations, succeed while others fail; and (4) implementing and sustaining agreements, which considers the strategies that result

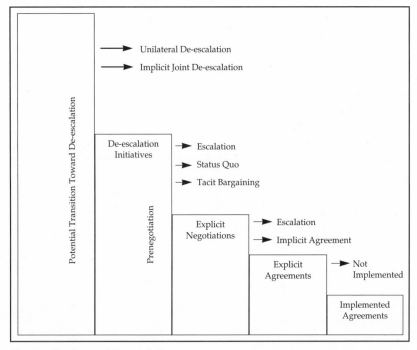

Fig. 8.4. The Steps of De-escalation

in long-term solutions. Kriesberg (1992) addresses these questions through detailed case analysis of de-escalation efforts in both the Arab-Israeli and U.S.-Soviet Union conflicts over a forty-year period. As his model allows for, de-escalation does not always follow the specified sequence—some efforts toward negotiation result in escalation, some negotiations lead only to implicit agreements, and some agreements are not implemented.

Closely related to de-escalation is *timing*, that is, recognizing the most propitious point(s) in the cycle of conflict for the parties or third parties to make de-escalatory moves. According to Kriesberg (1987), timing involves knowing when the parties are ready to move away from escalation or down from stalemate. Timing is important because inappropriate initiatives can be counterproductive. However, he contends that there is no one generally right time for such efforts, for receptivity depends on a host of conditions in the adversaries' domestic situations, their relationship, and the wider international context. In contrast, the more specific concept of *ripeness* does refer to the right time to undertake a de-escalatory effort in a particular conflict (Kriesberg 1991b). A conflict is ripe when the necessary but not sufficient conditions for de-escalation exist, and the added effort of a party or a third party initiates de-escalation.

Zartman (1985) stimulated much of the current interest in timing and ripeness by articulating the concept of a "ripe moment" for resolution, which accrues from a mutually "hurting stalemate" between the parties in combination with a recent or impending catastrophe. Thus the parties are in a costly deadlock and the prospects are that the situation will get worse. This mutual sense of futility must be combined with requitement (a belief that the other party will reciprocate a conciliatory move) and the perception of a way out, indicating that the issues in the conflict will be reduced (Zartman & Aurik 1991). At this point, the parties are likely to be receptive to the efforts of a third party and are predisposed to move into negotiations. Zartman (1985) also contends that third parties can help create the perception of a ripe moment through leverage. It is noteworthy that this contention is compatible with the contingency model, in which power mediation is hypothesized to be useful in controlling hostility and gaining an initial agreement at a high level of escalation.

After reviewing several analyses of timing and ripeness, Rubin (1991) concludes that the explanatory power of these concepts is qualified, for their effectiveness depends on a host of circumstances. However, he asserts there are multiple ripe moments and that there is likely no wrong time to attempt de-escalation. The real danger is that ripeness can be a trap, used as an excuse to passively wait for the ripe moment, rather than attempting to address an unacceptable situation. In contrast, Rubin (1991) advises looking for ways to create ripeness, one of which is creating incentives through exchanging information about underlying interests. Note that when this activity is undertaken by a third party, it constitutes one of the prevalent functions of ICR. If more attention was given to timing and ripeness, as Rubin suggests, we might have a better idea of when particular third party interventions could contribute to the creation of ripe moments.

The possibility of linking different intermediary activities to particular stages of escalation or de-escalation in international conflict has been raised by theorists other than Fisher and Keashly. Kriesberg (1991a) relates the four stages in his model of de-escalation (see above) to a range of mediating activities that can be carried out by various official and unofficial parties (e.g., providing good offices, reframing the conflict, suggesting new options, adding resources to settlement). Although Kriesberg maintains that each type of activity can occur at every stage in different forms, some activities are more prominent at certain stages in his presentation. Reframing the conflict through problem-solving workshops, for example, is linked primarily to stages one and two (initiating de-escalation and negotiations) while suggesting new options is more frequent in stage three (conducting negotiations and reaching agreement). Kriesberg concludes that unofficial intermediaries can be especially effective in the early stages of de-escalation, thus adding some support to the contingency model.

A contingency strategy is evident in a multimodal approach to intractable conflict proposed by Pruitt and Olzack (1995), who note there are several competing remedies in the domain of conflict resolution—all supported by some evidence. Following the experience of the field of psychotherapy, Pruitt and Olzack suggest that treatments should be matched to the specifics of the disorder and then followed up by other remedies to address related elements of the problem to ensure lasting change. In conflict resolution, this approach requires an understanding of the dynamics of conflict, which is provided by a systems model linking conflict to changes in five modes of human experience: motivation (M), affect (A), cognition (C), behavior (B), and social environment (E). These modes then become targets for remedies that need to be invoked at particular points and in specific sequences to de-escalate the conflict. The resulting combinations with supporting rationale is the "MACBE" model.

Highly escalated conflicts usually involve hostile elements in all five modes of experience (Pruitt & Olzack 1995), and these are described in social-psychological models of conflict escalation (e.g., Deutsch 1973; Fisher 1990; Rubin, Pruitt & Kim 1994). In a mildly escalated conflict, only one or two modes may be problematic, and improvements will follow interventions in one or two parts of the system. However, in intractable conflicts, interventions must address all elements of the system to change the situation and to prevent relapse. Otherwise conflict-inducing structures (residues) throughout the system will reassert themselves and re-escalate the conflict. This possibility is particularly true in intergroup conflict where powerful norms and the social environment support a competitive, less trusting, and more polarizing orientation.

Pruitt and Olzack identify seven "modules" of conflict intervention to be used selectively after diagnosis and combined into logical sequences, much like the contingency model. Interventions (identified here by numbers in parentheses) begin with the most common procedures of negotiation and mediation and follow a "discovery" order, in which each is used as necessary to remedy deficiencies in the preceding one(s). Negotiation and mediation (1) are designed to alter behavior (B), but failure to reach agreement implies insufficient motivation (M) to deal with the conflict. This situation raises the issue of ripeness, which Pruitt and Olzack see as the motive to escape the conflict. Thus third parties need to use pressure or enticements to induce bilateral ripeness (2). However, these actions and the ensuing ripeness may not be sufficient in a severely deteriorated relationship where trust, a type of cognition (C) is lacking. Hence the parties themselves (e.g., through unilateral conciliatory initiatives) or third parties (e.g., by engineering simultaneous concessions) need to foster the development of trust (3). However, even when this occurs, the parties or their representatives or both may lack the problem-solving skills to manage their differences effectively. Thus the intervention of choice is to provide training to develop negotiating, problem-solving, and related skills (4).

Nonetheless, negotiation or mediation will still be difficult if deeper issues such as frustrated basic needs are driving the conflict. Pruitt and Olzack point out that negotiation is typically directed toward solving a narrow set of concrete issues that predominate in the parties' thinking. Thus deeper analysis of conflict dynamics, including the perceptions, emotions, attributions, and motivations of the parties, may be necessary (5), especially to achieve longer-lasting solutions. Through methods such as problem-solving workshops (i.e., ICR), motives (M) can be illuminated, hostility (A) can be reduced, trust (C) can be enhanced, and escalatory behavior (B) can be identified and eliminated. However, win-win outcomes are not always available, and a final step of reducing the aspirations of the parties may be necessary (6). Over time the parties learn to resolve some issues and to live with those they cannot, thus adjusting their motivation (M) to deal with conflict in their relationship. Finally, there is the importance of restructuring the social environment (E) when that is possible (7). This can be accomplished, for example, by reducing the parties' contact with allies who may be working to maintain the conflict.

In applying the MACBE model, Pruitt and Olzack recommend a distinction between moderate and severe conflict. When conflict is moderately escalated, changes are usually required in only one or two elements of the system. Thus diagnosis followed by surgical treatment using only one or two of the modules will likely be adequate to restore a functional relationship. However, with highly escalated conflicts, all of the modules must be involved. To answer the question of how to sequence the modules, they turn to the contingency model of Fisher and Keashly, and draw parallels between the two models. For highly escalated conflicts, both models assume that the development of motivation to escape the conflict has to be the first step, and that conflict analysis needs to precede negotiation for there to be lasting solutions. In international conflict, this process often begins with unofficial, problem-solving interactions among coalitions of "doves" who lay the basis for future de-escalation, as with the role of the Dartmouth Conference in preparing the way for the end of the cold war. Pruitt and Olzack (1995) conclude that there is a logic to the sequencing in the MACBE model, and they make a case for conflict analysis at an early stage in de-escalation. Thus their analysis supports the rationale of ICR workshops with influential members of the parties.

Assessing the Utility of the Contingency Model

The contingency model has an innovative and appealing logic for addressing intergroup and international conflicts that have escalated to violence and intractability. It offers a simple, comprehensive, and prescriptive framework for de-escalating protracted social conflicts through the complementary sequencing of third party interventions. In a world beset by these types of conflicts, such a logic is seductive, especially for those who yearn earnestly for a more peaceful creation. However, the international system, including its connections to domestic politics, is an incredibly complex one—the most complex in which change agents such as third party consultants can work. As analyses by Kriesberg (1992) and others indicate, de-escalation in such a system is affected by numerous conditions and constraints, and initiatives can come from many different sectors and actors. As he points out, this may require "a broader view than that which considers conflict resolution technique as more or less effective under different circumstances" (15). At the same time, Kriesberg maintains that peacemaking needs to consider what methods are effective at different stages in a conflict. Hence even though the contingency model is a "bare bones" framework, it may offer a useful starting point for more detailed analyses and assessments of applications that are cognizant of the complexity of any given situation, and thereby cumulatively of the system as a whole.

The contingency model should be seen as a set of initial working hypotheses, to be assessed logically through theoretical analyses, and empirically through case studies as well as more rigorous methods. Such work is under way, particularly by younger scholars, who may be attracted by the newness and potential of the model. For example, Smith (1994) strongly endorses the logical distinction between pure mediation and power mediation, and contends that failure to make this distinction will compromise the validity of any study of third party effectiveness. On the empirical side, a number of case studies provide mixed but encouraging results (Keashly & Fisher 1996).

Keashly and Fisher (1990) applied the contingency model to the Cyprus conflict. The major events were charted over five decades and divided into the four stages of escalation. Third party interventions in the same periods were categorized according to the interventions in the model and juxtaposed with the events and stages. This analysis indicated the futility of power mediation at stage one and two in the escalation process where conciliation or consultation followed by pure mediation may have been more effective. Two applications of consultation in the form of workshops appeared to have some useful effects on the relationship in encouraging a return to stalled mediation. The failure of repeated mediation efforts may indicate the potential utility of consultation as the intervention of choice to follow successful peace-keeping. Thus, the model was useful in identifying why some interventions might have been unsuccessful, and what alternatives and combinations might have proven more effective.

Two recent analyses applied the contingency model to the bitter, sectarian conflict in Northern Ireland with limited success (Bloomfield 1995; Dawson 1991; see Keashly & Fisher 1996). These studies support the important premises of considering subjective elements in escalation and the utility of using escalation as the means for identifying appropriate interventions. However, they question the sequential nature of escalation, for conflict may cycle back and forth between stages through temporary de-escalation, a return to violence, and so on. Furthermore, they suggest that other indicators of escalation, such as additional parties and issues that change over time, need to be considered as cues in the matching process. Dawson's study also attempted to assess the effectiveness of the four different interventions proposed at stage four, and found that only peacekeeping had long-term utility. Power mediation and development aid evidenced short-term effects, while consultation efforts had no discernible impact. Besides difficulties in defining success and in mixing informal with formal interventions, the assessment of comparative effects in these studies is made problematic by the relative underdevelopment of consultation efforts (Keashly & Fisher 1996). Nonetheless, these studies raise important questions for further consideration and elaboration, while generally supporting the rationale of the model.

An endorsement of the contingency model is found in an application by van der Westhuizen (1993a, 1993b) to community level conflict in South Africa in the early 1990s. The analysis is limited to consultation and mediation, for other third party methods were not available. The community conflict was largely between local residents (supported by the African National Congress) and families inhabiting hostels earlier vacated by workers (supported by the Inkhata Freedom party). The conflict was ethnically linked, but more important was rooted in a rivalry over group identity, access to resources, and political power. The previous fifteen years had been marked by outbreaks of violence and work, school and consumer boycotts, during which time Inkhata recruited in the hostels. There were continuing incidents of violence between residents of the areas that escalated through the engagement of outside military support. Over a two-year period alone, 150 houses were destroyed.

Third party intervention was initiated by a team of consultants from the negotiation program of an ecumenical community development organization, two of whom were graduates of conflict resolution training in the U.S. After two months of preparation, the team organized a series of weekend workshops for representatives of the conflicting groups to tell their story about the history of the conflict—one for each group separately followed by a joint workshop. This consultation intervention involved instruction in problem solving followed by dialogue and conflict analysis. The third party constructed a single text analysis of the conflict, and the participants developed strategies for taking the outcomes back to their communities.

Unfortunately the reality of the conflict intervened dramatically with the bombing of a taxi stand shared by both groups, which killed several people. Taxi pick-up now became segregated by community and attacks and counterattacks escalated with more killings. At this point, both sides appealed to the consultants to intervene as mediators, for they were the only mutually trusted third party. The third party team convened an initial meeting to share perceptions, which while it evidenced mutual blaming, did serve as a premediation link. A subsequent two-day session was held for high level decision makers from the two communities and representatives of the taxi operators. After establishing a problem-solving atmosphere, the team divided the participants based on group affiliation to identify the main issues in the conflict as perceived by themselves and the other groups. From this information, the third party, now in the role of mediator, produced an integrated agreement, which the participants endorsed and agreed to present to their constituents. The agreement was ratified and a joint monitoring commission was established to oversee its implementation. This body, composed of one the mediators and a representative of each group, soon became the forum for dealing with subsequent incidents, thus preventing escalation of the conflict.

In the theoretical analysis of the interventions, van der Westhuizen (1993a) asserts that the consultation workshops were instrumental in improving the relationship between the conflicting groups right up to the leadership level. Thus, when a crisis erupted requiring mediation, the third party team was able to work on the substantive issues successfully. The analysis also supports the stage model of escalation as the conflict moved up to the level of mutual threats to survival, that is, destruction. Even at this stage, the mediators were able to work effectively on substantive concerns, because the consultation intervention had established a working relationship free of perceptual distortions and negative attitudes.

Conclusion

The taxonomy of third party interventions is useful to stimulate greater clarity of thinking in the domain of conflict management and resolution. It becomes even more beneficial when the various methods are linked to different conditions of conflict, as in the contingency model. However, whether the stage of escalation is the predominant cue or not awaits further theoretical development. Meanwhile the model serves as a source of helpful working hypotheses, even though it is questionable whether such a simple model of broad scope can be strictly applied. Clearly, the complex process of de-escalation requires further elucidation as does the matching process. Such work can then produce more sophisticated contingency models, assuming the basic rationale holds.

Support for parts of the model come from both laboratory studies and real world cases. The strongest element appears to be the use of consultation as a prenegotiation methodology. Successful examples are found in intergroup, intercommunal, and international conflict, and from these a broad theme emerges. ICR can reduce some of the subjective barriers and build working relationships, thus paving the way for more effective negotiations and agreements.

Leaving aside the question of contingency, it can be argued that ICR should be the first move in many situations of intense conflict. It is useful for providing a mutual analysis that yields a diagnosis on which further interventions can be based. In addition, ICR methods are a potential mechanism for inducing ripeness, and unlike power strategies, are not likely to induce additional resistances to movement. Thus ICR could usefully serve as part of a coordinated, multimodal approach to conflict de-escalation and resolution, with timing and sequencing determined by the conditions of each situation. Thus there is no question that the ultimate utility of ICR lies in its usage within the broader context of conflict management and resolution.

Part Three
The Prospects for the Future

9

Assessment
The State of the Art and the Science

A Review of Interventions

Interactive conflict resolution as a form of applied social science now spans thirty years, from the first Burton workshop in 1965 to a number of ongoing projects in 1996. Several reviews and "state of the art" assessments have been produced over this period (e.g., Doob 1975; Fetherston 1991; Fisher 1972, 1983, 1986, 1993a; Groom 1986; Hill 1982; Mitchell 1981). These have generally been carried out by sympathetic ICR scholar-practitioners, and have stressed the innovative nature and potential utility of the method based on a limited set of cases. The number of published interventions has steadily grown, particularly in the 1980s, thus allowing a more substantial and discerning review and analysis.

The primary source of information for the current review is published accounts cited in previous chapters. In addition, as noted in the Introduction, personal interviews were conducted with many of the leading scholar-practitioners in the field. The interview schedule was loosely structured and tailored during the interview to the experience and interests of the interviewee. At the same time, a general sequence of topics included the individual's background in coming into the field, their major contributions, their assessment of their work, and possible improvements they could make in their methodology. In addition, interviewees were asked what they saw as the critical issues facing the development of the field, how they would recommend overcoming these, and how they saw the future of problem-solving approaches.

As noted in the Introduction, the interview results have been supplemented by the author's participation in various meetings of ICR scholar-practitioners and symposia at scholarly conferences, particularly the annual meetings of the International Society of Political Psychology, which includes many professionals interested in ICR. Particularly since 1991 a series of sessions overviewed ongoing work and focused on the question of assessment (e.g., Babbitt 1994; Mandell 1993; Saunders 1992; Slim 1991). These events provide useful commentary on the state of the art as perceived by those in the field. Thus at no previous time has there been as broad an array of information on which to base an assessment of ICR practice, theory, and research.

The major, published ICR interventions in international conflict over the last three decades are described in table 9.1. Interventions that involve mainly dialogue with grass roots individuals or members of diasporas are not included. This is arbitrary, but partly justified because most dialogues do not have the objective of directly affecting the interaction of the parties. In addition, many dialogue projects go unpublished, making it difficult to adequately assess that line of work. The table covers most of the interventions that can be described as consultation, and that generally aspire to influence the relationship between the parties. Almost all deal with a two-party situation, even though some of the conflicts, such as the Middle East, involve multiple parties.

Table 9.1 covers seventy-six separate workshops, which likely make up the lion's share of consultation work in ICR from 1965 to 1995, as opposed to dialogue, education, or training. Many interventions flow from an institutional base in an academic setting created by the organizers for this specific purpose. Although the number of workshops may seem noteworthy, in reality it represents the initiatives of a few scholar-practitioners and their associates (Burton, Doob, Kelman, Azar, Volkan, Fisher, Saunders), suggesting that the expertise and credibility to mount ICR interventions is spread rather thinly. In contrast, there are more than three-hundred documented cases of mediation, and many more institutional bases and credible mediators available to the international system.

In duration, the interventions evidence a considerable range from two to fourteen days. However, most are three or four days, this reality being primarily determined by the many workshops organized by Kelman and the Dartmouth meetings cochaired by Saunders. The former usually involved weekend workshops of about two and one-half days combined with half-day preworkshop sessions with each group. Some twenty Dartmouth task force meetings lasted from three to four days. The longest workshops are found in the early work of Doob, lasting ten and fourteen days. In between the extremes, there is a common pattern of four- to five-day workshops, as expressed in the work of Azar, Fisher, and Volkan.

Table 9.1.
Major Interactive Conflict Resolution Interventions at the International Level, 1965–95

Study, Year, Duration	Parties	Third Party	Method of Assessment	Reported Outcomes
Burton (1969) 1965, 10 days (5 + 1, etc.)	Malaysia/ Indonesia/ Singapore*	Mixed team of social scientists	case study analysis	framework of settlement
Burton (1969) 1966, 5 days	Greek and Turkish Cypriots	Mixed team of social scientists	case study follow-up interviews	return to negotiations
Doob (1970) 1969, 2 weeks	Ethiopia/ Somalia/Kenya	American social scientists and trainers	case study postworkshop questionnaires	improved attitudes
Cohen et al. (1977), 1971, 3 days	Israelis/ Palestinians*	American and Canadian social scientists	case study analysis	increased understanding
Doob & Foltz (1973) 1971, 10 days	Catholics/ Protestants Northern Ireland*	American social scientists and trainers	case study postworkshop interviews	increased understanding plans for joint projects
Kelman (1992) 10 workshops 1982–92, 3 days	Israelis/ Palestinians*	American social psychologist and colleagues	case study postworkshop interviews	influence on political environment and discourse
Kelman & Cohen (1979) 1972, 3 days	India/ Pakistan/ Bangladesh	American and Canadian social psychologists	case study analysis	increased understanding
Fisher (1980) 1976, 2 days	India/Pakistan	Canadian social psychologist	pre- and post-interviews	improved attitudes
Cohen & Azar (1981) 1979, 2 days	Egypt/Israel*	American and Canadian social scientists	case study analysis	contribution to postagreement peace process
Julius (1991) 5 workshops, 1979–84, 5 days	Israelis/ Egyptians/ Palestinians*	American psychiatrists and social scientists	case study analysis	increased understanding
Azar (1990) 1983/84/85, 3 forums 4/4/3/ days	Britain/ Argentina	Mixed team of social scientists	case study analysis	increased understanding principles for settlement

continued

Table 9.1. *Continued*
Major Interactive Conflict Resolution Interventions at the International Level, 1965–95

Study, Year, Duration	Parties	Third Party	Method of Assessment	Reported Outcomes
Azar (1990) 1984/84, 2 forums 4/4 days	Lebanese communities*	Mixed team of social scientists	case study analysis	principles for united Lebanon
Azar (1990) 1985, 3 days	Sinhalese and Tamil Sri Lankans	Mixed team of social scientists	case study analysis	measures for reducing tension
Doob (1987) 1985, weekly meetings	Greek and Turkish Cypriots	American social psychologist	case study analysis	indeterminate/ ended
Chufrin & Sanders (1993) 1982–92, 20 meetings 3 to 4 days	Soviets and Americans*	Soviet and American scholar-practitioners	case study analysis	contributions to policy formation
Fisher (1991) 1990, 2 days	Greek and Turkish Cypriots	Mixed team of social scientists	postworkshop questionnaire	increased understanding
Fisher (1992) 1991, 4 days	Greek and Turkish Cypriots	Mixed team of social scientists	pre- and postworkshop questionnaires	peace building initiatives
Volkan & Harris (1992), 1992, 4 days	Russia/ Lithuania-Baltic Republics*	American scholar-practitioners	case study analysis	increased understanding action possibilities
Volkan & Harris (1993), 1993, 4 days	Russia/Baltic Republics*	American scholar-practitioners	case study analysis	increased understanding action possibilities
Fisher (1994) 2 workshops, 1993, 4 days	Greek and Turkish Cypriots	Mixed team of social scientists	pre- and postworkshop interviews	proposals for peace building initiatives
Saunders (1995) 1993–ongoing 12 meetings 3–4 days	Tajikistan government/ opposition*	American and Russian scholar-practitioners	case study analysis	increased understanding contribution to negotiations

continued

Table 9.1. *Continued*
Major Interactive Conflict Resolution Interventions at the International Level, 1965–95

Study, Year, Duration	Parties	Third Party	Method of Assessment	Reported Outcomes
Volkan (1995) 1994–ongoing 2 workshops 4 days	Russia/ Estonia-Baltic republics*	American scholar-practitioners	case study analysis	increased understanding action possibilities
Rouhana & Kelman (1994) 5 workshops, 1991–93 3 to 5 days	Israelis/ Palestinians*	Mixed team of social scientist–practitioners	case study analysis	formulations of issues prenegotiation input
Kelman (1995) 1994–ongoing 3 to 5 days	Israelis/ Palestinians*	Mixed team of social scientist–practitioners	case study analysis	understanding of difficult issues paranegotiation input

* These conflicts have shown some movement toward resolution.

Many of the earlier workshops were one-shot events, largely of a pilot nature to study the process and its initial effects. However, some occurred within an ongoing program of interventions, such as Kelman's work on the Israeli-Palestinian conflict. In addition, over time there has been a healthy development toward continuity. In some instances this has been achieved by participants returning along with new delegates (e.g., Azar, Julius, Chufrin & Saunders), while in other cases it results from a truly continuing workshop, though with some changes in participants (e.g., Rouhana & Kelman, Saunders & Slim). The continuing design is a recent development to be encouraged, especially for positive effects of a prenegotiation or paranegotiation nature.

In focus, most interventions deal with protracted social conflicts with international involvements as described by Azar, Burton, and others. These conflicts typically have a long history of antagonism between identity groups and go through repeated cycles of escalation and stalemate. Some are intercommunal or internal in scope, while others are interstate. In relation to identity groups, however, this is an almost arbitrary distinction, for most borders exist where armies collided and where peace treaties or colonial legacies determined a line. Although most of these conflicts have experienced periods of widespread violence or war in the recent past, some are in the early stage of escalation where large-scale hostilities can be prevented, such as between Russia and the Baltic republics. Typically the conflicts of interest have repeatedly resisted traditional methods of management. It is likely that this intractability has attracted the attention of ICR proponents wishing to try out their innovative methodology.

The national identity of the third party consultants is predominantly American, with British, Canadian, and Australian involvement as well. Thus ICR comes from a western European–North American base in its cultural proclivities and its adherence to the principles and goals of applied social science and practice. One exception is the work of the Dartmouth task force, where Americans and Russians have collaborated, first in addressing the spectre of the cold war, and secondly in applying their learnings to the Tajikistan conflict. In professional terms, the most frequent backgrounds are those of political science, international relations, and social psychology, although psychiatrists, lawyers, and retired diplomats are also involved. With regard to gender, the ICR field has been dominated by men in the early going and in the organizing of major consultation interventions. However, women professionals have played important roles in many of the projects, for example, in Kelman's work, and their presence is stronger in some recent efforts, such as Randa Slim's involvement in the Tajikistan work. Overall it appears that women have generally made more lead contributions to dialogue and training interventions than to consultation ones.

In the identity of participants, it is possible to roughly categorize these individuals in the degree of influence they are perceived to have on the decision making and policy formulation of the parties. Table 9.2 attempts to distinguish interventions by identifying their participants as preinfluentials (a term coined by Kelman), influentials, informal policy advisers, or informal representatives. Although the categories are bound to overlap to some degree, preinfluentials are typically younger, less politically connected individuals who are graduate students, young professionals, or lower-level political activists. Influentials are established professionals (academics, journalists, writers, parliamentarians, retired officers, former bureaucrats, or out-of-office politicians), who carry considerable weight in their societies in affecting public opinion or official policymaking or both. Informal advisers are a step closer to the decision makers in their groups or states, having direct access to the leadership, but not through official policy roles. Informal representatives carry the influence of advisers, but in addition are appointed by the leadership as informal delegates to the workshop or meeting. They may be in official or unofficial roles, but come in an unofficial capacity.

Table 9.2.
Participant Characteristics Categorized over 76
Workshops, 1965–95

Category	n	%
1. Preinfluentials	8	10
2. Influentials	19	25
3. Informal Policy Advisers	44	58
4. Informal Representatives	5	7
Total	76	100

Notes: Category 1 includes an estimated 5 workshops from the earlier work of Kelman 1992 as well as Cohen et al. 1977; Kelman & Cohen 1979; and Fisher 1980.

Category 2 includes an estimated 5 workshops from the later work of Kelman 1992 as well as Doob & Foltz 1973; Julius 1991; Azar 1990—Britain/Argentina); Doob 1987; and Fisher 1991, 1992, 1994.

Category 3 includes workshops by Doob 1970; Cohen & Azar 1981; Chufrin & Saunders 1993; Saunders 1995; Volkan & Harris 1992, 1993; Volkan 1995; Rouhana & Kelman 1994; and Kelman 1995.

Category 4 includes workshops by Burton 1969 and Azar 1990—Lebanon and Sri Lanka.

The analysis presented in table 9.2 indicates that preinfluentials make up a small proportion of participants (i.e., only eight interventions). Most of these were in the developmental period of the field and involved workshops more of a pilot nature, to try out and improve the methodology in a low risk, low cost manner. Categorizing five of Kelman's early workshops in this manner is arbitrary, but hopefully valid, for these involved a mix of preinfluentials and influentials. Similarly, workshops with appointed representatives are rare, mainly coming from the early work of Burton and his later collaborations with Azar. This outcome speaks to Burton's methodology, which is tied more closely to diplomatic practice, and geared more to creating alternatives for resolution in the sessions themselves. At the same time, it is clear that most practitioners have either chosen, or been required to choose, a less direct method of gaining participants.

Influentials are the participants in about one-quarter of the cases. These interventions occur over the entire period of development and involve various initiatives. What they have in common is the manner of selecting and inviting participants who carry weight in their societies, often with the tacit approval of the leaderships, but without their direction. More striking is the predominance, especially more recently, of informal policy advisers as participants. Almost sixty percent of the interventions are categorized this way, although one-half of these are attributable to the twenty meetings of the Dartmouth task force. A number of the leading ICR figures, including Kelman, Volkan, and Saunders, are moving in this direction, apparently to maximize utility, while maintaining a healthy degree of independence from the official domain.

In the methods of assessment given in table 9.1, most interventions provide only case study description and analysis to substantiate their claims of effectiveness. These analyses are based almost solely on the impressions of the third party, and are further limited by a reluctance to tape record sessions for reasons of confidentiality and feared constraints on participants. Table 9.3 demonstrates that almost ninety percent of studies relied on this minimal research strategy, whereas seven percent used some form of post-assessment and five percent a before-and-after design. In no instance was the more powerful control group design implemented, possibly indicating both the difficulty and inappropriateness of this method at the international level. Pre- and post-assessments are typically done through interviews and questionnaires, and it is difficult to understand why these simple and relatively nondemanding methods are not used more frequently.

The effects of interventions over the past thirty years are categorized in table 9.4, based on the reported outcomes in table 9.1 and the descriptions provided in previous chapters. A few interventions (thirteen percent) claim only increased understanding or improved attitudes by participants, and though this is a minimal outcome, it does indicate that this form of guided intergroup contact does not have negative effects on participants. This is an important finding, for many forms of interaction in such conflicts are characterized by aloofness, suspicion, or hostility, which simply reinforce existing stereotypes and behaviors. This minimal outcome is identified in almost all interventions, thus attesting to success in creating the conditions that allow par-

Table 9.3.
Research Characteristics 76 Workshops, 1965–95

Method of Assessment	n	%
1. Case Study Analysis Only	67	88
2. Post-assessment (including follow-up)	5	7
3. Pre- and Post-assessments	4	5
Total	*76*	*100*

Table 9.4.
Effects of 76 Workshops, 1965–95

Reported Outcomes	n	%
1. Increased Understanding/Improved Attitudes	10	13
2. Influence on the Peace Process	31	41
3. Contributions to the Peace Process (Documents, Plans, Initiatives)	13	17
4. Contributions to Negotiations (Analyses, Formulations, Frameworks)	20	26
5. Indeterminate	2	3
Total	76	100

Notes: Outcome categories are exclusive in terms of cases coded, but categories 2, 3, and 4 subsume changes in category 1, and categories 3 and 4 are more concrete expressions of category 2.

Category 1 includes Doob 1969; Cohen et al. 1977; Kelman and Cohen 1979; Fisher 1976; Julius 1991—5 workshops; and Fisher 1991.

Category 2 includes Kelman 1992—10 workshops); Chufrin & Saunders 1993—20 meetings; and Azar 1990—Sri Lanka.

Category 3 includes Cohen and Azar 1981; Azar 1990—Britain/Argentina, 3 forums; Azar 1990—Lebanon, 2 forums; Fisher 1992; Fisher 1994—2 workshops; Volkan and Harris 1992, 1993; and Volkan 1995—2 workshops.

Category 4 includes Burton 1969—2 workshops; Saunders 1995—12 meetings; Rouhana & Kelman 1994—5 workshops; and Kelman 1994.

Category 5 includes Doob and Foltz 1973 because of the controversy surrounding the reported outcomes; and Doob 1987 because of interdeterminate outcomes.

ticipants from conflicting groups to learn about each other in a positive manner.

In more substantial outcomes, many interventions (forty-one percent) can be interpreted as having a beneficial influence on the peace process, although these numbers come almost entirely from the work of Kelman on the Israeli-Palestinian conflict and Saunders on the U.S.-Soviet relationship. These conclusions rely on the evaluation of the third parties themselves based on follow-up contacts, feedback from participants, and changes in policy directions that are congruent with previous workshop discussions and outcomes. A more direct linkage is provided by the interventions (seventeen percent) that produced specific contributions that were fed into the peace process as principles for a settlement, plans for peacebuilding activities, initiatives to reduce tension, and so on. In situations where negotiations are ongoing between the parties, a considerable number of interventions (twenty-six percent) appear to have made direct contributions to the diplomatic process. Included are the early work of Burton, and the most recent work by Kelman and Saunders. These efforts have engaged in analyses of resistances, formulations of issues, and the creation of frameworks for settlement that by the very identity of the participants and their involvement in the negotiation process are deemed to have had influence. Thus work in ICR appears to be producing positive outcomes that are congruent with its basic rationale and objectives.

This overview also attests to the continuing vitality and consistent development of the field. There has been an ever-expanding application of the method, and more recent efforts show more continuity and direct connections with official peacemaking processes. At the same time, ICR continues to face critical questions in its applicability and effectiveness in the international arena. It is therefore important to address these issues, while working to identify the strengths and deficiencies of the method and its various approaches. What is required is an ongoing assessment of the state of practice, theory, and research, so that the field can realistically assess its current status and engage in further developments to reach its full potential.

Assessment of Applicability and Effectiveness

The *applicability* of ICR to the reality and complexity of international conflict was first raised by Yalem (1971) in his critique of Burton's initial work (see chapter 1). Yalem accurately perceived controlled communication as a social-psychological approach for altering the perceptions and attitudes of representatives of conflicting parties, so that reduced hostility might facilitate negotiations. However, he challenged the assumptions that international conflicts are primarily subjective and that its sources are to be found mainly in internal politics and decision making, rather than in the international system. In contrast, he posits that international conflict is a mix of objective incompatibilities and subjective distortions and faulty images; thus improved communication is only a necessary rather than sufficient condition for resolution. Yalem also contests the notion that concepts and procedures can be automatically transferred from the interpersonal and intergroup levels to the international one with its larger array of more complex variables. Yalem asserts that traditional diplomatic and legal methods will continue to be necessary to address intense international conflicts, and that controlled communication may serve as a useful supplement to these methods, rather than being a panacea.

Mitchell (1973) took up the challenge on behalf of the Burton group in responding to Yalem's critique. He counters the procedural questions that Yalem raises, and points out that proponents of the method, including Burton and Kelman, have indicated that it is not a substitute for negotiation, but a useful preparation. Mitchell argues that Yalem's view of the subjective nature of conflict is simplistic, that is, the misperceptions of the parties. In contrast, a complex view of subjective conflict includes values, such as security, that are not in limited supply, preferences for goals, which may be reordered, and reevaluations of costs. These elements often change, thus making conflict a highly subjective phenomenon, and allowing for changes in the parties' orientations, even though the objective incompatibilities remain.

In defending the use of analogous reasoning from other levels to support controlled communication, Mitchell (1973) distinguishes between the use of the method for altering perceptions and developing insights into a problem, and for resolving conflicts peacefully. In the first use, considerable experience and rationale from social psychology and group dynamics would justify the method as a means of attitude change and problem analysis. In the second use, transfer from other levels should occur unless international conflict proves to be fundamentally different from that in other domains. This does not appear to be the case, because various forms of domestic conflict also involve many complex variables and the use of power and threat. Thus findings from conflict analysis and resolution at one level can be useful at another one.

In a later and more extensive rationale for problem-solving methods, Mitchell (1981) affirms the subjectivist approach by stating that the opportunities for misperception, misinterpretation, and miscalculation in international relationships are endless, especially when there is a history of conflict. He elaborates further a number of other bases on which intercommunal and international conflict can be regarded as subjective. To the three noted above, he adds the multiple and often conflicting goals of the parties, the priorities of which change over time, and the potential transformation of the parties' definition of the situation, for example, through a joint realization of higher order goals. Mitchell notes that because traditional techniques of conflict management have typically attempted to simply stop disruptive behavior and obtain a compromise agreement, it falls to the newer innovative methods to more fully utilize the insights of the subjectivist approach and assist parties in reaching integrative resolutions.

Also bearing on applicability, Mitchell (1981) asserts that many academics and practitioners have charged that consultant peacemaking is impractical, ineffective, and untestable. (However, it is interesting to note that there are no concerted attacks in the literature since Yalem.) Practicality relates most strongly to applicability, and asks whether problem-solving approaches will ever be used much beyond interpersonal and intraorganizational settings. On closer examination, what are seen as inherent difficulties at the international level turn out to be a failure to grasp the essence of the approach or administrative inconveniences. According to Mitchell, most diplomats and international organizations are not informed about the approach or its differences from traditional methods. In addition, world society lacks an established organization identified with and able to offer consultation services. Mitchell further points out that difficulties in implementation are not impossibilities, and that many arguments about impractibility appear to arise from conservatism and caution rather than searching analysis. He also notes that the approach has been implemented at the international level with some success, a conclusion that can be drawn even more strongly today, as evidenced by tables 9.1 and 9.4.

The results of the interviews also bear on applicability, as most ICR practitioners remain optimistic about the method's potential utility. They generally believe that ICR is relevant to the international system, not as a panacea, but as a method that is valuable in its complementarity to existing practices such as negotiation and mediation. Most have not experienced resistance from parties and potential participants, who tend to see the confidential, low risk, research-orientated venture as providing a unique and possibly useful forum for interaction. Rather, they have experienced resistance from other scholars, decision makers, or funders who regard the approach as unrealistic, risky, and perhaps dangerous. These sentiments are based on a view that the method is simplistic and naive in comparison to the complexity of a power-based, anarchic system.

Given that the problem-solving approach to international conflict has shown only modest growth over the past three decades, one must suspect that there is considerable resistance by diplomats and decision makers. John Burton's failed attempts to establish a consultation base both through the International Studies Association and later through a group of middle powers at the United Nations would seem to indicate that realists in both academia and diplomacy are sceptical about the approach (Burton 1983; Burton & Mitchell 1986). Their hesitancy to expand beyond established ways is likely based on resistance to change as well as questions about the relevance of newer methods. Unfortunately applicability is the source of its own continuance. Realist opponents who are in decision-making positions in international organizations, governments, academia, and funding institutions will not approve of ICR projects, because they perceive them as unrealistic and inapplicable. Thus the proponents are not provided with opportunities to demonstrate applicability and utility, and the arguments of resistance are not challenged with evidence.

The second issue in assessing ICR is that of *effectiveness*, that is, does it work? Applicability merges into this, for it asks a priori whether in principle the method can be effective in the global domain. A response requires theoretical arguments about why the method should work, as well as an explication of how it should work. The first question is addressed more in the arguments above, while the second relates more directly to effectiveness.

Kelman (1972) at first identified the ultimate goal of workshops as feeding the changes and solutions generated into official policymaking. This *transfer* involves two elements: first, the individual changes (improved attitudes, new orientations) as a result of the workshop, and second, the influence of these changes on the policy process. Similarly, Mitchell (1981) distinguishes "internal effectiveness" on the participants from "external effectiveness" on the course of the conflict. Between the two comes the "reentry" problem, wherein participants with new insights and more cooperative orientations are subjected to social pressure and sometimes physical danger when they return to their home community or state.

Proponents of ICR are well aware that participants will encounter a wall of normative resistance upon their return, and often discussions are held toward the end of a workshop on the reentry process. They are also aware that the ability of participants to resist conformity pressures and to have influence on policymaking depends in part on their identity, stature, and political connections. Kelman (1972) suggested that the ideal participants are influential individuals at an intermediate distance from decision making, who are thus in a position to evaluate and influence policy, even though their role is not to formulate or implement it. His work on the Israeli-Palestinian conflict is an excellent example of involving participants of increasing influence who can affect policy decisions in various ways (see chapter 3).

Mitchell (1981) proposes a number of working hypotheses about reentry and transfer that attempt to identify the conditions fostering greater effectiveness. These deal with the degree of isolation of the workshop, the conservatism of the home environment, and the closeness of the participants' involvement in official decision making. He proposes that the closer participants are to decision making, the less likely they are to change their attitudes, but the greater will be the impact of any changes. Mitchell also identifies the final problem confronting effectiveness as utilization, that is, how insights and changes might be used in complex policymaking.

In the interviews, it was pointed out that there is no overall model of linkage between intervention outcomes and effects on policymaking about the conflict. Thus it is difficult to persuade sceptics that attitudinal and other changes in a few influentials could influence intraparty decision making in large collectivities. The difficulty of transfer and the need to conceptualize and document it are well taken by proponents. First, they assume that there is nothing inherent in small-group methods that should rule out possible effects. Much policymaking itself takes place in small, elite groups, though often taking into account a wide range of concerns and constituencies. Negotiation between parties is also a small-group process, with the negotiators being in a boundary role position not unlike participants in a workshop. Well-connected influentials could serve similar functions in an unofficial manner with the leadership that negotiators serve in an official manner, especially over a series of workshops. In addition, the mounting evidence summarized in tables 9.1 and 9.4 appears to indicate that ICR interventions do influence decision making and policy formulation. The question remains how, given that there is no detailed conceptualization of the ways in which workshop outcomes could tie in to policymaking processes and institutions at the international level. This question is true in general terms as well as across particular cases, where the complexity and variety of policymaking would be highly evident.

The study of foreign policy and international politics has a rich history in political science and international relations (e.g., Rosenau 1969). A wide range of factors influence foreign policymaking, both from the external system and the domestic context (Holsti 1992a). Internal factors include variables such as national attributes, government structure, public opinion, and the role of the bureaucracy. In many direct and subtle ways, these various influences come to bear upon the leadership of the state as it formulates foreign policy to guide its interactions with other significant actors. While international relations generally refers to all the various forms of interaction between different societies, international politics focuses on government-to-government interaction as driven by their foreign policies (Holsti 1992a).

The objective of ICR in international or intercommunal conflict is to influence the policymaking process and outcomes of the governments or leaderships involved, so that their interaction changes. Thus proponents need to think systematically about how the transfer process can bring insights and new orientations to bear upon decision makers. The first step is to identify the possible linkages of influence between ICR participants and various bodies that are involved in policymaking and implementation.

Lederach (1995a) provides a model of leadership in populations affected by protracted conflict that identifies three levels: (1) the top leadership comprised of political and military leaders who are highly visible and speak for their constituencies, (2) middle-range leaders who are respected and influential individuals from various sectors who are connected to the top leaders and the constituencies they represent, and (3) grass roots leaders in local settings who have understanding of the fear and suffering of the population and firsthand knowledge of the deep-rooted animosity of the conflict. Lederach sees problem-solving workshops as a middle-range approach to peace that provide an unofficial venue for midlevel leaders to analyze the conflict and create alternatives to adversarial interaction. Lederach's model helps clarify the role of ICR in peacebuilding and correctly situates it at an intermediate level of influence in society. Thus ICR is not geared to produce immediate agreements between top leaders, but to influence policymaking over time, partly by linking grass roots concerns with top-level action through the connections of midlevel influentials.

Figure 9.1 presents an initial attempt to provide a model of the potential transfer effects of ICR interventions on the policymaking and interaction of antagonists. The model deals with two parties, as do most interventions, but the proposed linkages would be similar with more parties, including additional, secondary parties who might become involved in the ICR process. For each party, a few important generic actors in policymaking are identified: a leadership, governmental-bureaucratic constituencies, public-political constituencies, diplomatic representatives, and unofficial diplomats, that is, those involved in ICR or other unofficial interactions. This level of generality is chosen so that both highly organized and institutionalized entities such as states are included, as well as less organized and structured collectivities such as insurgent groups.

What is central to policymaking are the basic functions and interactions of the various units. The leadership has primary responsibility for policymaking, but is dependent upon governmental and bureaucratic input, advice, and constraint. Although the complexity of these processes will vary widely, even among small and large states, the leadership usually receives policy analyses and options from relevant bureaucratic units, and is often responsible to some legislative body as well as a judicial arm of government, at least in the extreme. Thus the leadership may be both encouraged and constrained by governmental obligations, and will also receive bureaucratic input that may be a confused or limited outcome of complex bargaining among different units. Policy options may therefore be developed that serve the interests of particular units more than those of the group or state as a whole.

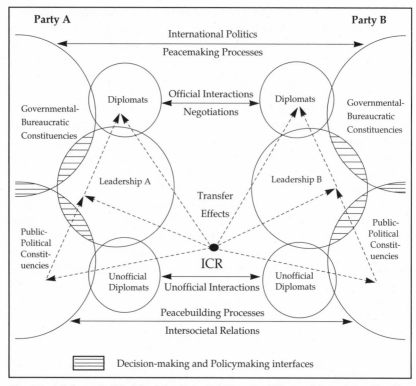

Fig. 9.1. A Schematic Model of the Potential Transfer Effects of Interactive Conflict Resolution

In the domain of public-political constituencies, the leadership to varying degrees will be sensitive to public opinion, while at the same time working to influence such opinion to conform with its own policy objectives. The role of nongovernmental organizations (NGOs), interest groups, and social movements will come to bear on policymaking, as will the ideology and platform of political parties, especially the one(s) directly connected to the leadership. In democracies, the governing party will usually face an organized and public opposition, while in all states and groups various elements and factions will be opposed to the leadership's policy directions. Thus there will be very important policymaking interfaces between the leadership and the governmental-bureaucratic constituencies and the public-political constituencies, as well as between the latter two, in electoral processes, lobbying efforts, policy input from NGOs to bureaucrats, and so on.

It is acknowledged that this functional overview and the model are simplistic, both in general terms as well as in relation to the complexity and uniqueness of any given party. In fact, it can be said that to really understand policymaking in any party requires a detailed case analysis of that collectivity in all its uniqueness. Nonetheless, the model represents an attempt to grasp the general essence of the policymaking structure and process, so that the possible relation of ICR interventions and effects to these can be identified, at least at a generic level.

The interactions between the parties are represented in the model both in general and specifically related to ICR. International politics refers to all forms of government-to-government interchanges, including peacemaking. Of particular interest are official diplomatic interactions that include negotiations between designated representatives who are accountable to their respective leaderships, either through bureaucratic channels or directly. Intersocietal relations refers to all manner of interactions between the public-political constituencies of the two parties, including peacebuilding in all sectors, such as commerce, religion, NGOs, the media, and so on. Unofficial interactions are specifically those involving unofficial diplomats, including ICR interventions with various types of influential participants.

The potential transfer effects of ICR are shown by the dotted arrows in the model. These relate initially to the identity of the participants in relation to the policymaking structures and processes in their respective parties. The least direct form of transfer is through preinfluentials or influentials who are connected to public-political constituencies in their communities. These would include, for example, young professionals, journalists, retired politicians, political activists, academics, NGO leaders, and so on. They could have influence on public opinion in their respective communities and on various bodies (think tanks, research institutes, the media, political parties) that interface with policymaking, either directly with the leadership or through governmental-bureaucratic constituencies. In relation to table 9.4, the most likely transfer effect from their involvement would be a positive influence on the peace process, for example, in broadening the image of the adversary, increasing expectations about the likelihood and desirability of a peaceful resolution, and developing options for conciliatory or tension-reducing moves. These types of effects would generally be more appropriate in the prenegotiation phase of conflict de-escalation.

When the participants are informal advisers who have access to decision makers, the linkage to the leadership is direct. In this case, positive influences on the peace process can occur in a more immediate fashion. In addition, tangible contributions to policymaking are possible, such as statements of principles underlying a settlement, plans for confidence-building measures, proposals for peacebuilding initiatives, and so on (see table 9.4). These contributions would likely receive serious consideration from the leadership given the stature and role of the participants, and could be implemented at the discretion of the leadership. In situations where negotiations are under way, relevant ideas could be passed on to the negotiators. In cases where there are no negotiations, the input might influence a policy decision to consider or to move into negotiation.

When participants are informal representatives, that is, appointed by the leadership to participate in an ICR intervention in an unofficial capacity, the linkage to policymaking is the most direct. The fruits of the exercise will be communicated immediately back to the decision makers, and they are likely to consider any ideas of merit in subsequent policymaking and for input into negotiations. When some participants are advisers to or representatives in the negotiations, the transfer effect could also be directly into that forum. In either case, tangible contributions could be fed into negotiations as joint analyses of interests, formulations of difficult issues, or frameworks for a settlement (see table 9.4). A paranegotiation function of ICR would be most efficacious when the intervention consisted of a continuing series of workshops with advisers to the leaders and the negotiators.

This conceptual overview of the potential transfer effects of ICR interventions provides a minimal rationale for the applicability of the method. As such, the model is worthy of elaboration, revision, and detailed application to particular cases. It could also serve as a rough guide for tracking the outcomes of interventions and assessing the effects on the parties' decision making and interaction. However, evaluating external effectiveness faces a multitude of barriers that may be only partly surmountable (see below).

Evaluation of Different Forms of Intervention

ICR workshop methods show much commonality as articulated in the model of third party consultation developed by Fisher (1972, 1976) and in the generic analysis provided by Mitchell (1981). Nonetheless, differences on a number of components distinguish the major forms of intervention—the Burton school, the Kelman group, the psychodynamic approach of Volkan, Julius, and Montville, and the work of Saunders and his colleagues. A complete analysis of differences is beyond the present scope, but some comments can be made on how the variants deal with the issues of applicability and effectiveness. These will identify some of the strengths and weaknesses of the various forms, but will also raise the possibility that certain variants might be more appropriate and effective under different conditions. Thus it is possible to conceive of a contingency model within ICR itself.

The Burton school is deemed to include original and continuing members of the Centre for the Analysis of Conflict (Burton, de Reuck, Groom, Mitchell, Banks) as well as later collaborators, most notably Azar, who have contributed to ICR. By and large this group has followed the method articulated by Burton (1969, 1987). A distinguishing feature is the direct connection to the leaderships of the parties, both in seeking support for the intervention and the delegation of unofficial, high level representatives to attend the meetings.

In Burton's earliest work, the representatives were in official roles, while his later statements indicate that they should be one step removed from decision makers, for example, parliamentarians, personal friends, or scholars. In either case, the nomination process makes these sessions more comparable to "off-the-record" interactions or "back-channel" negotiations in their connection to official diplomatic processes. Although appointed representative may carry the most influence with decision makers, they are also likely the most resistant to change. If a mutual breakthrough in orientations occurs, the "silver bullet" effects could be dramatic, but this is unlikely unless there is a series of workshops, as Burton (1987) notes.

In Burton's approach, the organizers of the intervention also report back to the leaderships, having at first sought their approval for it. This linkage has a number of potential functions, including assessing the value of further meetings and serving as a transition to negotiations. Burton (1987) maintains that the organizers must give special consideration to this transition throughout the process, thus underscoring his ultimate goal of resolving the conflict, first by agreements in principle and then by agreements on implementation.

The favored analysis in the Burton model has shifted from an emphasis on clearing up misperceptions and miscommunication to the centrality of human needs in conflict creation and resolution. However, the preferred outcome is the same—a redefined relationship based on functional cooperation and the political agreements that operationalize these. Thus the focus is on influencing decision makers, while ignoring the role of public and political constituencies in the policymaking process. The approach therefore assumes that leaders have considerable autonomy in the formation of foreign policy, and if this is not the case, the effectiveness of the method is compromised.

The Kelman model of interactive problem solving has shown a conscious and detailed concern with applicability and effectiveness throughout its development. Kelman (1972) provided a sophisticated discussion of the transfer process, while Kelman (1995) describes the contributions that unofficial conflict resolution efforts have made to the Israeli-Palestinian peace process. Kelman (1992) notes how workshops are linked to the ongoing political process by the selection of participants and the definition of agendas, both of which follow from an analysis of the current political situation. The objective is to generate inputs into the political dialogue within each party and the decision-making processes within and between them. These inputs are geared toward creating a political environment that is conducive to the transformation of the relationship and the resolution of the conflict.

To operationalize their model, Kelman and his colleagues have carefully selected influential and politically active representatives of the parties who are not in official decision-making roles. However, the participants have come with the tacit approval of the leaderships and are in a position to feed their learnings back into the political process (Kelman 1995). Participants need to have credibility, access to the political center, and be part of the mainstream of their communities, while at the same time committed to a negotiated solution. In the transfer model in fig. 9.1, Kelman's participants are likely a mixture of those who have influence with various public and political constituencies and those who have direct access to the leadership. As the credibility of his work has increased over the years, it is likely that the number with direct access has increased, as has the involvement of some individuals from official roles. Thus the transfer effects have been multiple and more directly linked to the leaderships as the work has matured.

Regarding effectiveness, Kelman has set realistic objectives over time with a sophisticated view of what can be accomplished at what point in the international system. Transfer effects are a complex, ongoing process requiring the third party to develop a close knowledge of the parties and to build and maintain diverse networks (Kelman 1995). Kelman identifies three contributions that his long-term intervention on the Israeli-Palestinian conflict has made to the peace process. One is the development of cadres of participants who have not only played various roles in influencing policy in both communities, but have been directly involved as advisers and negotiators in the official talks and in the back-channel discussions that led to the 1993 breakthrough. Second, the workshops produced substantive inputs, which were gradually infused into the two political cultures and on which negotiations were built. Third, the intervention over time contributed to the evolution of a new relationship and a political atmosphere that was conducive to negotiations.

Now that workshops are continuing alongside negotiations with relatively direct connections, Kelman's work continues to feed into the official process, particularly around exploring difficult future issues.

Thus the Kelman approach has worked toward all of the transfer effects identified in fig. 9.1 in a careful sequence of increasing influence over time. This helps explain the contribution that has been made to the transformation of Israeli-Palestinian relations and to the overall Middle East peace process.

The psychodynamic approach of Volkan and his colleagues has demonstrated increasing attention to the linkages between unofficial and official processes. The initial work on the Middle East conflict involved a mixed collection of influentials who appear to have been recruited primarily through professional connections and who were not directly connected to the leaderships, even though some were in official roles. Thus these individuals apparently came without the approval or knowledge of the decision makers and were under no obligation to report back to them. Given this, the potential transfer effects were directed mainly to public and political constituencies with a view toward developing peacebuilding activities rather than policy changes. It is therefore understandable that the primary outcomes were collaborative initiatives in the scholarly domain and an ongoing network for unofficial contact.

The later work of Volkan in the Baltic republics shows a definite concern with "crucial junctures" by which the findings from the workshops are reported to official decision makers in the hope that this will influence policymaking. The primary way of ensuring this connection was by inviting representatives who have access to decision makers or who are themselves members of the governments involved. The participant lists from the workshops shows the involvement of high level officials from government units directly concerned with interethnic and international affairs. Thus there was immediate awareness and scrutiny of ideas by official policymakers, and the action possibilities could be taken forward directly to the leaderships for further consideration.

It is also expected that a number of the participants were involved in official interactions between Russia and the Baltic republics, thus having a direct impact on negotiations. Therefore the potential transfer effects would be both through the leadership and directly into official negotiations. In addition, some of the action ideas that related to interethnic relations within the Baltic states could be taken forward in the public-political domain as well as the governmental-bureaucratic one. Thus, in principle, it appears that Volkan's current approach allows for all possible transfer effects, which could maximize the probability of having beneficial influences on the conflicts in question.

The work of Saunders and his colleagues in the Dartmouth Conference demonstrates an immediate, sustained, and direct concern with transfer to policymaking. The impetus for Dartmouth came from an official need to have an unofficial forum for communication, particularly during difficult periods in U.S.-Soviet Union relations. Thus the sessions carried the approval of both leaderships and were expected to focus on policy matters relating to the overall relationship. Furthermore, many of the participants have been individuals with policymaking experience or who are close to decision makers or both. In the Regional Conflicts Task Force, which Saunders has cochaired for more than ten years, participants typically met with government policy officials before the sessions as well as afterward to brief them on the outcomes.

Many of the policy directions that led to the initial transformation of the Soviet Union and to the demise of the cold war were developed in the task force in a spirit of mutual analysis and collaborative change. The impact of transfer effects to American-Soviet (now Russian) relations is impossible to ascertain, but the potential linkages went directly to both leaderships as well as likely penetrating some governmental-bureaucratic constituencies as well. Thus the intended and claimed outcomes of this sustained intervention are unofficial policy dialogue leading to changes in official policy when other factors are amenable. The ultimate outcome is a transformation of international politics between the parties.

In initiating the Tajikistan dialogue, the Dartmouth model was followed by gaining the approval (though tacit) of the parties and by seeking influential participants with connections to the various leaderships. The sessions focused on policy-relevant matters, including a shared conception of a future Tajikistan and a joint memorandum on a mutually acceptable negotiating process. The latter product was transmitted directly to officials in all parties and to the negotiating teams, which include three members of the dialogue. The complementarity of the two tracks is further demonstrated by the decision of the dialogue group not to deal with the same issues as negotiations, but to consider future issues and means of implementing an agreement and creating a civil society. The transfer effects have thus flowed directly to the leaderships and the official interactions among their representatives.

From this brief overview of the transfer effects of the major ICR approaches, a number of conclusions can be drawn. First, all the organizers show a sensitivity to policymaking in their design work, particularly in the selection of participants, the interface with the leaderships, and the formation of workshop agendas. It is clear that all approaches intend to influence policy toward the de-escalation and resolution of the conflict, and that each sees itself as supportive of official negotiations in a complementary manner. Not surprisingly, effective interventions are characterized by a series of continuing workshops, with mostly repeat participants and an ongoing connection to policymaking or negotiations or both. In some cases, the potential for influence has grown over time, as more influential participants are drawn in, and as multiple connections with policymaking are achieved. In all cases, an argument can be made, backed up with observations and impressions, that these continuing interventions have had a positive de-escalatory effect on the conflicts they addressed.

The State of Practice, Theory, and Research

The practice side of ICR shows a healthy variety of interventions and clients as depicted in table 9.1. A number of major players have developed their practice over time, and have come to share considerable commonality, even though their disciplinary backgrounds vary and their underlying explanations come from different theoretical bases. An important shift over time is from one-shot interventions to a carefully planned continuing series of workshops designed to have maximal impact on policymaking. There is also a trend toward involving informal policy advisers rather than simply influentials who have no direct access to decision makers. Another change is a shift in focus from producing creative alternatives for resolving the conflict to engaging in various collaborative activities for improving the overall relationship between the parties. What emerges is the continuing improvement of a promising social technology of conflict analysis and resolution that is increasingly demonstrating its applicability and effectiveness in addressing protracted social conflicts.

In theoretical development, the field presents a mixed picture. Most major proponents have produced descriptive theories that elucidate the elements of their approach in some relation to the phenomena of intergroup and international conflict. Fisher's (1972) model of third party consultation continues to capture the major components of the method at a generic level, while Kelman's theorizing describes many of the inherent dynamics and dialectics (Kelman 1992; Kelman & Cohen 1986). Most of the work presents a prescriptive "theory of practice," which proposes what procedures with what participants under what conditions will produce what outcomes.

As Mitchell (1993) points out, all practitioners aim to affect the conflict in: (1) an impact on participants (images, expectations, perceived options), (2) an outcome that can be reported back to decision makers (principles, proposals), and (3) an outcome in the longer term that brings about policy changes and diminishes the level of coercion. He identifies "micro-level theory" as concerned with the relationship between the structure and dynamics of the intervention and the impact on participants. At this level, much of the literature is not theoretical in the sense of clearly delineated hypotheses that link independent and dependent variables (Mitchell 1993). Examples of testable hypotheses are provided by Fisher (1983), Mitchell (1981), and Hill (1982), but such investigations are rare.

Another necessity is the creation of a "theory of understanding" that would more closely link the rationale and operation of ICR interventions to the conditions and dynamics of conflict itself. Mitchell (1993) coins the term "meso-level theory," which involves hypotheses about the outcome of interventions in relation to characteristics of the conflict in question. Example questions include: What are the most appropriate objectives for an intervention given the existing relationships in the conflict, and what is the most appropriate strategy when the adversaries themselves are subject to divisive internal conflicts? Such theorizing would greatly inform ICR practice, and yet there is very little scholarly focus on such ideas. As Hill (1982) points out, the modal assumption supported by workshop experience is that conflict is inherently subjective, but beyond that there is little hypothesis testing about what variations in methodology are more effective, especially in relation to what aspects of conflict.

It is concluded that theory development in ICR is rudimentary, when we define a theory as a set of testable propositions specifying the relationships among variables. What exists is a descriptive and normative sketch of a method and its anticipated outcomes, both immediate and long-term. Within this, differences among scholar-practitioners represent their professional backgrounds (e.g., social psychology, psychoanalysis, political science) and provide them with divergent explanations on why and how the methodology is effective. Furthermore, there is not much specification of relationships among variables within the models, for example, between attributes of the third party and the qualities of interaction between the delegates. Nor is there a detailed elucidation of how the outputs from a workshop are expected to flow through the participants into the policymaking process. What exists is a theory of practice that lacks an adequate theory of understanding, both about its internal functioning and its relationship to the phenomena it addresses.

With respect to research, table 9.3 shows almost a sole reliance on case study methods to document and evaluate ICR interventions. These are almost without exception single case studies, for there is very little comparative case analysis, such as Kelman (1972). There is also limited use of quantitative methods using questionnaires or interviews to tap the evaluations of participants and the changes they may have experienced. Furthermore, very few studies assess transfer effects back to the parties, the wider relationship and the conflict, and the few that do offer only anecdotal impressions as opposed to more systematic follow-up procedures and evidence. Although descriptive methods are useful for initially documenting the approach, they are not adequate for testing theoretical linkages or making inferences about effectiveness.

It must, however, be acknowledged that there are severe practical limitations and challenging ethical responsibilities in doing evaluation research on interventions in such complex and politically sensitive situations. ICR scholar-practitioners understandably prefer giving a higher priority to protecting the sanctity of the process and the anonymity of their participants than to the needs of research. They are generally against intrusive procedures such as tape recording, which can provide a valuable record for analysis, but which would likely raise participant fears about later attributions that could not be denied. There is a concern that demands for data collection may de-emphasize the practical importance of the work and may seem inappropriate to high level influentials. Extensive follow-up procedures risk identifying participants to hard liners in their group who could threaten them socially, economically, or physically. In addition, large-scale, multi-method research enterprises would be required to trace the process and outcomes of transfer effects on policymaking, assuming that enough of the information would even be made available. Finally, to place and gauge the effects of an ICR intervention in the multitude of causative factors that affect policymaking would be a conceptual and methodological task of immense proportion.

All of these factors limit research possibilities, even before the problem of acquiring funding for an evaluation component is addressed. Organizers often find they have enough trouble getting support for the intervention, let alone for a substantial research adjunct. Nonetheless, ICR is a method based in applied social science—an enterprise that has generally shown concern with documenting and evaluating its action component directed toward social change. It is therefore incumbent upon scholar-practitioners in the field to ask how they can increase the frequency and quality of their research.

Conclusion

The assessment shows ICR to be a robust but small interdisciplinary field with a limited number of major actors. Since 1965, interventions have developed from one-shot exercises to continuing programs with high level influentials, often in concert with official negotiations. Several different forms of intervention share common features and claim positive outcomes.

Applicability is partly demonstrated by three decades of successful experience, but is muted by the lack of ongoing scholarly debate. Although effectiveness is claimed through largely impressionistic evidence, its evaluation requires a much greater utilization of different research methods. The model of transfer effects provides a start toward understanding how ICR interventions may influence policymaking. Each of the major forms of ICR shows an understanding of transfer effects, and each works to maximize its influence on policymaking.

In the theory-research-practice triumvirate, practice is the most developed. Theorizing is ongoing but slow, and research is extremely weak. Thus ICR continues to be a promising social innovation, but there is a long way to go before its potential may be known let alone realized.

10

Critical Issues for Interactive Conflict Resolution
Barriers to Realizing the Potential

The applicability of interactive conflict resolution can partly be addressed by rational argument based on theoretical considerations. However, to fully address this issue and even moreso those of effectiveness and utility, it is necessary to have greater operationalization of the method on which to base conclusions. Without a much larger body of systematic, empirical evidence, it is simply not possible to know how influential and useful the method is. Unfortunately greater operationalization is not easy, for it depends upon the prior resolution of a number of critical, developmental issues. ICR interventions require the involvement of well-trained *professionals* who can handle difficult strategic questions and delicate ethical dilemmas and who have secure funding and a solid institutional base. In the current state of development, these requirements are very difficult to obtain. Thus the future of the field is in question.

Although the rationale and the need for ICR may seem obvious if not compelling, the method is largely underutilized and may even be in some danger of slow extinction as a social innovation. This is partly because sceptics appear to outnumber proponents and also are more likely to occupy positions of decision-making authority in academia, government, philanthropic foundations, and policy research institutes. Applicability thus encapsulates its own intractability in that proposed projects in ICR are seen as unrealistic or risky. Therefore they are denied operationalization, and consequently the very opportunity to demonstrate their applicability and utility! Nonetheless, achieving greater operationalization is paramount in the further development of ICR. However, this can happen only if some formidable obstacles are overcome.

First, in human resources, the number of skilled, knowledgeable, and ethically astute scholar-practitioners who are equipped to carry out the third party consultant role in the international domain is extremely small. Furthermore, these few pioneers have not created many protégés to carry on the work, because they face severe limitations in doing so. Partly because of realist resistances in both academe and government, there are few locations where adequate education and training are available and there are few identified roles for third party consultants in national bureaucracies or international organizations.

Second, there are severe limitations in funding for ICR, which affects not only the implementation of programs but also the development of human resources and institutional structures. Applied research and practice in conflict analysis and resolution is a very time-consuming, unpredictable, and somewhat risky enterprise, and may not fit well with the current priorities and requirements of major funding sources. Thus the scholar-practitioners who wish to carry the method forward through demonstration and action research are faced with a series of barriers that may make the full development of the method highly problematic if not impossible in the current era.

Third, with regard to organizational bases, there are very few strong institutional structures out of which ICR consultants can work. Many current practitioners are academics, who are subject to all of the demands and restrictions of that role, which make initiating programs or responding to requests for consultation difficult. For ICR professionals outside of universities, there are difficulties in credibility and financial support. In both cases, it is almost impossible for consultants to establish the organizational infrastructure and the human resource team that is required for effective long-term projects.

Training Professional Scholar-Practitioners

Training professional scholar-practitioners is a daunting task in any discipline, let alone a multidisciplinary field such as ICR. Scholar-practitioners are professionals who can integrate sophisticated theoretical understanding with advanced expertise in both research and practice in ways that increase personal and disciplinary effectiveness in all three areas of activity. Thus, through the work of scholar-practitioners, the domains of science and practice are mutually enriched, and both conceptual knowledge and its application to real-world problems are extended. Protracted social conflict is both a social phenomenon and a social problem and as such should be amenable to the methods of applied social science. The question is whether it is possible to train scholar-practitioners in ICR who can analyze conflict using concepts from social science and can help address it using social-scientific methods of research and practice.

Formal education for scholar-practitioners typically involves some years in a professional college at a university or in graduate training often to the doctoral level. Although baccalaureate training equips one to function as a professional practitioner, for example in law, nursing, or engineering, scholar-practitioners in these and other disciplines, such as psychology, social work, or organizational development, typically hold graduate degrees. True scholar-practitioners are rare in the social sciences. There are many scholars, but few scholar-practitioners in universities, and many practitioners, but few scholar-practitioners in government, business, and so on.

After initial education, scholar-practitioners also engage in lifelong learning through continuing professional education to keep abreast of new conceptual developments and practice methods. The challenge is not only to have a wide grounding in conceptual knowledge but also the ability to apply this knowledge through professional practice in their domain of interest. Thus the scholar-practitioner requires theories of understanding about relevant phenomena, theories of practice about how to intervene effectively, and the expertise and skills required to do so.

The pioneers and senior scholar-practitioners in ICR have had no professional training institutions to attend or formal educational programs to prepare them for this specific role. They brought formal education in some related profession or discipline to bear on analyzing and resolving social conflict. Thus they have tended to approach the problem from the perspective of and with the biases of their respective profession or discipline—psychiatry, law, psychology, diplomacy, political science, or whatever. Their limited formal training combined with the complexity of the field and institutional resistances have made it very difficult to develop training experiences for the next generation of ICR consultants.

Some of the pioneers have trained a few protégés, and some of these individuals are now working on intercommunal dialogue projects and other forms of ICR. Some senior ICR practitioners have also been able to establish formal training programs that work to operationalize the scholar-practitioner identity. For example, the establishment of the doctoral program in conflict analysis and resolution at George Mason University, through the efforts of John Burton, Chris Mitchell, Dennis Sandole, the late James Laue, and others, is a landmark development in conflict resolution, with positive outcomes for ICR. Similarly, the work of Herbert Kelman at Harvard University, in establishing the Program in International Conflict Analysis and Resolution, is a useful step in the direction of scholar-practitioner training in ICR (see chapter 11).

Unfortunately few newcomers can yet work at the level of their mentors on protracted social conflicts in a consistent and influential way. Thus, after thirty years of existence, the field is limited in establishing a second generation of scholar-practitioners who can further develop the innovation. Hopefully, this problem will be rectified if the critical issues described here can be successfully managed.

One possible reason for a shortage of training programs in ICR is that present consultants disagree on the potential or necessity of training and on the nature of desirable programs. In the interviews with senior scholar-practitioners, several stated that the role is simply too complex and demanding to train for. Thus stringent selection is the way to generate consultants. In other words, individuals from various backgrounds must be found who possess the requisite human relations, organizational, and diplomatic skills, adequate knowledge about conflict and conflict resolution, an ability to act professionally, a pragmatic ability to adapt to difficult, rapidly changing situations, and an openness to evaluate and learn from their experience. The implication is to set up institutions for practice and select individuals from a wide range of disciplines and professions to become involved in operationalizing ICR. Given that there would be no generic preparation, a team approach to consultation would take on added importance so that strengths and deficiencies of different members would compensate for each other.

More interviewees considered training a serious and manageable issue, although there was no consensus on the components of an ideal program. Few ICR consultants have taken up the matter in their work or writings. One exception is a brief outline that I developed some time ago of the type of training sequence that might be required for third party consultants (Fisher 1976). The first element is theoretical knowledge at a number of levels of human social functioning, that is, an understanding of how individuals, groups, organizations, communities, societies, and the international system operate. This material is generally covered with different explanations and emphases in all of the social sciences and related disciplines. One core area is theory and research on social conflict, its causation and escalation, and methods of addressing it, including philosophical underpinnings.

In human relations skills, trainees should participate in experiential workshops in interpersonal communication, group processes, consultation as a professional practice, and intergroup problem solving. Direct practice would take place within an apprenticeship model in which beginning consultants would serve as team members addressing low intensity conflicts before being involved in more intense, protracted ones. Close supervision and evaluation would enhance skill acquisition and professional development throughout the sequence.

Extending this design to prepare ICR consultants at the inter-communal and international levels would require a multidisciplinary program linked to a number of the social sciences and humanities. Professional graduate programs in international affairs, of which there are about a dozen in the United States and Canada, provide one possible institutional venue for the development of specialized training in ICR. Students would require core courses in international conflict analysis and resolution as well as a sequence of practical experiences that would prepare them for a junior consulting role.

Most interviewees who favored formal training would respond to this general design positively. The importance of a broad and deep theoretical base was emphasized, so that interventions are grounded in an understanding of social structures and processes related to the conflict in question, and not simply a reenactment of techniques learned in other situations. The necessity of skill training to operationalize the practice side of ICR was supported. This training can at first be accomplished through experiential training exercises and simulations that involve participation of and feedback to trainees.

The need for an apprenticeship approach came out quite strongly, involving a staged professional development track integrated with conceptual preparation and continuing theoretical integration. Involvement would follow a progression beginning with observation of consultation sessions followed by debriefing with the consultants, move to coconsulting experiences in a partial and junior role, and finally to coconsulting on an equal and senior basis, including the chairing function.

The conceptual learning complement to this practice sequence would involve a continuing professional seminar, in which trainees and supervising senior consultants would discuss cases in an analytic, comparative, and integrative fashion. Finally, a supervised internship in an institute or program carrying out ICR work would serve as the crowning experience in initial professional development. The graduate would then be in a position to offer his or her services to the public.

Unfortunately interviewees identified difficulties in implementing training programs for ICR consultants. First, it is difficult to select individuals who are likely to be successful at the task. Academic competence can be assessed, but it is difficult to first de-select individuals whose personality dynamics or interpersonal style makes them incompetent or even dangerous in implementing the role. For example, individuals with a high need for power or control, or who exhibit cognitive rigidity or cultural prejudices, or who attempt to deceive and manipulate others, and so on, should not be allowed to move through a training program. This is a problem faced by all professional educational programs, and is managed with some degree of success. However, ICR has not addressed this issue with practicing consultants, let alone those in training.

Another difficulty is a contradiction between some trainee expectations and the realities of protracted social conflicts and ICR interventions. Some interviewees commented on the inappropriate expectations of students who want to be trained quickly in a set of techniques that they can then apply to whatever conflict they want. This superficial demand for a "bag" of generalizable process skills ("tricks") must be countered by admonitions for the acquisition of theories of understanding and practice from which the strategies and activities of intervention are forged. Particularly at the intercommunal and international levels, trainees must acquire the knowledge, the analytical skills, and the process skills necessary to appreciate the complexity of such conflicts and to intervene appropriately, effectively, and responsibly. Thus completing the kind of professional education sequence outlined above, given the dearth of training programs, is extremely difficult at present.

A further restriction is limited opportunities to intervene in protracted social conflicts, for few consultation efforts in ICR are ongoing. Furthermore, such interventions are high risk endeavors in which trainees should not be allowed to gain practice experience at the expense of the welfare of the participants or the program itself. Thus some ways need to be developed for appropriate trainee involvements in low risk situations. For example, dialogue workshops with members of the diasporas of conflicting groups as participants and with senior consultants as supervisors could provide beneficial training experiences for trainees. Students could be involved not only as observers but could also rotate through the third party panel to gain experience in a lower intensity situation.

An example of meaningful involvement by graduate students in international affairs in a consultation workshop on the Cyprus conflict is provided by Fisher (1991). This workshop, described briefly in chapter 7, brought together Greek Cypriots and Turkish Cypriots living in Canada who maintained their interest in the conflict and in their respective communities. The workshop provided an opportunity for some apprenticeship experience by the students within the context of a class in international mediation and problem solving. Thus students had read many of the core works in ICR and were familiar with the third party consultant role. In addition, they took part in a weekend training workshop in communication skills, group processes, and conflict management with a view to helping them prepare for the consultation workshop. In the sessions, the class group formed an outer "horseshoe" of observers around the core discussion group. In each quarter-day session, two students joined the third party panel, while one regular member dropped off to become an observer. The workshop was also observed by a social psychologist skilled in group processes, who provided later feedback to the panel and the students. After the workshop, the class met to discuss reactions and the comments of the process observer. Thus this was a powerful form of experiential learning, to which students are seldom exposed.

In conclusion, ways must be found for developing training programs for scholar-practitioners in ICR. Creative thinking and long-term commitment will be necessary to overcome limitations and to produce future generations of ICR consultants who can then work to protect and expand this promising social innovation.

The Catch-22s of Funding

"Catch-22" is a term coined by author Joseph Heller (1955) in his true-to-life novel about American military personnel flying bombing missions from a small Mediterranean island in World War II. The missions were extremely dangerous and the casualty rate was very high. The only way to avoid duty according to policy was to claim some form of insanity. However, if you did so, it demonstrated that you were actually sane, for it was crazy to fly the missions. Thus "catch-22" of policy was invoked. If you pleaded insanity or demonstrated in some way that you were crazy, it merely confirmed you were normal and fit for combat. Catch-22 has since come to indicate paradoxical situations with no apparent rational solution.

In ICR, the catch-22s generally play out as follows. To do the work you need funding. However, to demonstrate that you deserve funding, you need to do some of the work, because this convinces funders you can meet their requirements and produce positive effects. Because you cannot do the work, because you do not have funding, you cannot demonstrate that you deserve funding. There is nowhere to go. This predicament plays out in several ways in the funding process.

Individuals working in ICR tend not to write about their problems in obtaining funding. One exception is Leonard Doob, who has outlined the difficulties in working to obtain funding for the workshop on the Horn of Africa (see chapter 2). Doob (1970) at first met a solid wall of resistance to his proposal from major American foundations, which while expressing enthusiasm for the project, refused support because the idea was too politically sensitive and because they assumed that neither the governments involved nor potential participants would agree to become involved. (Catch-22: "We would like to support this project, but we know it will never get off the ground; therefore we will not support it." Of course, Without funding, it cannot get off the ground.) Fortunately, Doob was able to obtain initial funding from Yale University to demonstrate the feasibility of the plan, which he did by visiting the countries and obtaining approval of two of the three governments and by identifying participants. In gaining involvement, Doob had to promise that the money would not come from the United States government.

The demonstration of feasibility, however, failed to convince the foundations to provide support. Although the project continued to be seen as intriguing and having potential for reducing the tragic costs of the conflict, it was nonetheless a delicate matter, and could proceed only with State Department approval. (Catch-22: "We would be willing to fund this project if you had government approval, but because you do not have it and will not get it, we cannot provide support." Of course, Doob did not want to seek formal government approval, because the political baggage could jeopardize the project.) Nonetheless, Doob informally broached the idea with State Department officials and received tacit approval and a willingness to communicate this to foundations. However, when this was made known to foundation representatives, other reasons for nonsupport came forward—the project is not in line with our mandate, it is too risky, it is too sensitive, and so on, even though almost all expressed enthusiasm for it in principle.

After much hesitation and consternation, Doob then applied to government sources for funding, partly because two agencies had expressed interest in the project. However, the proposal was turned down, partly because recent activities of the Central Intelligence Agency had made any American intervention in Africa highly sensitive. Also, independent of this situation, one official indicated that the proposal was denied because it was feared that government sponsorship in general would harm the initiative. (Catch-22: We would like to fund you, but we believe this would harm your project, so we cannot support it." Of course, Without support the project never happens.)

About one year after initial contact, the third government indicated its approval, and with the backing of the United Nations Institute for Training and Research, Doob was able to gain funding from two American and one British source. However, during this long delay, one of the governments withdrew its consent, owing to an impending election.

The funds were returned and the invitations to participants were withdrawn. After the election several months later, approval looked likely, and the project was reinstituted with all haste. Yale University again provided up-front money, and the previous supporters agreed to provide funds if the project became a reality. (Catch-22: "We will provide support, but only if you can demonstrate that the project will happen as planned." Of course, Without lead support the project cannot get beyond planning.) Doob then visited the three capitals to confirm support and to repeat the task of inviting participants. Unfortunately a workshop site that had been offered by UNITAR was by this time unavailable, and an alternate location had to be found in short order. Then arrangements had to be made for the almost thirty organizers, trainers, and participants to depart from several locations on three continents and to arrive in the same location simultaneously!

Given all of these hoops and hurdles embedded with one catch-22 after another, it is amazing that the Fermeda workshop was ever held. The persistence and ingenuity of the organizers in marketing the idea, in overcoming resistances, in adapting to changing circumstances, and in regrouping in the face of frustrating contradictions and defeats is truly laudable. One wonders how many other worthwhile projects have never gotten off the drawing board due to the catch-22s of funding, not to mention the many defensible reasons for withholding support. On the brighter side, Doob (1987) notes that it was easier to gain funding for the Northern Ireland and Cyprus initiatives, because in the former the work on the Horn of Africa had been published and, in the latter, officials in both communities provided assurances to a foundation that the workshop could conceivably aid in negotiations.

Difficulties in obtaining funding for consultation programs were raised consistently in the interviews with senior scholar-practitioners. Almost without exception, consultants have been prevented from initiating interventions, often in cases where the request came from the parties themselves, and have had to spend an inordinate amount of time and effort to obtain funding when they were successful in doing so. An added difficulty is convincing funders to provide an adequate amount so that a better-than-puny intervention could be carried out.

There are a number of unique characteristics of ICR that interact with the identity and requirements of funders to make the acquisition of support an arduous and tenuous process at best. Interventions with high level representatives is a delicate and risky business that should be carried out with limited publicity. In situations of protracted conflict, any intervention of significance is almost bound to offend some constituency on one side or the other. Philanthropic foundations understandably do not like negative publicity and are more predisposed to support research or development work that is likely to be perceived as good or at least benign by all parties. When projects go well, funders legitimately bask in some of the glory and are affirmed in their mandate. Action research that intervenes in a volatile political situation carries greater risks of critical reactions and hence is less desirable. When success is achieved, positive publicity may still be limited owing to the confidential nature of the enterprise.

Because of the impartial nature of consultation, almost all scholar-practitioners are loathe to seek government funding. Any government carries political baggage and even in cases where a government may be seen as impartial to the conflict, some constituency on one side or the other may read in bias or self-interest that contaminates the intervention and harms the consulting relationship. American consultants in particular have been very reluctant to follow this route, and have done so only when all other available avenues to save an intervention were exhausted. In addition, governments are sensitive to and are targets of both internal and external political pressure, so that like foundations, they are reluctant to engage in a process that might elicit negative responses from anyone. Hence governments are much more likely to support less risky policy research.

A third source of funding—charging for services—is also seen by most consultants as inappropriate. Protracted social conflicts often involve parties of unequal power and wealth, and the question of how to distribute costs would be difficult and delicate. Furthermore, acquiring support from either or both sides will likely induce concerns or perceptions of third party bias on one or both sides, thus hampering or scuttling the intervention. Private sources on both sides of a conflict could be approached for donations if this was handled in a balanced and cautious fashion with clear and open communication among all. However, the consultant will again be hampered by spending more effort in fund-raising than is realistic or possible.

The scholar-practitioner of ICR is typically faced with a further set of perplexing and frustrating catch-22s, that is, contradictions between the nature of the work and the expectations or requirements of funders. In situations of protracted social conflict, much entry and contracting work is required before the parties are willing to commit and the program of interaction can be designed and implemented. However, few if any funding sources see this prework as a legitimate activity for support. In the words of one interviewee, "no one understands the importance of talking about talking." A large effort is required to secure the commitment of the parties and participants, which funders often require before they will consider providing support. The prework provides no products and no guarantees that the project will move forward. On both counts, funders are understandably reluctant to make an investment that may yield few of the usual payoffs, especially in comparison to deserving proposals from other fields.

Another problem is that funders often invoke requirements, such as public commitments from the parties or the submission of detailed action plans, that are incongruent with the low publicity, high flexibility nature of the work. In many cases, the parties would not come if a public statement of intent was required. It is also difficult for consultants to provide funders with the usual assurances on positive outcomes and documentation that they require. Given the newness of the method and the complexity conflict, it would be irresponsible for consultants to communicate an expectation of positive outcomes to funders. Given the confidential nature of the work, it would be unethical of consultants to promise detailed documentation and follow-up that might hamper practice or place participants at greater personal risk.

To be fair, from the perspective of funders, interventions in ICR may at times look like presumptuous and potentially ill-fated escapades created by harebrained academics. They are being asked to provide considerable sums of money so that a "social scientist-practitioner" (whatever that is!) who lacks any official credentials can travel to troubled parts of the world meddling in politics and diplomacy. They are asked to provide start-up funds with no guarantee of continuation when they have many detailed, practical, and useful proposals sitting on their desks. They are asked to fund a high risk intervention that has no assurances of success, which if it did occur couldn't be publicized anyway! Little wonder that funders have reservations about this work as it has often been proposed and implemented.

For all these reasons on both sides, ICR consultants often find themselves at variance not only with most program definitions but also with the proposal and report requirements of most major funding sources. This problem is compounded because funding is a critical issue that affects the development of the method, both in human resources and institutional bases. That is, without adequate funding, consultants in ICR cannot operate effectively at the project level. Thus they cannot provide training opportunities for developing consultants, or further develop their theory of practice. In addition, they cannot gain support for institutional bases, for they have not been able to demonstrate the utility of their work. On all counts, ICR is caught in a suffocating dilemma. Some remedies will be considered in chapter 11.

It should be noted that the funding situation seems to be slowly improving, at least since Doob's experience in the 1960s. A number of scholar-practitioners have acquired support for a continuing program of workshops. However, the number is small in comparison to the larger pool of ICR professionals who are interested in and capable of mounting useful interventions.

Barriers to Institutionalization

The question of institutionalizing ICR received a positive response from interviewees, depending on how it is done. A number expressed the concern that the field has been initiated by a small cadre of committed individuals and may be in danger of extinction or modification if it is not institutionalized as a unique social innovation. Most see an institutional base as providing greater legitimacy, credibility, and consistency than operating as an individual consultant or "academic entrepreneur." Institutionalization also increases the probability of funding and provides a venue for training and professionalization. In addition, it can provide greater flexibility for consultant activities, assuming that some or all of their salary requirements would be provided by the institution.

Many ICR consultants are academics and are thereby subject to the demands and restrictions of a faculty member's role. They have to blend the requirements for consultation work into a resource system that is already underfunded and overstretched in meeting its basic teaching, research, service, and administrative demands. Furthermore, the teaching and supervisory duties of a full-time faculty position are not easily rearranged or rescheduled. In contrast, the demands of an ICR project can be intense and unpredictable, requiring much effort and critical involvement at certain points for the project to survive or to respond to fast-breaking realities. Protracted social conflicts ebb and flow, and a positive climate that might support a consultation intervention at one juncture may evaporate in weeks or months. Often, requests for consultation that are received have to be declined or postponed owing to the teaching or administrative necessities of the moment.

For consultants who operate outside of universities, other problems arise. They may spend so much of their time soliciting funds or seeking legitimacy that they don't have adequate time to devote to the work itself and thereby their long-term viability is threatened. Also, because they are more dependent for their survival on "client satisfaction," they may be drawn by the parties to provide informal conciliation or mediation rather than consultation, because most participants see the conflict in substantive terms and want to make gains on tangible issues of importance to them. They will thus influence the third party in this direction in the hope of gaining support for their preferred settlement, and the unique potential of ICR is lost.

The comments of interviewees on institutionalization were not uniformly positive; some pointed out that it can have disadvantages in comparison to the "independent academic entrepreneur." The research and scholarly character of the academic allows parties and participants to enter into the process with a less official and more ambiguous orientation from which they can defend their involvement. The informal aspect may also help move participants away from the usual adversarial behavior and influence attempts associated with formal structures, where they have a judge or an audience to play to.

Based on his experience, Kelman (1991a) comments on potential disadvantages to institutionalization. He suggests that publicly identifying ICR in a formal manner might reduce the ambiguity of the enterprise (as a combined research and political activity) which allows the parties to take part with flexibility. The ability and freedom of the consultant to contribute to the political process might also be lessened, because an institution might find this a more difficult and vulnerable role. Institutionalization could also reduce the contribution of the personal factor through which the relationship between the individual consultant and the representatives of the parties is very important to success. In addition, ICR should not be institutionalized if this means delegating critical tasks such as entry and contracting to less experienced and lower status coworkers. A senior and respected consultant needs to be involved in all phases of the process. Finally, an institutional base might reduce flexibility to work on different conflicts, for an institution carries the international reputation of its country more strongly than an individual consultant and may be rejected on that basis.

It follows that the nature of institutionalization becomes paramount, so that potential costs can be minimized while the benefits are maximized. Thus many questions must be asked before proceeding. Can an institution be designed that provides for flexibility and the degree of ambiguity required for ICR work? Can roles be structured so that consultants can respond appropriately, and, if necessary, immediately to requests for service? Can roles be defined so that personal contact of parties with experienced consultants is maintained, while junior colleagues fulfil other important role demands and gain experience and exposure at the same time? Can institutions be developed that are seen as semiindependent from their national identities? And finally, as mentioned by one astute interviewee, can an institution for ICR be designed that puts most of its resources into service delivery rather than the maintenance of its own bureaucracy? Some answers will be provided in chapter 11 by proposing an ideal model for institutionalizing ICR.

There have been attempts at institutionalization in the broader field of conflict resolution over the past three decades, mostly small research centers in universities. These have met with mixed success, partly because the individual scholars are not freed from their full load of university demands and the center thereby exists in name but not with uniquely dedicated human resources. Fortunately, the late 1980s witnessed a resurgence of interest in conflict resolution centers in universities, partly as a result of some forward thinking and support by major foundations (see chapter 11).

The myriad problems that innovative, applied, multidisciplinary centers can run into is illustrated in a detailed account of the life and death of the world's first center for research on conflict resolution at the University of Michigan from 1956 to 1971 (Harty & Modell 1991). This center was at the leading edge of conflict research and peace activism with the dual hope of establishing a comprehensive theory of human conflict and of developing a new profession of advisers on national security policy. Its limited success in these areas as well as institutional, political, and economic problems led to its demise. In particular, Harty and Modell (1991) indicate that the rationale for closing the center was based on deficiencies in both scholarly productivity and external financial support. I was a graduate student at Michigan in 1971 and participated in the unsuccessful attempt to save the center. In my judgment, the closure also appeared related to the perceived audacity of the center in strongly supporting and in fact providing its offices as the headquarters of a 1970 student strike, initiated by black students to redress their grievances, that shut down the university for the first time in its history. The leadership of the center had ignored the old adage about not biting the hand that feeds you.

Another problem exists with university-based centers. The professional practice side of such centers, if it exists, is constantly threatened, because the university environment provides much stronger support for scholarly research on conflict and methods of resolution than for action research with an element of direct involvement by the researcher. In other words, universities are generally not as understanding or supportive of the practitioner side of the ICR consultant's identity. Thus it is not surprising that existing centers are influenced toward conceptual or descriptive research by administrators and colleagues as well as by the reduced practical difficulties of such work. For centers that do perform an active consulting role, it is a constant struggle to maintain the internal and external support necessary. Fortunately some success stories exist (see chapter 11).

There have also been attempts to institutionalize ICR as a professional service that could be offered to conflicting parties in the international arena. Most notably among these are the efforts of John Burton in trying to interest different institutions in supporting the development of a conflict resolution service that would in some way parallel official diplomatic activities. In 1983, Burton organized a session on facilitated conflict resolution at the annual meeting of the International Studies Association, and though there was some interest, could not persuade the organization to serve as a focus for developing an international service of facilitators (see Burton, 1983). During his time at the University of Maryland, Burton and Edward Azar established the Council for the Facilitation of International Conflict Resolution, which was composed of some one hundred scholars, diplomats, and other practitioners with interests in the problem-solving approach. The role of the council, besides providing a list of potential panel members for workshops, was to make facilitation more available to parties engaged in protracted social conflict and to encourage international organizations to use problem solving. Unfortunately, with Burton's departure and Azar's premature retirement and untimely death, the council was never able to operationalize its goals.

John Burton tried for many years and in different ways to interest the United Nations in the problem-solving approach. A number of informal overtures to various UN bodies, including the secretary-general's office, the United Nations Institute for Training and Research, and the United Nations University were unsuccessful. One proffered reason for this lack of interest was that only the UN Security Council should deal with conflict resolution, and that it did so through its resolutions—these *were* "conflict resolution" in the real world.

Undeterred, Burton used his diplomatic connections with the Australian Mission at the UN to organize a meeting of the UN ambassadors of fifteen "middle powers" in June 1986 (Burton & Mitchell 1986). The rationale was that middle powers, such as Australia, Canada, Egypt, India, Nigeria, Norway, and Poland, could play a special role in world affairs by using their influence independently of the superpowers and by supporting the problem-solving approach to conflict resolution. Although there was some interest in these possibilities, the ambassadors generally supported the traditional role of the UN and the power-realist approach to international relations. A second meeting with UN representatives present reaffirmed the view that only the UN Security

Council and office of the secretary-general should be involved in conflict management activities. One wonders how many other overtures to expand the options for dealing with destructive international conflict have been rejected by those with traditional views in positions of influence.

Thus the road to institutionalization is long and arduous. However, it is clear that the potential of interactive conflict resolution can never be realized unless it becomes more than a part-time activity of a handful of independent scholar-practitioners based largely in universities. For this to happen, the developmental issues of training, funding, and institutionalization need to be simultaneously and effectively addressed. Ideas and activities for moving in these directions are discussed in the next chapter.

11

Challenges for Practice and Policy

To improve its prospects for the future, interactive conflict resolution has to develop strategies for gaining greater control over its destiny. Applicability and effectiveness need to be addressed through changes in the standard operating procedures of ICR scholar-practitioners, funders, administrators, and diplomats. These changes also need to address funding, training, and institutionalization, wherein lie the impetus and rationale for the further development of the field.

Besides mounting carefully managed, continuing programs of intervention with influential, informal representatives, ICR professionals should invest greater energy in developing high quality demonstration projects that take the research side of the enterprise much more seriously. Such projects would be less threatening to funders and decision makers and would be more compatible with the usual requirements of funders. ICR scholar-practitioners should continue to establish interdisciplinary centers for practice, research, and theory development, and in doing so should build collaborative relationships with funders, administrators, and diplomats. These centers would deal with institutionalization and would provide a venue for training future generations. Finally, individuals working in ICR should initiate efforts toward the professionalization of the field. This would provide a forum for many worthwhile activities, such as further defining the profession, providing professional development experiences, and initiating a continuing dialogue with funders.

This chapter will elucidate these challenges for practice and policy. An action research agenda will be proposed that draws on knowledge and skills in research design, measurement and analysis, and program evaluation. Some examples will be provided of research work in ICR that demonstrates movement in useful directions. The desired characteristics of institutional bases for ICR will be enumerated and some existing centers for research and practice will be described. Lastly, a rationale for professionalizing the field will be discussed, and some possible functions and activities will be proposed. By meeting challenges in these areas, ICR can demonstrate its utility and improve its prospects for becoming a central method in the wider domain of conflict management and resolution.

The Research Agenda

The review in chapter 10 indicated a number of deficits in ICR research that restrict our ability to conclude that interventions are effective. Although there are serious limitations on doing research in this area, the almost sole reliance on case study impressions is reminiscent of how the field of traditional diplomacy assesses its effectiveness. Surely as applied social scientists we can do better, even though ICR interventions suffer from many of the same restrictions as diplomatic practice in sensitive situations, for example, the need for quietness if not secrecy, the protection of sources, and the confidential nature of the enterprise. The question is how to proceed.

Rouhana (1993), who has worked closely with Kelman, raised a number of concerns about the field, and proposed an initial framework for moving the research agenda forward. He noted that there is great variety in the goals of different interventions, that the appropriateness of various models is unclear, and that no approach has demonstrated its effectiveness. To evaluate ICR interventions, he proposed a framework that comprised three questions, each of which has relevant sources of evidence. First, does the process really happen? For example, do the participants really learn about each other, and do they produce joint ideas based on this learning? This question could be addressed by studying workshop transcripts made from notes taken during the sessions. Second, do attitudinal changes occur in the participants and do these last beyond the workshop? Sources of evidence here include the writings and statements of participants after the workshop. Third, do the changes in attitudes and behavior affect the larger societies through the reports, writings, and other activities of participants? Data relevant to this question could be obtained through interviews with participants and other actors. Rouhana thus provides a very useful overview of how to address many of the research deficiencies that plague ICR.

The strategy of the research agenda proposed here is for ICR proponents to devote greater attention to high quality demonstration projects that take the research side of the enterprise very seriously. That is, programs of consultation need to be appropriately developed in the context of ongoing monitoring and involvement in the conflict, as articulated for example by Azar (1990), and need to include a research component that addresses a range of questions, including those posed by Rouhana (1993). Questions of a theoretical nature should also be addressed, such as those raised by Hill (1982), who proposed a shift in strategic emphasis within the field to less political and more experimental interventions.

The strategy would place less emphasis on politically directed interventions with high level representatives and more on workshops of an educational nature involving influentials who appreciate and are not put at risk by the research demands of the program. Both research orientated and politically directed workshops could be organized to focus on the same conflict in the same time frame, or the demonstration work could come first to build the credibility of the third party and the process. On the practice side, demonstration workshops would provide a useful peacebuilding function within and between the adversarial societies, but would not affect policymaking in the short term. They would also allow for more involvement by younger ICR professionals in ways appropriate to their lesser experience. In addition, the research component would provide useful roles for graduate students and junior colleagues who might otherwise be excluded. Thus, in developing the field, the payoffs would be great.

To initiate consideration of the strategy, it is useful to think in broad questions of *research design*. In simple terms, an ICR intervention is an experiment in which a composite independent variable (the workshop) is predicted to affect a range of dependent variables (knowledge, attitudes, behaviors, transfer effects, policymaking). The effects of the independent variable can thus be assessed through a number of design options. One is simply a posttest on the dependent variables, but that provides no basis of comparison, so it is impossible to conclude that the intervention affected outcomes. A stronger but still weak design is a before-and-after comparison on the same measures, which are chosen to reflect the dependent variables. Unfortunately, because the intervention is not the only factor that might affect the dependent variables over the period of the workshop, any differences between pre- and post-measures cannot be attributed with confidences to the independent variable.

The highest level of rigor is achieved with the control group design, wherein a group equivalent to the participant group does not take part in the workshop, but is also assessed before and after the intervention. Thus any differences between the groups on dependent variable measures at the postassessment can be attributed to the independent variable, that is, the workshop. In addition, there are quasi-experimental designs that can be used to tease out the effects of the independent variable.

For demonstration projects the minimum research design that should be used is the before-and-after comparison. Unless there are dramatic events in the conflict or other identifiable factors that occur during the intervention, there could be some confidence that changes were attributable to the program. However, another, more rigorous design may be feasible—a delayed control group design, wherein a pool of participants is selected, but only half are randomly assigned to take part in a workshop, although all are given a preassessment. After the workshop, another assessment occurs and serves as the postcomparison between the groups. Then the control group takes part in a second workshop, and can also be assessed at the end in a before-and-after design. This design not only provides for a strong evaluation of the intervention but also involves the initial control group as full participants in the enterprise, with benefits on all sides.

Another way of looking at design is to draw on the interdisciplinary field of *evaluation research.* Applied social scientists have developed a range of methods for determining if a social program is achieving the benefits that were intended. Thus, if we regard ICR interventions as consultation programs, we can apply the different forms of program evaluation to these. At first, we note whether the objectives of a program are well-specified, plausible and measurable, the activities in the program are clearly delineated, and the logical linkages between the two are stated and are reasonable. If these preconditions for evaluation are not met in program planning, then a conceptual analysis known as "evaluability assessment" needs to be done to identify deficiencies. Further program development is then carried out until the preconditions are deemed to be in place. To my knowledge, such a process has never been explicitly carried out in ICR.

Another form of program evaluation, known as "process evaluation," monitors the activities of the program to see if they are being implemented as intended. If they are not, then one can hardly expect the program to attain its objectives. In ICR interventions, this would mean, for example, assessing the role of the third party in implementing essential functions, such as diagnosing the conflict, as well as the behavior of participants in engaging in necessary interactions, such as dialogue or joint planning. Process evaluation can be based on information from various sources, including observations or recordings of activities, comments from program staff, and information gathered from participants. In ICR, process evaluation should also include an assessment of the internal conditions established in the workshop, such as improved communication or development of trust, which are essential to the subsequent effects on outcomes.

Assuming that preconditions are met, and activities are adequately implemented, "outcome evaluation" is then used to assess the effectiveness of the program in meeting its objectives. Drawing on the research designs noted above, outcome evaluation asks whether the independent variable caused changes in the dependent variables. Information from various sources can measure different variables through both qualitative and quantitative methods. Participants can be interviewed, or answer questionnaires, or complete attitude scales or other instruments. Decision makers can be interviewed about the impact of any ideas that were transferred from the workshop by participants. Writings and public statements by participants or related policymakers can be scrutinized to reveal transfer effects. Third party panel members can provide their impressions of any changes they observed in participants. Thus there are many ways to gauge the effects of ICR interventions, and all are underutilized. Greater emphasis on research at all stages could lead to a powerful combination of process evaluation, outcome evaluation, and "transfer evaluation" to comprehensively assess the effectiveness and utility of ICR.

These ideas for ICR research are drawn from a traditional social science perspective known to applied researchers (e.g., Fisher 1982b). Newer approaches to social research, informed by perspectives such as community psychology and the feminist critique, call for the reduced treatment of research participants as objects of study, and greater attention to participative and collaborative research strategies. Thus participants should be involved in planning research studies that satisfy their needs for knowledge, and should be regarded as collaborators in the implementation, analysis, and reporting processes. The research process then becomes one of joint inquiry, rather than one wherein ICR scholar-practitioners look for ways to answer the question of effectiveness on their terms.

Some of the roots of the collaborative approach go back to the concept of *action research* enunciated during the 1940s in applied social psychology and other fields. This approach called for collaboration between scholars, practitioners, and lay people, and was designed to assist in the planning of actions to address social problems as well as to evaluate the effects of those actions. Some forms called for those taking action to be involved in the research process from the very beginning, so that their motivation to bring about social change was increased at the same time as the research was improved. Action research can be seen as a forerunner of evaluation research as well as more participative and qualitative approaches.

Applied to ICR, action research would call for greater involvement of participants and possibly other members of the groups involved. Programs would be planned with more input and control of participants and a research collaboration would be set up to monitor and evaluate the process and its outcomes. Besides some form of pre-, post-, and follow-up assessments, discussion time during the workshop would be devoted to research questions, and postworkshop meetings would be held to further gauge effects from the participants' point of view. This approach would rely much more on participants' needs in planning workshops, and on their shared experiences in evaluating them. Designs would likely put more emphasis on process evaluation rather than outcome evaluation. However, there is no inherent incompatibility between a collaborative approach and the more rigorous research designs and methods of assessment. In fact, a fusion of the two would likely produce the most powerful research outcomes for ICR.

To illustrate some elements of the strategy, two recent ICR interventions will be described, each having a research component embodying various of the above suggestions. The first is a women's Israeli-Palestinian workshop organized by members of the Harvard Program on International Conflict Analysis and Resolution (PICAR). The second involves two conflict analysis workshops on the Cyprus conflict, organized by the author to follow on from two earlier workshops described in chapter 7. The first illustration follows a participative approach in its research component; the second demonstrates how a rigorous assessment of initial outcomes can be obtained through traditional social scientific methods.

The women's Israeli-Palestinian workshop was organized in 1993 by women members of PICAR by drawing on the Kelman group's experience in arranging previous workshops (see chapter 3). The organizers were partly interested in whether the interaction would be different for women participants working with third party panel also composed of women (Babbitt & Chataway 1993). The invitees represented a range of women influentials, some of whom had been involved in previous workshops. The research component was framed as a joint enterprise between participants and consultants.

Thus, rather than proceed with preworkshop interviews, the consultants integrated questions on expectations, hopes, and concerns into the single party, preworkshop sessions. Participants also discussed additional topics, such as where they found it hard to understand the other group, and how their identity as women affected their experience. The panel had planned for separate caucuses during the workshop to track the research questions, but the intensity and flow of the interaction precluded this. As an alternative, the organizers studied the transcript of the workshop to assess the nature of the interaction among participants. They also devoted part of the last session to evaluation, asking questions such as what were the most significant points in the workshop and what had each side learned about the other group. In addition, follow-up interviews were carried out to ascertain whether participants used any ideas from the workshop, whether they established any new or different relationships as a result, and so on.

Hence various probes were employed to tap into the experience of the participants to allow them to share what was meaningful and what was lasting about the workshop. Much of this probing was done in a participative and collaborative fashion within the workshop itself. The design therefore illustrates how a research component can be blended into the practice side in ways that are more complementary and less obtrusive than traditional approaches.

The two 1993 workshops on the Cyprus conflict were part of a project to stimulate peacebuilding efforts between the two communities on the island (Fisher 1994a). An earlier workshop had identified general areas where intercommunal cooperation would be beneficial, including business, social research, and education. In subsequent consultation with associates in both communities and representatives of the UN mediation effort, it was decided to focus on the role of education in the conflict and its potential resolution.

The participants (ten in each workshop) were influential educationalists from various settings and roles with a wide range of experience in the educational systems of the two communities. The agenda included the role of education in maintaining the conflict, the potential role of education in reducing the conflict, and possible areas and projects for intercommunal cooperation in education. After the two workshops, all participants met together with an intercommunal steering committee (formed to foster unofficial cooperation between the sides) to merge their ideas and develop plans for joint peacebuilding projects.

From a research perspective, various methods were used to assess the experience and the outcomes of the workshop as seen by participants. First, part of the closing session elicited evaluative comments from participants, who spoke about increased understanding of the other community and the conflict. They also experienced an increased awareness of the similarities between the communities and the common elements of Cypriot culture. Most important, they identified mutual empathic realizations about the deep fears and basic needs that drive the conflict, and a joint understanding that the concerns of both sides must be addressed to establish a renewed relationship.

Second, participants completed an evaluation questionnaire, which assessed their reactions to and assessments of the workshop.

This included rating scales (with comments) on satisfaction, usefulness, and tension level, as well as open-ended questions on learnings about the conflict or the other side, the third party role, strengths and possible improvements in the workshop, and any additional comments. Thus, along with a descriptive report on the workshops (Fisher 1994a), the questionnaire results served mainly as a process evaluation. The feedback on the workshops was generally very positive, with high average ratings and supportive comments on the helpfulness of the third party and the usefulness of the workshop as a unique and valuable learning experience.

The third element in the research component consisted of structured, personal interviews with each participant before and after the workshop. The preinterview covered their expectations in reasons for attending, concerns, and anticipated achievements. The postinterview asked about reactions to the workshop in perceived effects and accomplishments, communications with others about the experience, and involvement in peacebuilding activities. In addition, the major part of both interviews asked questions about the relationship between the communities (including the causes of and current issues in the conflict), perceptions of the other community (including its primary motives and concerns), and ways of improving the relationship toward a realistic ideal. These questions are presented in fig. 11.1 to illustrate the attempt to gain a broad, qualitative picture of the perceptions of participants. The postinterview also asked questions about changes in the respondents' perceptions of the other community or the relationship as a result of the workshop experience.

To transform the respondents' answers into a manageable and consistent picture, a set of rating scales and coding categories was developed. These are shown in fig. 11.2 organized into the three main areas of questioning on the relationship and the conflict, the other community, and ways of improving the relationship. A rating manual was devised giving definitions of each dimension, and a research assistant was trained to transform the interview responses, which had been transcribed from audiotapes, into scores on the rating scales and coding categories. The dimensions were developed from conceptual knowledge in social psychology and conflict theory that identifies areas important in analyzing and resolving intergroup conflict. Higher postscores on these dimensions would indicate increased awareness of elements driving the conflict, a more sophisticated view of the other group, and a greater appreciation for a collaborative, multistrategy approach to improving the relationship.

Unfortunately various practical difficulties were experienced in arranging the interviews in the time available and this precluded gaining

The Relationship Between the Two Communities

1. With respect to the conflict between the two communities, what do you see as the main causes of the disagreements and hostilities?
2. How would you describe the present relationship between the two communities?
3. What do you see as the major issues in the conflict?

Perceptions of the Two Communities

1. How would you describe the other community in general terms?
2. Why do you think the other community is approaching the relationship and the conflict in the way that it is? What factors do you think lead it to behave in the way that it does?
3. What do you see as the main concerns of the other community? To what extent do you think these concerns are justified?

Improving the Relationship

1. Are there any ways that you think relations between the two communities could appropriately be improved?
2. Are there any areas of cooperation or common goals that you think the two communities might share?
3. What kind of ideal relationship would you like to see between the two communities? Please comment on the qualities that you think would be important in such an ideal relationship.

Fig. 11.1. Core Interview Questions from the Cyprus Workshop Project

a complete set of pre- and post-transcripts. Partly as a result, the statistical analyses on the rating dimensions failed to show significant changes, although the qualitative responses demonstrated outcomes congruent with workshop objectives. To overcome such difficulties, it would be useful to engage an external evaluator to conduct interviews and to manage other aspects of the research component. An external evaluator could also form a research team with some of the participants, thus infusing a collaborative approach while at the same time maintaining a systematic and rigorous evaluation. Future ICR interventions should seriously consider this combined strategy to improve the quality of research that is being conducted in the field.

Interdisciplinary Centers for Research and Practice

Institutionalization was discussed in chapter 10, and questions were raised about whether means can be found to maximize the effectiveness of institutional initiatives. This issue also links to that of train-

Relationship Dimensions

R1: Awareness of Joint Causality:

  Scale: 1 no awareness of causality whatsoever
          2 low awareness: total responsibility to one
          3 moderate awareness: most attributed to one
          4 high awareness: shared responsibility
          5 very high awareness: joint responsibility

R2: Awareness of Both Internal and External Causality:

  Scale: 1 no awareness of causality whatsoever
          2 low awareness: internal or external only
          3 moderate awareness: some mix of factors
          4 high awareness: a range of factors
          5 very high awareness: factors at all levels

R3: Awareness of Reciprocal Escalating Behaviors:

  Scale: 1 no awareness of reciprocal escalation
          2 low awareness: single sequences
          3 moderate awareness: general principle
          4 high awareness: continuing escalation
          5 very high awareness: autistic hostility or malignant so-
             cial process

R4: Differentiation of the Relationship:

  Scale: 1 no indication of differentiation
          2 low differentiation
          3 moderate differentiation: both dimensions and character-
             istics
          4 high differentiation
          5 very high differentiation

R5: Differentiation of Issues:

  Scale: 1 no differentiation of issues
          2 low differentiation: small number basic issues
          3 moderate differentiation: basic and additional issues
          4 high differentiation
          5 very high differentiation

Other Community Dimensions

O1: Degree of Other Group Differentiation versus Stereotypy:

  Scale: 1 no awareness of variety at all
          2 low differentiation; stereotypy present
          3 moderate differentiation; some subgrouping
          4 high differentiation; considerable subgrouping
          5 very high differentiation

continued

O2: Internal versus External Attribution:

    Scale: 1 no awareness of external causation
              2 low awareness; primarily internal attributions
              3 moderate; a mix of internal and external
              4 high awareness; leaning toward external
              5 very high awareness; predominantly external

O3: Degree of Relational Empathy:

    Scale: 1 no acknowledgment of other's concerns
              2 acknowledgment but little understanding
              3 moderate understanding
              4 high understanding and appreciation
              5 very high; suspension of judgment

O4: Degree of Justification for Concerns:

    Scale: 1 no justification whatsoever
              2 some justification of concerns
              3 moderate justification
              4 high justification
              5 very high justification

O5: Degree of Respect and Trust for the Other Group:

    Scale: 1 no indication of respect or trust
              2 low respect/trust
              3 moderate respect/trust
              4 high respect/trust
              5 very high respect/trust

Improving the Relationship Dimensions

I1: Ways of Improving the Relationship:

    Scale: 1 no ways identified
              2 low
              3 moderate
              4 high
              5 very high

I2: Degree of Problem-Solving Mode:

Scale: 1   no evidence of problem-solving mode
              2 low degree
              3 moderate degree
              4 high degree
              5 very high degree

I3: Areas of Cooperation:

    Scale: 1 no areas or goals identified
              2 low
              3 moderate

continued

```
            4  high
            5  very high
     I4: Qualities of an Ideal Relationship:
     Scale:  1  no positive qualities indicated
            2  low
            3  moderate
            4  high
            5  very high
  I5: Collaborativeness of the Ideal Relationship:
     Scale:  1  no indication of collaborativeness
            2  low collaborativeness
            3  moderate
            4  high
            5  very high
```

Fig. 11.2. Rating Scales and Coding Categories from the Cyprus Workshop Project

ing, in that institutional bases would house the projects in which apprentices could gain experience by enacting ancillary roles. Along with these considerations, the responses of the ICR scholar-practitioners in the interviews provided ideas for developing an ideal model to anchor practice and research in the field.

The ideal institutional base is seen as a university-affiliated, semi-independent, nonprofit, interdisciplinary center for ICR focusing on protracted intercommunal and international conflicts. These characteristics each carry a supporting rationale.

The university affiliation and academic identity bestows credibility and legitimacy, and communicates a concern with conducting research, developing professional practice, and creating and disseminating knowledge in an impartial manner. This base immediately distinguishes ICR from diplomacy, even though the two are complementary. The university connection also links the center with its most appropriate pool of human resources—faculty and graduate students in the social sciences and related disciplines with expertise and interests in conflict resolution. Some members can be recruited to enact the scholar-practitioner role while others can serve in supportive capacities, such as regional specialists. Conflict analysis and resolution cross disciplinary boundaries, especially at the complex level of the international system, and a center that engages in these activities needs to be interdisciplinary in every respect. In a university setting, cross appointments can be used to affiliate members in different ways that serve their needs while at the same time providing resources for the center.

In training, the center would be linked with graduate programs in applied social science and hopefully in conflict resolution itself. Students could complete internships as part of their professional training through the center and could also work as assistants supported by project grants and other funds. University affiliation would carry some financial support from the institution, including a salary component for faculty members with teaching and other responsibilities. In addition, some student assistants could be supported by university scholarships or by research grants of faculty.

A primary part of core funding would hopefully come from the university to ensure continuity and legitimacy. In addition, the center would seek support from a wide range of sources, including governments, research councils, foundations, and private donors. However, the center needs to have control over the management of its funding, so that only "clean" money is used on specific projects where the parties might be biased against particular sources, such as government. The center would need to operate semi-independently in securing funds and would have to invest significant energy in fund-raising. Thus it would need to establish good relationships with funders, and be sensitive to their concerns, requirements, and priorities.

The semi-independent nature of the center carries additional advantages. The center would often need to take action quickly to respond to the cyclical nature of protracted social conflict, both in mounting interventions with influentials and in initiating demonstration projects at propitious moments. In all cases, there will be unforeseeable, immediate challenges that must be dealt with in a direct and autonomous fashion. There may not be time to discuss options with some higher authority, especially a cumbersome one, when an intervention program or its effectiveness hangs in the balance. Thus the center must develop its own operating procedures, ongoing sense of priorities, and contingency plans, and have the independence to move on its own as required. However, accountability to a higher body, such as a university, has the advantage of inducing sober thinking in times of crisis and of maintaining an ultimate arbiter of professional conduct. This accountability is important from an ethical point of view and adds to perceived credibility.

The nonprofit nature of the center is essential to preclude dependency on the marketing of its services. A business approach at the intercommunal and international levels is inappropriate and dangerous. The services offered must not be provided to the highest bidder, but on a *pro bono publico* basis, free from extraneous considerations. The functions of ICR must be carried out with the freedom to operate and the exercise of judgment unfettered by concerns about impression management related to continued financial support from clients. This condition is especially true when one party in the conflict is in a position to provide more financial support than the other. The impartiality and autonomy of the third party should not be compromised by a need to make a profit from the services it provides.

It is conceivable that locations other than universities could provide a home for ICR, although they would not have all the same advantages. Government-supported research institutes, such as the International Peace Research Institute in Oslo, Norway (PRIO), could certainly house a program in consultation. PRIO has carried out some limited consultation programs and remains interested in developing this service (see chapter 6). The Canadian Institute for International Peace and Security initiated a program of consultation on the Cyprus conflict, but this sponsorship was ended by the premature abolition of CIIPS by the Canadian government (see chapter 7). Action research with policy relevance often falls within the mandate of such institutes, and the personnel to carry out the work can be assembled on either a project or an ongoing basis. These institutes often maintain linkages with government departments and nearby universities and can assemble teams of scholar-practitioners partly from such sources. These institutes have the legitimacy and credibility to carry out ICR work, and may have access to continuous, guaranteed funding from government, although the political baggage of such funding needs to be considered carefully. The middle powers, such as Canada, India, Sweden, and Zimbabwe, might be in a good position to sponsor ICR work, for they are strong supporters of multilateral cooperation and often serve as intermediaries.

International nongovernmental organizations (INGOs) could also play a role in organizing ICR interventions. International Alert (based in London, England), the Institute for Multi-Track Diplomacy, and Search for Common Ground (both in Washington, D.C.) have all embarked on some activities in training and dialogue that come under the ICR rubric. A primary problem for INGOs, however, is the uncertainty of continuous funding and the difficulty of organizing the breadth and depth of scholar-practitioner expertise that is required for long-term consultation programs. Also, along with research institutes, these actors are not as well poised to serve a training or professional development function for junior colleagues, although they certainly can provide internship and other experiences for graduate students from academic programs. The final difficulty that INGOs and research institutes sometimes face is adequate credibility and legitimacy, which more readily flows to a university-affiliated center. However, INGOs have the advantage of flexibility and adaptability, which the more conservative and cumbersome university base often lacks.

In the long term, the institutionalization of ICR functions within international governmental organizations is a feasible and desirable option. The UN and regional organizations have a history of peace-making and peacekeeping, rather than interactive peacebuilding. They have only recently demonstrated an interest in conflict resolution, and have not been receptive to unofficial diplomacy, although this may be changing. There is no inherent reason why these organizations could not develop a consultation service to work on relationship issues with member states embroiled in intercommunal or international conflict. It would, however, require a shift in identity and priorities for them to begin mixing official and unofficial diplomacy, and the manner of do-ing this would need careful consideration. This shift would involve a new variant of ICR, wherein an official actor offered informal, un-official forms of interaction in an off-the-record manner. This variant of ICR would require the engagement of scholar-practitioners with the necessary knowledge base for conflict analysis and the human-relations skills for facilitating productive dialogue and confrontation, areas in which diplomats have not traditionally been trained. None-theless, there is no a priori reason why such a variant could not be developed.

One compelling reason for advocating university-based centers is that only the academic-professional environment is likely to provide for the integration of theory, research, and practice. For maximum util-ity, the field must link these three pillars of knowing and doing in a manner like the applied social sciences. In articulating the identity of applied social psychology, for example, Fisher (1982b) has stressed the importance of having research and practice based in theory, of using both practice and research outcomes to inform theory development, and of using research skills to evaluate practice.

Building on action research, Argyris, Putnam, and Smith (1985) ar-ticulate the approach of "action science," designed to generate useful and valid knowledge of the world, while at the same time contributing to theories of action that help change it for the better. Thus action sci-ence is about theoretically based social change, brought about by action scientists collaborating with participants in a critical inquiry into social problems and social practice. It thus requires public reflection and pub-lic experimentation to improve social practice.

University-affiliated centers for ICR would be in the best posi-tion to operationalize action science in conflict resolution. Theoretical knowledge about the sources and processes of conflict can be orga-nized, further developed, and fed into both the creation of interventions and a general model of practice. Theories of understanding will thus guide practice and inform the development of theories of practice. In turn, practice outcomes will reflect back on theories of understanding of conflict and models of intervention. Research skills can be used to assess theoretical propositions and also to evaluate practice interventions in ways that reflect back on underlying theory. The connections are many and varied, and will result in a powerful integration that can move the field forward. Only a university-based institution is likely to garner the support and assemble the human resources required to capitalize on the potential interconnections among theory, research, and practice.

As noted in previous chapters, a few university-affiliated centers already exist. Although these are concerned with conflict resolution in wider terms, they also serve as bases for ICR interventions. In addition, there are a few INGOs that are engaging in ICR practice, usually with the participation of scholar-practitioners from academic settings. A brief description of some of these initiatives follows, with the qualification that the list is illustrative rather than exhaustive. The number of such institutions will likely grow in the future, as ICR becomes a more accepted form of practice.

Centre for Conflict Analysis, University of Kent, Canterbury, U.K.

The original Centre for the Analysis of Conflict (CAC) was established by John Burton and his colleagues at University College London in 1965 to provide an institutional base and network of scholar-practitioners for the continued development of their form of ICR (see chapter 1). The nonprofit unit was supported by grants from foundations and offered a consultancy service in reconciliation through problem solving to parties in destructive conflicts. With the move of Burton and A. J. R. (John) Groom to the University of Kent, the Centre was reestablished there in 1978. After Burton's departure in 1982, the Centre functioned more as a research network, particularly on international mediation, and ICR work waned, although some members, especially Groom, took part in other initiatives. Members are primarily faculty at Kent and the London School of Economics and Political Science, with support provided by graduate students in international relations at Kent. In 1989, the unit was reorganized under a changed title (CCA) to recognize the incorporation of a new generation of scholar-practitioners. Recently, the Centre has mounted a project focusing on the Moldova conflict, and has held three workshops with more on the drawing board.

Institute for Conflict Analysis and Resolution,
George Mason University, Fairfax, Virginia, U.S.A.

Originally established in 1981 by Bryant Wedge and his colleagues as the Center for Conflict Resolution with the objective of training professionals in conflict management (Wedge & Sandole 1982; see chapter 5), this unit was expanded and directed more toward ICR work by Burton and Chris Mitchell (see chapter 1). ICAR now offers both a master's and a doctoral program on conflict analysis and resolution, and involves students along with faculty in field projects through the Applied Theory and Practice Program, which evolved out of the Conflict Clinic founded by James Laue. ICAR faculty have taken part in a number of ICR projects, including ones focusing on Northern Ireland, South Africa, and the Basque conflict in Spain. ICAR faculty, especially Chris Mitchell, have been involved in a number of projects organized by other ICR consultants.

Program in International Conflict Analysis and Resolution,
Harvard University, Cambridge, Massachusetts, U.S.A.

The work of Herbert Kelman and his colleagues on the Middle East conflict has proceeded for many years through the sponsorship of the Center for International Affairs at Harvard University. Recently the Kelman group formalized their operation more succinctly through the establishment of PICAR, directed toward the broader goal of understanding protracted intergroup conflict and the processes for resolving it. The primary interest of PICAR is the development of Kelman's approach of interactive problem solving and the main focus continues to be the Israeli-Palestinian conflict, which is now being addressed through the paranegotiation strategy of a continuing working group (see chapter 3). PICAR is also directing attention to Northern Ireland, racially diverse communities in the U.S., and native communities in Canada. PICAR is composed of faculty and graduate students from various departments at Harvard and nearby universities, with social psychology being the main discipline.

Department of Peace Studies, University of Bradford, Bradford, U.K.

This unique department was brought into being in the mid-1970s through the efforts of Adam Curle, a longtime peace educator and researcher and a well-known Quaker mediator (see chapter 5). One of the first academic programs in peace studies, Bradford now offers degrees at the bachelor's, master's, and doctoral levels. Bradford's programs encompass conflict analysis and resolution at all levels from the interpersonal to the international. It has shown increasing interest in destructive intergroup conflict, and has recently established a Centre for Conflict Resolution. This practice unit functions with a professional staff and is directing its attention to a number of protracted conflicts, including Northern Ireland, Sri Lanka, and former Yugoslavia. The degree to which it follows an ICR approach should soon be apparent.

International Peace Research Institute (PRIO), Oslo, Norway

This base for peace research was initiated as a government department in 1966, but soon became an independent unit with support from various sources. PRIO has an interdisciplinary, international staff who do research in several areas, but with particular interest in ethnic conflict. Thus the institute has sponsored meetings, conferences, and projects on a number of protracted social conflicts, including consultation sessions on Sri Lanka (see chapter 6). PRIO gives priority to increasing the competence of local actors, and its ongoing interest in ICR is therefore likely to take a collaborative approach.

Search for Common Ground, Washington, D.C., U.S.A.

This NGO was founded by John Marks in 1982 to advance his "common ground" approach in which opposing parties enter into dialogue and hopefully move toward cooperative action. Some of Marks's early work involved televised dialogues between proponents and opponents of controversial social issues, such as abortion. This work continues in situations of protracted social conflict, including South Africa and Macedonia, but the organization has added an array of other methodologies to its work, including training in conflict resolution and the formation of working groups focusing on particular aspects of a conflict. Common Ground has recently organized a broad initiative focusing on the Middle East conflict, which consists of a core working group of high level influentials and experts from over a dozen countries, augmented by working groups in the critical areas of economic cooperation, security, and conflict resolution. Besides its own staff, Common Ground engages ICR scholar-practitioners in its various projects.

International Alert, London, U.K.

Founded as an INGO in 1985 by the late Martin Ennals with a primary concern about human rights abuses, IA has come to focus more broadly on the prevention and resolution of violent intercommunal conflicts. IA has intervened in more than twenty such conflicts with various ameliorative activities, including training in conflict resolution. Modal activities consist of conciliation, fact-finding, and informal mediation, and the foci have included Sri Lanka, South Africa, the Philippines, Fiji, and several former republics of the Soviet Union, including Georgia and Tartarstan. Thus IA has developed a role as an unofficial international body in ways that complement official activity and that involve elements of ICR practice, particularly in training workshops with participants from conflicting groups.

Institute for Multi-Track Diplomacy, Washington, D.C.

IMTD was established in 1992 by John McDonald and Louise Diamond, based on their combined experience in official and unofficial peacemaking processes, to implement their innovative systems approach to peacebuilding (see chapter 5). It concentrates on informal but systematic professional and citizen efforts to bring about peace in divided, conflict-ridden societies, including Cyprus, Israel, and Liberia. A major project has been a bicommunal conflict resolution training program focusing on different target groups in Cyprus and carried out in collaboration with the Conflict Management Group and the NTL Institute. Other ICR work includes dialogue sessions on the Tibetan and Ethiopian conflicts. IMTD engages ICR scholar-practitioners in its projects, and provides internships for students from graduate programs in conflict resolution.

These illustrations demonstrate the vitality and diversity of ongoing ICR efforts that are necessary to establish the field. These initiatives show a healthy mix of university-based and INGO variants, but it is unfortunate there are not more academic bases, primarily because of the theory-research-practice payoffs. The apparent shift to INGO initiatives in the 1980s may be partly due to the difficulty of establishing innovative ICR units in relatively conservative and cash-strapped universities. The collaborative approach taken by most INGOs of involving academics helps produce well-rounded teams, as well as interventions that may be subject to closer evaluation and that might eventually make theoretical contributions. The skills of the INGO staff can be blended with the knowledge and research expertise of their academic colleagues to the mutual benefit of all. Unfortunately the overall extent of institutionalization is a drop in the bucket compared to the problem.

Professionalization of the Field

The case was made in chapter 7 that third party consultation and ICR constitute a new form of professional practice, and as such, are subject to ethical codes of conduct in both research and service. One issue is whether ICR is simply an extension of several existing professions into a specialized and shared method of practice, or whether it constitutes a new and distinct profession, though with various disciplinary bases. The first option would argue that mature professionals (lawyer, psychologist, diplomat, psychiatrist) simply add ICR to their repertoire of concepts and skills in ways compatible with their professional base. The second option calls for the development of a specialized profession, which while drawing on several existing professions, constitutes a new area of endeavor. The stance taken here is that ICR should be treated as a new profession with multidisciplinary roots and should engage in professionalization activities to advance both its competence and its credibility.

Most definitions of a profession share a number of characteristics, including a knowledge base, a concern with societal welfare, and ethical standards of conduct (see chapter 7). Also noted are a responsibility to advance the knowledge of the profession and a pride in its worth and in applying its knowledge and skills. The link to institutionalization is clear, in that interdisciplinary centers for theory, research, and practice are required to advance the knowledge base and contribute to the training and socialization of new members. What ICR needs to address is whether it collectively wishes to aspire to being a new profession, and if so, how to foster that development.

The decision to create a new profession should not be entered into lightly, for there is an array of pros and cons. Schon (1983), among others, points out how the professions are experiencing a crisis of confidence, at least in American society. Once regarded as the possessors of extraordinary knowledge to manage important elements of the quality of life, professions are increasingly seen as less than effective in producing intended results and as abusing their autonomy and power. Rather than applying leading edge knowledge to solve societal problems, professionals are increasingly seen as applying short-term technological fixes that have negative side effects. Rather than working to contribute to social well-being, professionals are perceived as promoting their own interests and failing to police themselves adequately. Thus along with challenging the professionals' claim to extraordinary knowledge and effectiveness has come questioning of their right to determine who should practice in their areas of expertise.

Professions have traditionally sought the power to decide who should be identified as possessing their particular knowledge and skills. Three levels of such accreditation can be distinguished, although there is no consensus on terminology (Fisher 1982a). Registration often means the voluntary identification of individual professionals with associations concerned with educational and organizing functions. Certification involves statutory registration and regulation of the use of the profession's title (e.g., clinical psychologist, professional engineer) as determined by the professional association. Licensing usually extends certification to include specific practices that are legally restricted to members of the profession. Although the primary rationale for certification is protection of the public, critics argue that it is an exclusionary process that restricts competition and uses inadequate measures of competence, such as advanced degrees (e.g., Gross 1978; Koocher 1979).

In the domestic arena, alternative dispute resolution (ADR) in North America is currently engaged in a debate over the desirability of certification and the setting of qualifications for practice (Morris & Pirie 1994). The growing interest and use of dispute resolution methods encompassing various forms of mediation (victim-offender, family, environmental) has been accompanied by calls for defining competency and setting standards for mediators through professional associations. Although the need for high quality dispute resolution is widely supported, the collection edited by Morris and Pirie (1994) raises some sobering questions: Is the current level of knowledge sufficient to support standardization of qualifications; Is professionalization driven by concerns for consumers or by motives for prestige and power; what could be the negative effects of professionalization (e.g., normalizing culturally biased methods)? A general strategy for approaching many of these issues is provided in a recent report by the Society for Professionals in Dispute Resolution (SPIDR 1995).

ICR at the intercommunal and international levels must eventually ask many of the same questions as those raised by ADR. However, first we must recognize that ICR is less developed than its domestic counterparts, particularly in professional associations and institutions that support the practice. Thus any steps toward professionalization should be limited, and geared to the definition and development of the field in associational and educational terms, rather than to regulatory activities.

In ICR, there exist only a few loose networks of people who work together, a few institutions dedicated to the practice, and some connections through wider professional societies and associations. There is no organized focus to help address the developmental issues and challenges that face the field. Thus a starting point for professionalization is to simply find ways for more scholar-practitioners at all levels of interest and experience to come together and build on their common experiences and shared aspirations for the field.

As ICR moves toward professionalization, it is essential to be wary of the potential disadvantages, while working to maximize the advantages. Schon (1983) suggests that leading practitioners who may question their profession's capability, at the same time exhibit a high degree of artful competence in what they do. The challenge is to reflect *on* one's practice and *in* one's practice to gain a better sense of it and to subsequently improve it. What would be useful in ICR at this stage is a collectivity of such "reflective practitioners," who share their experiences and their "knowing-in-action" (to use Schon's terms) toward the goal of initiating professionalization activities.

It is proposed that the associational needs of the emerging profession of ICR could best be served by a formal network that is interdisciplinary, intergenerational, and international. In the past few years, a number of moves have occurred in this direction, but have yet to come to full fruition. After discussions at meetings and conferences during the early 1990s, a group of younger scholar-practitioners formed an initial network. Organizing meetings were held at the annual meetings of the International Society of Political Psychology (ISPP), whose membership includes many individuals with ICR interests. Formal network meetings have now been held at each ISPP conference since 1992, and there has been much discussion about the nature and functions of such an association. There is strong support for activities such as communication, support, and learning, coupled with a hesitancy about moving toward any form of regulation. Another theme is that the network should not be a completely new organization, but should constitute itself as an interest group within an existing association.

Thus the Network for Interactive Conflict Resolution (NICR) has slowly evolved in association with ISPP, but with membership open to scholar-practitioners who are not members of ISPP. A working meeting at the 1993 ISPP conference constructed several core functions for NICR, including: defining and developing the field, professionalization, development and training, collaboration in research and training, financial resourcing, and keeping in touch. Based on these functions, the purpose of NICR is to contribute to the definition, development, and professionalization of the field of interactive conflict resolution through communication and support among members, the professional development of scholar-practitioners, and active collaboration between members in both research and practice.

The membership list for NICR comprises more than a hundred individuals from various disciplines, institutions, and countries, and ranges from graduate students in conflict resolution to senior professionals. A directory survey has been completed with a view to formalizing membership. Unfortunately it has not been possible to identify an existing institutional base that is able and willing to serve as a location to house the network. Thus the work of organizing is being carried on by a volunteer group broken down into different committees operating without dedicated resources, which unfortunately is not a viable option for long-term survival. Nonetheless, the network model appears to be the approach favored by those in the field, and has the potential for accomplishing many objectives relevant to the professionalization of the discipline.

Several initiatives could be undertaken by an established ICR network to address the developmental issues articulated in chapter 11 and to meet the current challenges of research, institutionalization, and professionalization. One major event would be a continuing annual conference on the identity of the field and the major issues facing its development. This could set the stage for several working conferences addressing different areas.

A meeting on funding should be held with a representative ICR group with the purpose of initiating a dialogue with representatives of funding organizations, primarily the major philanthropic foundations and granting agencies. These dialogue sessions would bring forward the defining elements of ICR in comparison with the proposal and reporting requirements of funders to see if adjustments on both sides could result in greater compatibility.

On research, a working conference of primary actors in ICR should be held to discuss the difficulties and resistances to both theory-relevant research and evaluation research. This might lead to a continuing series of training sessions on how to adapt research methodology to the particular nature of ICR interventions, which would be especially valuable for individuals entering the field.

On the practice side, it would be valuable to offer training workshops on ICR methods at meetings such as ISPP, so that younger professionals could enhance their knowledge and skills in designing and implementing interventions. Finally, it would be useful to hold a major conference on institutionalizing the field, with representatives from the different ICR centers as well as scholar-practitioners who are considering such initiatives. This conference could result in a sharing of experiences and an increased commitment to build the necessary bases.

Possible professionalizing activities in ICR are thus many and varied, but require human and financial investments. At what point scholar-practitioners in the field can convince funding and other institutions to support such initiatives remains to be seen, and is unfortunately subject to some of the same catch-22s that plague intervention proposals. Nonetheless, the need for developing the field is compelling, and it falls to proponents to convince others that the rationale has merit, and that ICR can significantly assist in coping with the horrendous problems of protracted social conflict.

Conclusion

It would be ideal if the research, funding, training, institutionalization, and professionalization agendas could move forward together in some degree of coordination, for they are inextricably linked within the development of the field. The demonstration research strategy offers ways of overcoming funding resistances and provides opportunities for trainees and less experienced professionals. Institutional bases are essential for training and also to build credibility and cooperative relationships with funders, administrators, and diplomatic practitioners. In addition, ICR centers could explore and develop collaborative relations with other university-based institutes and INGOs concerned with human rights and international development, for these are becoming increasingly interested in conflict resolution as both a preventative and remedial measure. Most important, institutional bases for ICR can provide support for communities of reflective practitioners who are dedicated to understanding and improving the practice. Such communities can engage in research and theory development to support the practice, and can link with similar communities in the common pursuit of professionalizing the field. In these ways, interactive conflict resolution can meet the challenges it faces and move toward fulfilling its unique potential. The prospects are promising.

Conclusion

The State of the Field: A Chapter Review

The need for developing creative approaches to conflict analysis and resolution continues to intensify and is not likely to decrease in the near future. Protracted social conflicts between identity groups are increasing in all parts of the world, and though there are some abatemates of violence, there are few resolutions. These conflicts seem largely resistant to traditional forms of conflict management. Thus the domain of international peace and security is incomplete, and requires methods of conflict resolution to move toward the attainment of common security. Interactive conflict resolution can play an essential complementary role alongside existing approaches toward reaching this goal.

The creativity of John Burton in launching ICR was in part based on his unwillingness to accept either the political dogma of the cold war or traditional international relations theory. His contribution was based on a constant questioning, challenging, and searching for a new frame of understanding. The creation of ICR was as much a discovery as it was a planned event, but that does not detract from its significance. Burton's initial forays in ICR were followed by the continuing development of his method, and by the creation of a broad conception of a political system based in human needs theory. On all counts, Burton has provided a rich legacy on which to build the field.

The courageous and yet questionable application of powerful methods of human relations training to intense conflicts by Leonard Doob and his colleagues remains something of an enigma in the field. The difficulties that were experienced in the Fermeda and Stirling workshops might have been prevented by a number of improvements, including pilot applications of the methods, more careful screening of participants, and so on. It is also possible that these methods, especially Tavistock training, involved more of a cultural or class gap or both between trainers and participants than other forms of ICR.

Among all of the contributors to ICR, Herbert Kelman must be acknowledged as the current master. His approach of interactive problem solving is embedded in a sophisticated understanding of the social psychology of international relations. He has provided a detailed theory of practice linked to the real world through his continuing efforts on the Israeli-Palestinian conflict, which have made an important contribution to the peace process. Kelman has given serious attention to the transfer question in the learnings that participants communicate back to their communities and leaderships. In addition, his unique emphasis on substantive policy analyses has most likely made a further contribution to the de-escalation of the Middle East conflict. At the same time, Kelman acknowledges the limitations and complementarity of ICR within the wider context of international conflict management and resolution.

The contributions of Edward Azar to ICR were embedded within a humanistic approach to international relations, which blew like a fresh breeze through a realist-dominated discipline. His model of protracted social conflict is a creative integration of political science, conflict resolution, and development theory that has profound implications for how such conflicts are to be addressed. At the same time, the PSC model is a generic one whose propositions do not necessarily fit all of the destructive intergroup conflicts in the world today. Nonetheless, Azar's legacy lies in the conceptual link between conflict resolution and international development, and on the pragmatic side, in his efforts that helped de-escalate the conflict in Lebanon.

In the development of ICR, there has been a coincidental fusion of unofficial diplomacy and the psychodynamic approach, largely through the identities of persons such as Bryant Wedge, Joseph Montville, and Vamik Volkan. However, the structure of intervening is not unique to psychiatry, and is more likely to follow a generic model of consultation. In addition, the implications of a psychoanalytic interpretation of intergroup relations are like those of other disciplines. Regardless of underlying theory, the interventions of most unofficial diplomats in ICR look similar, and are showing a healthy tendency toward continuing efforts. This tendency is partly through the influence of experienced diplomats such as Harold Saunders, who relate the unique contributions of unofficial processes with official policymaking. A broad context for ICR efforts is provided by John McDonald and Louise Diamond in their systems approach of multitrack diplomacy.

Projects in intercommunal dialogue attest to the growing vitality of ICR and also provide a valuable testing ground for developing methodology and expertise. There is no generally accepted model for dialogue interventions, but a healthy eclecticism that focuses on various conflicts, with some preponderance of the Arab-Israeli one. This work is valuable, for dialogue is a key element of ICR—it is essential to conflict analysis and a prerequisite to problem solving, negotiation, and reconciliation. A number of useful efforts, including those by Richard Schwartz, and by Richard Chasin and Margaret Herzig, are attempting to capture the core of dialogue in a generalizable methodological statement.

The model of third party consultation provides a framework for ICR practice by specifying each of the major components. The model captures much of the reality of ICR interventions, and provides a guide for third party functioning. The processes and outcomes specified by the model have received initial support from different research studies. Casting ICR as a form of professional practice highlights the centrality of ethical conduct and the need for continuing professionalization. Much like domestic mediation is now experiencing, ICR will have to ask whether it constitutes a new profession and whether standards for practice should be developed.

The contingency approach to conflict resolution provides an opportunity for innovative problem-solving methods to take their place alongside more traditional ones. The strongest rationale and the most evidence exists for the prenegotiation function of ICR, as demonstrated for example in Kelman's work. Within a contingency framework, the potential of ICR is to facilitate de-escalatory policies and initiatives. However, so many factors determine de-escalation that a model based solely on third party interventions is incomplete and simplistic. Nonetheless, parts of the model are gaining empirical support, and it thus may capture some of the reality of relationships between third party interventions and conflict de-escalation.

ICR evidences a healthy and growing variety of applications and generally positive outcomes based largely on consultant and participant impressions. Applicability has been addressed pragmatically by the more than seventy-five successful interventions over the past thirty years. Theoretically, this question needs to be answered in a more sophisticated manner than the initial model of transfer in chapter 9. Effectiveness remains only partially addressed, and there is a need for more frequent, high quality evaluation research on ICR interventions. A developing theme is that an ongoing series of pre- or paranegotiation workshops can have beneficial effects on the peacemaking process.

The critical issues facing ICR identify the requirements for establishing a professional field of practice, that is, training, funding, and institutionalization. Training has no shortage of enthusiastic trainees, but few systematic programs and only a few mentors are available. Funding has motivated applicants and some interested grantors, but only a formal, written or an incidental, personal connection between the two. Receptivity of funders to ICR appears to have improved over time, but the field is still a small player in international security. Institutionalization of ICR is slow, but encouraging, particularly on the INGO side. There is some room for long-term optimism, in that the reality of destructive conflict will slowly convince funders, governments, universities, and other centers of power to provide the resources necessary to deal with these terrible situations effectively, in part through ICR interventions.

In challenges for the field, it is essential that the research agenda not be allowed to wither away in the press for practice. On the contrary, the research stream of ICR must be strengthened considerably to bring rigor and credibility to the work. The appropriate tools are found in action, demonstration, and evaluation research, but their use requires professional discipline and dedicated funding. Improved research should go hand in hand with the establishment of institutional bases, especially in university settings. At the same time, the development of institutional initiatives is essential to move the field forward—INGOs often have greater freedom to be creative than university-based centers. Professionalization can best follow a networking process that builds the field slowly and addresses issues interactively. The same values and skills that underlie ICR as a practice should support its development as a profession.

Mapping the Field

The rich and growing profusion of conflict resolution activities may appear to demonstrate more confusion than order in the world of peacebuilding. However, the various ICR interventions described in the different chapters can be organized using a number of underlying dimensions. These include the identity of the participants (preinfluentials, influentials, unofficial advisers, informal representatives), the form of the intervention (dialogue, reconciliation, training, consultation), the objectives (individual changes in attitudes or skills, development of creative solutions, contributions to negotiations, input into policymaking), and the relationship of the intervention to formal processes, particularly negotiation (pre-, para- or post-negotiation).

Thus the different forms of ICR can be situated within the wider domain of the approaches to peace defined in the Introduction: peacekeeping, peacebuilding and peacemaking. Fig. C.1 presents the three approaches as overlapping circles in conjunction with three broad phases of conflict management: pre-settlement, negotiations, and post-

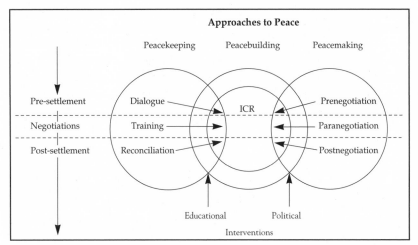

Fig. C.1. Forms of Interactive Conflict Resolution in Relation to the Approaches to Peace

settlement. Two major types of ICR interventions are distinguished by their objectives and by their location at the intersections of peacebuilding with peacekeeping and peacebuilding with peacemaking. Extending Kelman's (1986; chapter 3) distinction on the dual purpose of workshops, *educational interventions* are those directed primarily to individual changes in attitudes or knowledge, while *political interventions* are geared to having some impact on public opinion and policymaking regarding the conflict. This parallels to some degree, Foltz's (1977) distinction between "process-promoting" versus "problem-solving" workshops noted in chapter 2, the former providing new abilities and knowledge to participants with the latter focusing on possible solutions to the conflict.

At the interface of peacekeeping with peacebuilding, the escalation and violence of the conflict has temporarily been controlled, and the peacebuilding agenda is one of attempting to rebuild war-torn relationships and societies. Thus the overlap of ICR with peacekeeping raises the possibility of working with individuals and NGOs in an informal manner to reduce hostility and rebuild trust and understanding. The form of predominant intervention will generally vary with the phase of conflict management. In the pre-settlement phase, dialogue interventions are useful for getting antagonists to talk again and share their differing perceptions of the conflict and each other. In the negotiation phase, training interventions can be valuable to impart conflict resolution strategies and skills that support integrative rather than adversarial bargaining. The more that these strategies and skills are infused into the communities at large, the more likely they will come to characterize the formal negotiation process. Finally, when settlement does occur, ICR interventions as reconciliation can engender healing between individuals from the two sides. In protracted social conflicts, settlement is only the beginning of rebuilding the relationship between the parties. Reconciliation is an underdeveloped and underpublished form of ICR, but is evident in the work of some scholar-practitioners, such as Joseph Montville and Eileen Borris, and some religious organizations (see IMTD 1995; Johnston & Sampson 1994), and is one of the main thrusts of the new UNESCO Culture of Peace Program (UNESCO 1995).

At the interface of peacemaking and peacebuilding, formal interactions are occurring between the parties, while at the same time various interactive and developmental initiatives can be taken. The overlap of ICR with peacemaking occasions the use of the political interventions as consultation with various influentials, advisers, and representatives. In the pre-settlement phase before negotiations, these interventions would be cast as prenegotiation, attempting to clarify needs, interests, and positions and overcome the resistances to negotiation. In the negotiation phase, ICR shifts to paranegotiation work, typically as a continuing workshop to analyze particularly thorny issues and future issues before they hit the table. In the post-settlement phase, workshops can be directed toward the many postnegotiation issues of detailed implementation and of rebuilding the wider relationship. This postconflict peacebuilding can also focus on creating ideas for social and economic reconstruction.

The distinctions provided in this map are not entirely clear-cut, but they do provide a conceptual apparatus for clarifying the various forms of ICR in relation to the wider processes of peace work and conflict management. In reality, the three approaches to peace are often ongoing at the same time, but this analysis sees peacebuilding as the bridge between peacekeeping and peacemaking, in line with the contingency approach (chapter 8). Further rationale is provided by Fisher (1993b) wherein peacebuilding is seen as essential to bring about deescalation through addressing relationship issues and the frustration of basic needs that drive the conflict. As fig. C.1 indicates, various forms of ICR have a useful role to play at each phase of de-escalation. In addition, the complementarity among variants of ICR and traditional methods of conflict management is apparent.

Questioning the Field

ICR must deal with a number of critical issues and challenges if it is to attain acceptable levels of applicability and effectiveness. Besides

training, funding, research, institutionalization, and professionalization, ICR must also address serious issues about its cultural identity
and its relation to the nature and management of protracted intergroup
conflict. Questions must be asked about the cultural generalizability of
ICR, about the nature of the conflicts it can best address, and about the
realistic level of outcomes that can be attained in these situations.

The Question of Cultural Generalizability

The foremost proponent of ICR, John Burton, and presumably
other scholar-practitioners in the field, see the core methodology of
conflict analysis and problem solving as having a very wide range of
applicability across conflicts and across cultures. Burton and Sandole
(1986) cast the emerging field of conflict resolution as based in generic
theory that implies universal patterns of behavior and explanations
that transcend institutional, racial, and cultural differences and are applicable at all levels of social analysis. The generic theory underlying
conflict resolution involves a paradigm shift from the settlement of
conflict through control by authority to resolution by the parties themselves through problem solving. This shift is paralleled by a refocusing
away from the power of social institutions toward the needs of individuals, besides group interests and cultural values, as the important
elements to be addressed. Rather than conflict being related to the al-
location of scarce resources, the new paradigm emphasizes the individual using all means available and working through the identity
group to pursue basic needs.

The generic theory and universal nature of conflict resolution
has been questioned most strongly by cultural anthropologists Kevin
Avruch and Peter Black. In an initial response to Burton and Sandole
(1986), Avruch and Black (1987) noted the lack of emphasis given to
cultural influences in determining human behavior. They also expressed difficulty in locating the apparent paradigm shift underlying
conflict resolution, seeing the emphasis on human needs as simply another expression of functionalism, ostensibly because societies could
reach consensus on how to cooperatively satisfy basic needs at a satisfactory level, thus creating social harmony.

A systematic critique is offered by Avruch and Black (1990), contending in part that Burton's human needs approach denies culture its
important contributing role and leads to processes of conflict resolution that appear to be culture free and universally applicable. Thus
the problem-solving approach appears to render culture irrelevant, an
outcome that anthropologists and many other social scientists would

find highly problematic. Furthermore, the cultural dimensions of the problem-solving process itself are not available for study.

There are numerous definitions of culture and even groupings of definitions that emphasize one aspect over others. For present purposes, culture can be seen as the shared values, beliefs, norms, and behaviors that are central to the adaptation and identity of a distinct people or other social unit. Culture is therefore pervasive and powerful in determining how a group sees the world and what its priorities in living are. Cultural differences, expressed partly through value conflict, are an important element in many intergroup conflicts (Fisher 1990). Thus any approach to conflict resolution should not deal with culture lightly, seeking to downplay or bypass its effects either in the causation of conflict or its management.

Furthermore, how conflict itself is perceived and responded to is an element of culture, and different cultures will have varying views and ways of dealing with conflict, both internally and externally. In alternative dispute resolution, Lund, Morris, and Duryea (1994) studied applying the standard mediation models and practices to the cultures that are found in North America. They concluded that all conflict involves culture and that intervenors who work across cultures must understand the role that culture plays in defining and addressing conflict. In addition, dominant procedures and skills should be tested for their usefulness in different cultures. In a similar vein, Lederach (1995b) challenges the notion of simply transferring conflict resolution technology across cultures. With regard to training interventions, he distinguishes a traditional *prescriptive approach* from his proposed *elicitive approach*. The former attempts to apply concepts and skills from one culture (usually American) to another culture with some adaptation, while the latter draws on the cultural knowledge and resources in the host setting to discover and create models to deal with differences.

Ross (1993a) elucidates "the culture of conflict," which refers to a society's particular constellation of norms, practices, and institutions associated with conflict. Culture thus defines what people care about, what they will enter into a dispute about, how they will confront the issues, and what institutional processes will be used. Interpreting conflict as cultural behavior is useful in explaining why disputes over similar issues are managed differently in different cultures and also sheds light on successful management strategies.

On the management of conflict, Ross (1993b) concludes that failures in addressing destructive conflict are typically due to ignoring important psychocultural elements, such as antagonistic interpretations, while attempting to impose a settlement through authority or coercion. Greater success would be achieved by first dealing with dispositional elements, particularly needs and fears, before addressing substantive interests and their related positions. Thus Ross's analysis supports the use of ICR approaches, including prenegotiation and problem solving, but it does so in a way that is cognizant of the importance of culture.

The debate over culture has prompted Burton and others to clarify their position. In an initial response to Avruch and Black (1987), Burton and Sandole (1987) point out that it matters little whether generic patterns of human behavior are genetic or cultural. In either case, it is possible to develop a generic conflict resolution approach that is applicable across cultures and social levels. Burton (1990a) goes further in acknowledging the importance of culture, that is, the dynamic of cultural preservation in all ethnic conflict. However, he contends this is because culture is a "satisfier," that is, a means to achieve needs for identity and recognition.

Burton (1990a) also acknowledges that cultures deal with conflict differently, and that cultural differences can be important substantive issues in intergroup conflict. However, he contends that culture should not influence the problem-solving process, which needs to cut across cultures in a culturally neutral manner. Part of the motivation for innovative approaches is that most cultures, according to Burton, handle conflict in an authoritative, coercive, and if necessary, violent manner. In contrast, conflict resolution seeks a generic process that is based on universal abilities of logical analysis and problem solving, thus not favoring one culture over another. Although third parties need to be sensitive to cultural aspects, culture as such is not important in analysis and resolution.

Avruch and Black (1991) further raise the question as to what role culture should play in explanations of conflict and in methods for its management. They contend that conflict is neither a universal, invariant phenomenon nor completely idiosyncratic to specific situations. Thus it is a middle-range phenomenon in which culture—a group level concept—should be analytically powerful. However, how culture enters into interactive analysis and resolution needs to be further clarified and determined. Questions need to be asked about how the parties conceptualize conflict and what expectations they have about conflictual behavior. This approach would result in an "ethnoconflict" theory that would precede attempts at intervention.

Avruch and Black (1991) propose that case analyses from a cultural perspective would be very useful in understanding the relationship between conflict resolution and culture in three different contexts: cross-cultural, intercultural, and transcultural. In the first, case analyses have proven useful for revealing the local understandings of conflict and for making comparisons across cultures (see, for example, Avruch, Black &

Scimecca 1991). In the second context, much work needs to be done as existing analyses are often based on a simplistic notion of culture, looking for "national styles" that come forward in intercultural interaction such as negotiations (see, for example, Binnendijk 1987). What is required is a deeper understanding of the two parties' ethnoconflict theories and how they are expressed in intercultural behavior. The transcultural perspective focuses on understanding processes that are applicable to a wide range of cultures—the concern of universal problem-solving approaches. However, Avruch and Black (1991) point out that such universality should not be assumed on the basis of generic theories of human behavior, but needs to be approached through immersion in cross-cultural and intercultural work. This should eventually yield commonalities across cultures in modes of conflict resolution, and reveal the cultural dimensions of these modes at the same time.

The challenge for third party intervenors in situations of intercultural conflict is elaborated by Avruch and Black (1993). They contend that the ethnotheories that the parties bring to the interaction as well as their preferred techniques for resolution—their "ethnopraxis"—may be very different. The first task for the third party is to perform a "cultural analysis" that elucidates the cultural dimensions of the situation. This task requires getting beyond one's own cultural perspective and its value judgments to a deeper understanding of the cultural meaning of behavior relevant to the intercultural interaction. Such an analysis would preclude proponents of problem solving from reducing culture to mere custom, or from assuming that cultural differences are trivial because all people reason the same way and can thus engage in the analytic, problem-solving process. In the usual case where the third party's culture is different from each of the parties, the intercultural elements are maximized, and the intervenor must function as an interpreter among all three cultures.

In practical terms, the situation is further complicated—or perhaps partly resolved—by the proposition that the problem-solving setting creates its own culture, which is entered into by all the parties. This idea has some parallel in international diplomacy, which Avruch and Black (1993) acknowledge has to some degree its own culture, based on transcultural commonalities. Similarly, ICR seeks to create a social situation with its own values, norms, and behaviors, which are communicated and recommended to participants. Thus all parties enter into a "transcultural island" and engage in a mutual analysis and a joint problem-solving process, which Burton (1990a) regards as culture neutral. Black and Avruch (1989) see the emergence of a "metaculture" and acknowledge that participants would achieve shared meaning within it. However, this raises for them a further challenge for third parties—the necessity of a cultural analysis of this metaculture. In general terms this has already been done through the commonalities found in the various ICR theories of practice. However, it is not typically done in a formal way in specific interventions. Thus, although ICR consultants are usually sensitive to cultural dimensions, especially differences among all the parties, there is seldom a cultural and intercultural analysis before the intervention or an analysis of the metaculture.

The metaculture of ICR workshops admittedly comes from a common cultural base, that of the western European–North American world. Much has been written about how the individualistic, materialistic, achievement-orientated, egalitarian culture of the West differs from more the traditional, collectivist, hierarchical, harmony-seeking cultures of other parts of the world. Conflict resolution and ICR are an invention of the Western world, embedded in this host culture. At the same time, Burton (1990a) and others point out that the common approaches to handling conflict in the West are authoritative, adversarial, and coercive. Thus problem solving is not embedded in Western culture as a practice, and its processes are often more compatible with conflict management approaches in other cultures, particularly Third World and indigenous ones. It is apparent that cultural analyses would be extremely valuable in gaining greater clarity on these differing positions.

Concern is being raised as dispute resolution and conflict resolution begin to export their methods to other parts of the world. For example, Rubenstein (1992) has questioned the influx of North American dispute resolution professionals into eastern Europe and the former Soviet Union to assist struggling democratic regimes develop processes to manage intergroup conflicts, from labor-management problems to ethnic hatreds. He questions whether these training and advising activities equip the local people to resolve their problems, or whether they are forms of cultural imperialism that serve the interests of the intervenors and the dominant elites with whom they are aligned. To the benefit of ICR, however, Rubenstein suggests that what might be appropriate are conflict analysis and resolution approaches that allow the parties to identify their own needs and develop new systems to address them.

Paul Salem (1993) of the American University of Beirut offers a critique of Western conflict resolution from a non-Western, primarily Arab, perspective. He identifies a number of hidden assumptions that are not culturally generalizable and makes suggestions toward a macrocultural framework. Salem's comments generally revolve around seeing the West as a stable, successful and satisfied part of the world that now values order, peace, and nonviolence. Thus there is a lack of appreciation for the importance of struggle to achieve justice, which is still seen as necessary by many in the Arab world. The Western approach to conflict resolution is optimistic—a sense that problems can be solved in collaborative ways and suffering thereby reduced. This contrasts with the view that struggle is often worth the costs and that some conflicts may be inherently unresolvable. For these and other reasons, Salem concludes that Western conflict resolution theories and methods will need to undergo considerable adaptation to be useful in the Arab world.

These examples underscore the importance of the cultural analyses recommended by Avruch and Black. Rather than assuming the cultural generalizability of ICR based on limited experience, scholar-practitioners should take the cultural question much more seriously. This would involve more systematic and detailed analyses of the cultures involved before intervention, a clearer explication of the workshop metaculture with its underlying values and premises, and realistic expectations about how participants will react to the metaculture.

At the same time, ICR consultants generally operate with cultural sensitivity and respect for the host societies to make their own decisions about how they handle their conflicts. In addition, the method has achieved success partly because the metacultural island it creates is not foreign to the westernized elites who typically participate. As Avruch and Black (1993) point out, in a world marred by violence and suffering, caution should not be an excuse for inaction, but cultural analyses are recommended precisely because the stakes are high. It is clear that ICR should give greater attention to how culture enters in, with the anticipation that will improve both the practice and the theory.

The Question of Conflict and Its Resolution

The primary focus of ICR has been violent and prolonged conflicts between identity groups rather than interstate warfare. For Azar, these are protracted social conflicts (PSCs) based in ethnic hostilities crossed with developmental inequities that have a long history and a bleak future. For Burton, these are deep-rooted conflicts that result from the frustration of basic human needs that are nonnegotiable, although their satisfiers can be. For Kelman, these are existential conflicts that are close to intractable because they are perceived as threatening the very survival of the identity groups in question. The continuing development of ICR has added to the variety of such conflicts that have been addressed.

The most intense and destructive PSCs are a subset of the many intergroup conflicts that beset all parts of the world. In a ground-breaking piece of research, the Minorities at Risk project, Ted Robert Gurr, a political scientist, and his colleagues have provided an illuminating study of the various forms and levels of ethnopolitical conflict (Gurr 1993). This global survey identified more than 230 communal groups with a distinctive identity based on culture, most of whom collectively suffer systematic discrimination and have engaged in political mobilization to defend their interests.

Of most interest here are the some eighty groups called "ethnonationalists," who are relatively large, regionally concentrated identity groups who enjoyed autonomy in their history and pursue separatist goals in the present. Also of interest are the more than eighty "indigenous peoples," who are the conquered descendants of the original inhabitants of an area, many of whom are now oppressed by the state and typically live in peripheral regions. Also included in Gurr's study are "ethnoclasses" (culturally distinct minorities descended from slaves or immigrants), "militant sects" (defined by religion), and "communal contenders" (minorities that compete for power in the state arena).

Through combinations of historical conquest, state building, migration, and economic development, many of these groups have become politically and economically disadvantaged, and engage in political or military activity to seek redress of their grievances. The study generally finds that the more culturally distinct minorities are from the dominant group in a society, the more they experience economic and political inequalities, particularly if they are ethnonationalists or indigenous peoples.

In conflict behavior, more than two hundred of the communal groups in Gurr's (1993) study have resisted their inclusion in states that are dominated by other groups. Forms of resistance have included non-violent protest, violent protest, and rebellion, in decreasing order of frequency. Since the 1950s, all three forms of communal conflict have increased considerably, with the most dramatic change being a fivefold increase in rebellion by ethnonationalist groups by the 1980s. Indigenous peoples also show marked increases in political action in both nonviolent and violent protest. Both of these types of groups tend to look for ways to leave the state or to gain greater autonomy from it. Of all the conflicts occurring, the most severe are guerrilla or civil wars that are highly destructive and protracted. Almost all of these some forty conflicts are in the Third World.

Gurr's (1993) explanation of ethnopolitical protest and rebellion shows a number of similarities with Azar's (1990) theory of PSCs.

However, Azar's model is a general one, involving a dominant and subordinate group within the state structure and a generic process of escalation, whereas Gurr's theorizing takes account of different types of disadvantaged communal groups and different patterns of protest. In general, Gurr's model sees disadvantaged communal groups with a unique identity and degree of cohesion carrying forward their grievances through political mobilization. How this translates into protest and rebellion varies considerably, but the state plays a key role through its policies of repression or accommodation. External factors, such as military and developmental assistance and the contagion of communal activism, also affect the course and intensity of the conflict. The bottom line is that weak states that attempt to assimilate, control or exploit communal minorities, especially ethnonationalists, have found themselves in protracted and mutually debilitating conflicts.

The Minorities at Risk study provides strong support for the need and focus of ICR. The factors and trends that Gurr (1993) enumerates lead to the conclusions that ethnopolitical conflict is pervasive and will be with us for a long time. Most states are multiethnic mixtures and dozens of intergroup conflicts are at various stages of development and expression. Thus there is a continuing need for methods to address these situations. In addition, the most severe and protracted of these conflicts, involving ethnonationalists and indigenous peoples, are the most resistant to traditional methods of management and are the typical focus of ICR. This is in part, as Gurr (1993) points out, because these groups tend to seek secession or autonomy, options that are resisted most strongly by state governments. In contrast, other communal groups are more likely to seek redress within the framework of a pluralist society.

In the management or resolution of ethnopolitical conflicts, Gurr (1993) sounds a more positive note than analysts who see such situations as intractable or close to it. The evidence from his project indicates that many communal groups have achieved some form of acceptable accommodation between their interests and those of the state. This achievement is especially true in the Western democracies; however, even in the Third World, where protracted conflicts abound, many ethnopolitical schisms have been managed successfully. Options include agreements for regional autonomy, power sharing along communal lines, and policies of pluralism or multiculturalism that respect collective rights. These options are not always implemented adequately or successfully, but they provide potential arrangements for distinct identity groups to manage their relations within the same political framework. The challenge is how to get there, especially when there is a long history and a current expression of coercion and violence for dealing with differences.

Recently I have articulated a set of generic principles for resolving intense and protracted intergroup conflicts between identity groups (Fisher 1994b). These principles (fig. C.2) are based in humanistic values and the approach of planned social change, and are supported by experience in social scientific research and practice, including that related to ICR. The principles are proposed as general laws that state the relationships among the relevant variables and that provide a basis for social action. They are organized into the phases of conflict analysis, conflict confrontation, and conflict resolution, which are seen as developmental and sequential, at least at first, although later recycling among phases is likely. The phases of analysis and confrontation prescribe and capture much of what goes on in ICR interventions, *and* what is typically ignored in traditional and adversarial methods of conflict management. The phase of conflict resolution emphasizes the development of social policies and societal structures that will transform the conflict between identity groups into a new or renewed relationship that includes mutually acceptable processes for addressing group interests and managing intergroup differences.

The principles of conflict resolution enumerate some of the common characteristics of resolution found in the ICR literature, such as mutually acceptable, enduring outcomes that address basic human needs. They also identify in general terms the political arrangements that will provide for the ongoing management and regulation of intergroup differences over the long term, for these are not resolvable in some ultimate sense. These types of arrangements typically recognize the distinct identity of communal groups and their political right to some degree of power and autonomy to protect and enhance their culture. This can be accomplished by building conflict resolution processes into societal decision making and policy formation, and by creating political structures that involve power sharing.

From this perspective, multiethnic societies would be well advised to look toward policies of pluralism or multiculturalism and structures of power sharing or federalism to deal effectively with intergroup conflict. Pluralism involves acceptance of differences and mechanisms that provide for economic and political equality across members of different groups. Multiculturalism builds on pluralism to develop policies and programs that promote self-respect and pride within distinct cultural groups and mutual respect and harmony among groups. Power sharing involves some apportioning of political power among different communal groups, so that they can manage their own cultural affairs and enter into joint decision making at the state level, often with some rights of veto. Federalism is a constitutional structure whereby communal groups that are geographically concentrated can have a degree of re-

A. Principles of Conflict Analysis

1. Conflict analysis must focus on the sources and types of conflict and the interaction and escalation that have brought the conflict to its present state.

2. Conflict analysis must distinguish needs, values, interests, and positions in relation to the major issues in question.

3. Conflict analysis must focus on the perceptions, cognitions, needs, fears and goals of each party and allow for the exchange of clarifications, acknowledgments, assurances, and potential contributions between the parties.

4. Conflict analysis requires clear and honest communication in which parties remain sensitive to common errors in perception and cognition and develop empathic understanding of each other.

5. Conflict analysis can be facilitated by a skilled and impartial third party consultant, who enhances motivation, improves communication, regulates the interaction, and aids diagnosis by drawing on relevant social science concepts.

B. Principles of Conflict Confrontation

6. The parties must engage in face-to-face interaction under norms of mutual respect, shared exploration, and commitment to resolution without a fixed agenda but a progression of topics.

7. Conflict confrontation must take place under the facilitative conditions of intergroup contact, including equal status, high acquaintance potential, positive institutional supports, a cooperative task and reward structure, and the involvement of competent and well-adjusted individuals.

8. The interaction must incorporate the qualities of productive intergroup confrontation, including open and accurate representation, recognition of intragroup diversity, integration of both parties' knowledge and skills, sensitivity to cultural differences and power imbalances, and persistence and discipline to attain mutually acceptable outcomes.

9. Confrontation must follow the strategies of collaboration, including seeing the conflict as a mutual problem to be solved and working to maximize the gains of both parties.

10. Confrontation must follow the stages and meet the criteria of effective intergroup problem solving and integrative bargaining.

B. Principles of Conflict Resolution

11. Conflict resolution must transform conflicts in an enduring manner, rather than settling disputes or suppressing differences.

12. Conflict resolution requires a range of complementary methods appropriate to the issues and the stage of conflict escalation.

continued

13. Conflict resolution must address basic human needs and must build the qualities of sustainable relationships between groups.

14. Conflict resolution must be infused into decision-making processes and political structures to prevent the causation and escalation of unnecessary conflict.

15. Conflict resolution must create structural mechanisms involving equality among identity groups, multiculturalism, and federalism as appropriate to each situation.

Source: Fisher 1994b.

Fig. C.2. Principles for Resolving Intergroup Conflict

gional autonomy through local government, while cooperating with other such units at the state or federal level. Power is thus shared between the levels of government, with the federal structure generally taking most responsibility for matters relating to international relations.

It is the conceptual work of the sociologist, the political scientist, and the constitutional lawyer to generate the detailed definitions and various possible operationalizations of pluralism, multiculturalism, power sharing, and federalism. And it is the practical work of policymakers, community leaders, and politicians to create and implement systems that will survive on the ground. As social policies and political structures, these will need to be tailored to the specific requirements of the groups and state in question—there is no one model of these options that can be transferred from one experience to another.

It is the job of the conflict resolution specialist, particularly ICR scholar-practitioners, to develop methods by which contending identity groups can come to understand and address their situation, and move toward jointly creating the kind of relationship and society that they want. Through the knowledge and skills that assist in implementing the principles of conflict analysis, confrontation, and resolution, ICR consultants can provide a unique and necessary complement to the work of many other professionals. This providing will result in conflict resolution and ICR not being seen as some idealistic and unattainable dream world, but as a practical and necessary tool to improve the quality of life on this planet.

Prospects for the Future

The analysis and evidence in this book indicate that ICR has a lead role to play in conflict resolution and in the attainment of peace and security. This is not a central role, such as must be played by negotiations, peace agreements, social policies, and constitutional arrangements, but it is an essential preparatory role that can pave the way for these more substantive elements. In some cases, in a less chaotic future world, ICR will also play a preventive role besides a de-escalatory one. In all cases, ICR's role will be complementary to other methods at both the societal and international levels. That in no way, however, decreases the significance of ICR as a social innovation nor the importance of fully developing its potential.

This book has presented various ICR applications, some mixed but generally positive evaluations, and a number of approaches sharing a core methodology—in short, much experience and evidence to build on. There are a number of exciting leading edges in dialogue and consultation work as well as other forms of ICR such as training programs. Therefore, the prospects for the field are good, but will be realized only if several requirements are met, revolving around the necessity of establishing ICR as an interdisciplinary, professional field of practice. This involves a heavy agenda: the acquisition of a more secure funding base, the establishment of quality training programs, the development of a serious research track, the building of appropriate institutions, and finally, the establishment of a professional network.

The conclusion is that interactive conflict resolution needs to open many more doors and build many more partnerships before its prospects can be satisfactorily developed and its full potential can be realized. If this can be accomplished, the field will then be able to fulfill its legitimate and essential role in the management of destructive intergroup and international conflict.

Works Cited
Index

Works Cited

Alevy, D. I., B. Bunker, L. W. Doob et al. 1974. "Rationale, Research, and Role Relations in the Stirling Workshop." *Journal of Conflict Resolution* 18: 276–84.

Alker, H. R., and F. L. Sherman. 1982. "Collective Security-Seeking Practices Since 1945." In *Managing International Crises*. Edited by D. Frei, 113–45. Beverly Hills, Calif.: Sage.

American Psychological Association. 1992. *Ethical Principles of Psychologists and Code of Conduct*. Washington, D.C.: Author.

Argyris, C., R. Putnam, and D. M. Smith. 1985. *Action Science: Concepts, Methods, and Skills for Research and Intervention*. San Francisco, Calif.: Jossey-Bass.

Avruch, K., and P. W. Black. 1987. "A Generic Theory of Conflict Resolution: A Critique." *Negotiation Journal* 3: 87–96.

———. 1990. "Ideas of Human Nature in Contemporary Conflict Resolution Theory." *Negotiation Journal* 6: 221–28.

———. 1991. "The Culture Question and Conflict Resolution." *Peace and Change* 16: 22–45.

———. 1993. Conflict resolution in intercultural settings: Problems and prospects. In *Conflict Resolution Theory and Practice: Integration and Application*. Edited by D. J. D. Sandole and H. van der Merwe, 131–45. Manchester, U.K.: Manchester Univ. Press.

Avruch, K., P. W. Black, and J. A. Scimecca, eds. 1991. *Conflict Resolution: Cross-cultural Perspectives*. New York: Greenwood Press.

Azar, E. E. 1970. "The Analysis of International Events." *Peace Research Reviews* 4(1): 1–113.

———. 1972. "Conflict Escalation and Conflict Reduction in an International Crisis: Suez, 1956." *Journal of Conflict Resolution* 16: 183–201.

———. 1978. "From Strategic to Humanistic International Relations." In *Thinking the Unthinkable: Investment in Human Survival*. Edited by N. Jamgotch, ix–xv. Washington, D.C.: Univ. Press of America.

———. 1979. "Peace Amidst Development." *International Interactions* 6: 123–43.

———. 1980. "The Conflict and Peace Research Data Bank (COPDAB) Project." *Journal of Conflict Resolution* 23: 143–52.

———. 1983. "The Theory of Protracted Social Conflict and the Challenge of Transforming Conflict Situations." *Monograph Series in World Affairs* 20 (No. M2): 81–99.

———. 1985. "Protracted International Conflicts: Ten Propositions." *International Interactions* 12: 59–70.

———. 1986. "The Lebanon Case." In *International Conflict Resolution: Theory and Practice.* Edited by E. E. Azar and J. W. Burton, 126–40. Brighton, U.K.: Wheatsheaf.

———. 1990. *The Management of Protracted Social Conflict.* Hampshire, U.K.: Dartmouth Publishing.

———. 1991. "The Analysis and Management of Protracted Conflict." In *The Psychodynamics of International Relationships. Volume II: Unofficial Diplomacy at Work.* Edited by V. D. Volkan, J. V. Montville, and D. A. Julius, 93–120. Lexington, Mass.: Lexington Books.

Azar, E. E., and J. W. Burton, eds. 1986. *International Conflict Resolution: Theory and Practice.* Brighton, U.K.: Wheatsheaf.

Azar, E. E., and W. Eckhardt. 1978. "Major World Conflicts and Interventions, 1945 Through 1975." *International Interactions* 5(4): 203–40.

Azar, E. E., and N. Farah. 1981. "The Structure of Inequalities and Protracted Social Conflict: A Theoretical Framework." *International Interactions* 7: 317–35.

Azar, E. E., P. Jureidini, and R. McLaurin. 1978. "Protracted Social Conflict: Theory and Practice in the Middle East." *Journal of Palestine Studies* 8(1): 41–60.

Azar, E. E., and C. I. Moon. 1986. "Managing Protracted Social Conflicts in the Third World: Facilitation and Development Diplomacy." *Millennium: Journal of International Studies* 15: 393–406.

Azar, E. E., and A. F. Pickering. 1990. "The Problem-Solving Forums: The Falklands/Malvinas Islands." In E. E. Azar, *The Management of Protracted Social Conflict,* 82–108. Hampshire, U.K.: Dartmouth Publishing.

Babbitt, E. 1994. "Applications of Interactive Conflict Resolution to Peacebuilding and Peacemaking." Symposium at the annual scientific meeting of the international Society of Political Psychology. Santiago de Compostela, Spain. July.

Babbitt, E., and C. Chataway. 1993. "An Israeli-Palestinian Women's Workshop." Paper presented at the annual scientific meeting of the International Society of Political Psychology. Cambridge, Mass. July.

Bales, R. F. 1950. *Interaction Process Analysis: A Method for the Study of Small Groups.* Reading, Mass.: Addison-Wesley.

Banks, M. ed. 1984. *Conflict in World Society: A New Perspective on International Relations.* New York: St. Martin's Press.

Bargal, D. 1992. "Conflict Management Workshops for Arab Palestinian and Jewish Youth—A Framework for Planning, Intervention, and Evaluation." *Social Work with Groups* 15(1): 51–68.

Bargal, D., and H. Bar. 1988. "Anticipatory Socialization for Participants of Conflict Management Workshops Involving Arab and Jewish Israeli Youth." Paper presented at the third annual Kurt Lewin Conference. East Hanover, N.J. September.

———. 1992. "A Lewinian Approach to Intergroup Workshops for Arab-Palestinian and Jewish Youth." *Journal of Social Issues* 48(2): 139–54.

―――. 1994. "The Encounter of Social Selves: Intergroup Workshops for Arab and Jewish Youth." *Social Work with Groups* 17(3): 39–59.

Barston, R. P. 1988. *Modern Diplomacy.* London: Longman.

Becker, C., L. Chasin, R. Chasin et al. 1992. "Fostering Dialogue on Abortion: A Report on the Public Conversations Project." *Conscience* (Fall): 1–12.

Benjamin, A. J., and A. M. Levi. 1979. "Process Minefields in Intergroup Conflict Resolution: The Sdot Yam Workshop." *Journal of Applied Behavioral Science* 15: 507–19.

Berman, M. R., and J. E. Johnson, eds. 1977. *Unofficial Diplomats.* New York: Columbia Univ. Press.

Bernards, R. 1994. Personal communication.

Birnbaum, R. 1984. "The Effects of a Neutral Third Party on Academic Bargaining Relationships and Campus Climate." *Journal of Higher Education* 55: 719–34.

Binnendijk, H., ed. 1987. *National Negotiating Styles.* Washington, D.C.: Foreign Service Institute, Department of State.

Black, P. W., and K. Avruch. 1989. "Some Issues in Thinking About Culture and the Resolution of Conflict." *Humanity and Society* 13(2): 187–94.

Blake, R. R., and J. S. Mouton. 1961. *Group Dynamics: Key to Decision Making.* Houston, Tex.: Gulf.

―――. 1984. *Solving Costly Organizational Conflicts.* San Francisco, Calif.: Jossey-Bass.

Blake, R. R., H. A. Shepard, and J. S. Mouton. 1964. *Managing Intergroup Conflict in Industry.* Houston, Tex.: Gulf.

Bloomfield, D. P. 1995. "Towards Complementarity in Conflict Managment: Resolution and Settlement in Northern Ireland." *Journal of Peace Research* 32: 151–64.

Boehringer, G. H., V. Zeruolis, J. Bayley et al. 1974. "Stirling: The Destructive Application of Group Techniques to a Conflict." *Journal of Conflict Resolution* 18: 257–75.

Bonoma, T. V. 1975. *Conflict: Escalation and deescalation.* Beverly Hills, Calif.: Sage.

Breslow, M. 1987. *Dialogue Toward Israeli-Palestinian Peace.* Syracuse, N.Y.: American Coalition for Middle East Dialogue.

Brett, J. M., S. B. Goldberg, and W. Ury. 1980. "Mediation and Organization Development." *Proceedings of the Thirty-third Annual Meeting of the Industrial Relations Association,* 195–202. Madison, Wis.: Industrial Relations Research Associates.

Brockner, J., and J. Z. Rubin. 1985. *Entrapment in Escalating Conflicts: A Social Psychological Analysis.* New York: Springer-Verlag.

Burke, W. W. 1974. "Managing Conflict Between Groups." In *Theory and Method in Organization Development: An Evolutionary Process.* Edited by J. D. Adams, 255–68. Arlington, Va.: NTL Institute.

Burton, J. W. 1965. *International Relations: A General Theory.* London: Cambridge Univ. Press.

―――. 1967. "The Analysis of Conflict by Casework." *Yearbook of World Affairs,* 20–36. London: Stevens and Sons.

————. 1968. *Systems, States, Diplomacy, and Rules.* London: Cambridge Univ. Press.

————. 1969. *Conflict and Communication: The Use of Controlled Communication in International Relations.* London: MacMillan.

————. 1972. *World Society.* London: Cambridge Univ. Press.

————. 1979. *Deviance, Terrorism, and War: The Process of Solving Unsolved Social and Political Problems.* New York: St. Martin's Press.

————. 1983. International Problem Solving Organization: A Continuing Seminar and an International Facilitating Service. Paper presented at the annual conference of the International Studies Association. Mexico City. April.

————. 1984. *Global Conflict: The Domestic Sources of International Conflict.* Brighton, U.K.: Wheatsheaf.

————. 1985a. "Second Track Diplomacy: History and Practice." Paper presented at the Foreign Service Institute. Washington, D.C. February.

————. 1985b. "National Security and Regional Settlements." Address at George Mason Univ. Fairfax, Va. December.

————. 1987. *Resolving Deep-rooted Conflict: A Handbook.* Lanham, Md.: Univ. Press of America.

————. 1990a. *Conflict: Resolution and Provention.* New York: St. Martin's Press.

————, ed. 1990b. *Conflict: Human Needs Theory.* New York: St. Martin's Press.

————. 1992. "Conflict Provention as a Political System." Paper presented at George Mason Univ., Institute for Conflict Analysis and Resolution. Fairfax, Va. June.

————. 1994. "Conflict Analysis: Its Past and Future—Changing Assumptions and Their Implications (An Introspective Account)." Unpublished manuscript.

Burton, J. W., and F. Dukes, eds. 1990a. *Conflict: Readings in Management and Resolution.* New York: St. Martin's Press.

————. 1990b. *Conflict: Practices in Management, Settlement, and Resolution.* New York: St. Martin's Press.

Burton, J. W., and C. R. Mitchell. 1986. *The Role of Middle Powers in Conflict Resolution.* Fairfax, Va.: Center for Conflict Resolution, George Mason Univ.

Burton, J. W., and D. J. D. Sandole. 1986. "Generic Theory: The Basis of Conflict Resolution." *Negotiation Journal* 2: 333–44.

————. 1987. "Expanding the Debate on Generic Theory of Conflict Resolution: A Response to Critique." *Negotiation Journal* 3: 97–99.

Center for the Study of the Mind and Human Interaction. 1995a. "Methodology for Reduction of Ethnic Tension, and Promotion of Democratization and Institution Building." Charlottesville, Va.: Center for the Study of the Mind and Human Interaction.

————. 1995b. A psychopolitical workshop. Parnu, Estonia. October 10–13, 1994. Charlottesville, Va.: Center for the Study of the Mind and Human Interaction.

Chasin, R., and M. Herzig. 1988. "Correcting Misperceptions in Soviet-American Relations." *Journal of Humanistic Psychology* 28(3): 88–97.

————. 1993. "Creating Systemic Interventions for the Sociopolitical Arena." In *The Global Family Therapist: Integrating the Personal, Professional, and Political.* Edited by D. Berger Gould and D. Hilleboe DeMuth, 149–92. Boston: Allyn and Bacon.

Chinoy, M. 1975. "How Not to Resolve a Conflict." *New Society* 33(September), 513–16.

Chufrin, G. I., and H. H. Saunders. 1993. "A Public Peace Process." *Negotiation Journal* 9: 155–77.

Cohen, S. P. 1994. Personal communication.

Cohen, S. P., and E. E. Azar. 1981. "From War to Peace: The Transition Between Egypt and Israel." *Journal of Conflict Resolution* 25: 87–114.

Cohen, S. P., H. C. Kelman, F. D. Miller et al. 1977. "Evolving Intergroup Techniques for Conflict Resolution: An Israeli-Palestinian Workshop." *Journal of Social Issues* 33(1): 165–89.

Cousins, N. 1977. "The Dartmouth Conferences." In *Unofficial Diplomats*. Edited by M. R. Berman and J. E. Johnson. 45–55. New York: Columbia Univ. Press.

Crockett, W. J. 1970. Appendix 3. "The Parliamentary Group and the T-Group." In *Resolving Conflict in Africa: The Fermeda Workshop*. Edited by L. W. Doob. 193–99. New Haven, Conn.: Yale Univ. Press.

Curle, A. 1971. *Making Peace*. London: Tavistock.

———. 1986. *In the Middle: Non-Official Mediation in Violent Situations*. Oxford, U.K.: Berg.

———. 1990. *Tools for Change: A Personal Story*. London: Hawthorn Press.

Davidson, W. D., and J. V. Montville. 1981–82. "Foreign Policy According to Freud." *Foreign Policy* 45(Winter): 145–57.

Dawson, G. E. 1991. "Third Party Intervention in Northern Ireland: Assessing the Value of a Contingency Model Approach." Unpublished master's thesis. Carleton Univ., Ottawa, Ont.

de Reuck, A. V. S. 1974. "Controlled Communication: Rationale and Dynamics." *The Human Context* 6(1), Spring: 64–80.

de Reuck, A. V. S., and J. Knight, eds. 1966. *Conflict in Society*. London: J. and A. Churchill.

Deutsch, M. 1973. *The Resolution of Conflict: Constructive and Destructive Processes*. New Haven, Conn.: Yale Univ. Press.

Dialogue Conference Between Jewish and Palestinian American Women. 1989. *Summary Report*. Dialogue Conference Between Jewish and Palestinian American Women. June.

Dialogue Project Between American Jewish and Palestinian Women. 1990. *Report of Second Dialogue Conference*. Dialogue Project Between American Jewish and Palestinian Women. February.

Diamond, L., and R.J. Fisher. 1995. "Integrating Conflict Resolution Training and Consultation: A Cyprus Example." *Negotiation Journal* 11: 287–301.

Diamond, L., and J. McDonald. 1991. *Multi-track Diplomacy: A Systems Guide and Analysis*. Grinnell, Iowa: Iowa Peace Institute.

Doob, L. W. 1974a. "The Analysis and Resolution of International Disputes." *Journal of Psychology* 86: 313–26.

———. 1974b. "A Cyprus Workshop: An Exercise in Intervention Methodology." *Journal of Social Psychology* 94: 161–78.

———. 1975. "Unofficial Intervention in Destructive Social Conflicts." In *Crosscultural Perspectives on Learning*. Edited by R. W. Brislin et al., 131–53. New York: Wiley.

———. 1976a. "A Cyprus Workshop: Intervention Methodology During a Continuing Crisis." *Journal of Social Psychology* 98: 143–44.

———. 1976b. "Evaluating Interventions: An Instance of Academic Anarchy." In *Aboriginal Cognition: Retrospect and Prospect.* Edited by G. E. Kearney and D. W. McElwain, 54–68. Canberra, Australia: Australian Institute of Aboriginal Studies.

———. 1981. *The Pursuit of Peace.* Westport, Conn.: Greenwood Press.

———. 1986. "Cypriot Patriotism and Nationalism." *Journal of Conflict Resolution* 30: 383–96.

———. 1987. "Adieu to Private Intervention in Political Conflicts?" *International Journal of Group Tensions* 17: 15–27.

———. 1993. *Intervention: Guides and Perils.* New Haven, Conn.: Yale Univ. Press.

———, ed. 1970. *Resolving Conflict in Africa: The Fermeda Workshop.* New Haven, Conn.: Yale Univ. Press.

Doob, L. W., and W. J. Foltz. 1973. "The Belfast Workshop: An Application of Group Techniques to a Destructive Conflict." *Journal of Conflict Resolution* 17: 489–512.

———. (1974). "The Impact of a Workshop upon Grass Roots Leaders in Belfast." *Journal of Conflict Resolution* 18: 237–56.

———. 1975. "Voices from a Belfast Workshop." *Social Change* 5(3): 1–3, 6–8.

Doob, L. W., W. J. Foltz, and R. B. Stevens. 1969. "The Fermeda Workshop: A Different Approach to Border Conflicts in Eastern Africa." *Journal of Psychology* 73: 249–66.

Druckman, D., and B. J. Broome. 1991. "Value Differences and Conflict Resolution: Familiarity or Liking?" *Journal of Conflict Resolution* 35: 571–93.

Druckman, D., B. J. Broome, and S. H. Korper. 1988. "Value Differences and Conflict Resolution: Facilitation or Delinking?" *Journal of Conflict Resolution* 32: 489–510.

Duffy, G., and N. Frensley. 1991." Community Conflict Processes: Mobilization and Demobilization in Northern Ireland." In *International Crises and Domestic Politics: Major Political Conflicts in the 1980s.* Edited by J. W. Lamare, 99–135. New York: Praeger.

Duhul, Y. J. A. 1970. "Appraisal by a Somali." In *Resolving Conflict in Africa: The Fermeda Workshop.* Edited by L. W. Doob, 38–56. New Haven, Conn.: Yale Univ. Press.

Eshete, A. 1970. "Appraisal by an Ethiopian." In *Resolving Conflict in Africa: The Fermeda Workshop.* Edited by L W. Doob, 83–103. New Haven, Conn.: Yale Univ. Press.

Fetherston, A. B. 1991. "The Problem-Solving Workshop in Conflict Resolution." In *Peacemaking in a Troubled World.* Edited by T. Woodhouse, 247–65. Oxford, U.K.: Berg.

Ferguson, C. K. 1970. "Appraisal by a Trainer." In *Resolving Conflict in Africa: The Fermeda Workshop.* Edited by L. W. Doob, 123–35. New Haven, Conn.: Yale Univ. Press.

Fisher, R. J. 1972. "Third Party Consultation: A Method for the Study and Resolution of Conflict." *Journal of Conflict Resolution* 16: 67–94.

———. 1976. "Third Party Consultation: A Skill for Professional Psychologists in Community Practice." *Professional Psychology* 7: 344–51.

———. 1977. "Toward the More Comprehensive Measurement of Intergroup Attitudes: An Interview and Rating Scale Procedure." *Canadian Journal of Behavioural Science* 9: 283–94.

———. 1980. "A Third-Party Consultation Workshop on the India-Pakistan Conflict." *Journal of Social Psychology* 112: 191–206.

———. 1982a. "The Professional Practice of Applied Social Psychology: Identity, Training, and Certification." In *Applied Social Psychology Annual*. Vol. 3. Edited by L. Bickman, 25–55. Beverly Hills, Calif.: Sage.

———. 1982b. *Social Psychology: An Applied Approach.* New York: St. Martin's Press.

———. 1983. "Third Party Consultation as a Method of Conflict Resolution: A Review of Studies." *Journal of Conflict Resolution* 27: 301–34.

———. 1986. "Third Party Consultation: A Problem-Solving Approach for De-escalating International Conflict." In *Toward a World of Peace: People Create Alternatives.* Edited by J. P. Maas and R. A. C. Stewart, 18–32. Suva, Fiji: Univ. of the South Pacific Press.

———. 1989. "Prenegotiation Problem-Solving Discussions: Enhancing the Potential for Successful Negotiation." In *Getting to the Table: The Process of International Prenegotiation.* Edited by J. G. Stein, 206–38. Baltimore, Md.: Johns Hopkins Univ. Press.

———. 1990. *The Social Psychology of Intergroup and International Conflict Resolution.* New York: Springer-Verlag.

———. 1991. *Conflict Analysis Workshop on Cyprus: Final Workshop Report.* Ottawa: Canadian Institute for International Peace and Security.

———. 1992. *Peacebuilding for Cyprus: Report on a Conflict Analysis Workshop, June 1991.* Ottawa: Canadian Institute for International Peace and Security.

———. 1993a. "Developing the Field of Interactive Conflict Resolution: Issues in Training, Funding, and Institutionalization." *Political Psychology* 14: 123–38.

———. 1993b. "The Potential for Peacebuilding: Forging a Bridge from Peacekeeping to Peacemaking." *Peace and Change* 18: 247–66.

———. 1994a. *Education and Peacebuilding in Cyprus: A Report on Two Conflict Analysis Workshops.* Saskatoon, Sask.: Univ. of Saskatchewan.

———. 1994b. "Generic Principles for Resolving Intergroup Conflict." *Journal of Social Issues* 50(1): 47–66.

Fisher, R. J., P. R. Grant, D. G. Hall et al. 1990. "The Development and Testing of a Strategic Simulation of Intergroup Conflict." *Journal of Psychology* 124: 223–40.

Fisher, R. J., and L. Keashly. 1988. "Third Party Interventions in Intergroup Conflict: Consultation Is *Not* Mediation." *Negotiation Journal* 4: 381–91.

———. 1990. "Third Party Consultation as a Method of Intergroup and International Conflict Resolution." In R. J. Fisher. *The Social Psychology of Intergroup and International Conflict Resolution,* 211–38. New York: Springer-Verlag.

———. 1991. "The Potential Complementarity of Mediation and Consultation Within a Contingency Model of Third Party Intervention." *Journal of Peace Research* 28: 29–42.

Fisher, R. J., and J. H. White. 1976a. "Intergroup Conflicts Resolved by Outside Consultants." *Journal of the Community Development Society* 7: 88–98.

————. 1976b. "Reducing Tensions Between Neighborhood Housing Groups: A Pilot Study in Third Party Consultation." *International Journal of Group Tensions* 6: 41–52.

Foltz, W. J. 1977. "Two Forms of Unofficial Conflict Intervention: The Problem-Solving and the Process-Promoting Workshops." In *Unofficial Diplomats.* Edited by M. R. Berman and J. E. Johnson, 201–21. New York: Columbia Univ. Press.

Forster, C. L. 1990. "Group Moderators of the Effects of Third Party Consultation and Mediation." Unpublished master's thesis. Univ. of Saskatchewan, Saskatoon, Sask.

French, W. L., and C. H. Bell. 1995. *Organization Development* (5th edition). Englewood Cliffs, N.J.: Prentice-Hall.

Gabel, M., and E. Frisch. 1991. *Doing the Right Things.* Philadelphia, Pa.: World Game Institute.

Galtung, J. 1976. "Three Approaches to Peace: Peacekeeping, Peacemaking, and Peacebuilding." In J. Galtung, *Peace, War, and Defense: Essays in Peace Research II,* 282–304. Copenhagen: Christian Ejlers.

Glasl, F. 1982. "The Process of Escalation and Roles of Third Parties." In *Conflict Management and Industrial Relations.* Edited by G. B. J. Bomers and R. B. Peterson, 119–40. Boston, Mass.: Kluwer-Nijhoff Publishing.

Grant, P. R., R. J. Fisher, D. G. Hall et al. 1990. "The Intergroup Conflict Simulation." In R. J. Fisher, *The Social Psychology of Intergroup and International Conflict Resolution,* 117–42. New York: Springer-Verlag.

Groom, A. J. R. 1986. "Problem Solving in International Relations." In *International Conflict Resolution: Theory and Practice.* Edited by E. E. Azar and J. W. Burton, 85–91. Brighton, U.K.: Wheatsheaf.

Gross, S. J. 1978. "The Myth of Professional Licensing." *American Psychologist* 33: 1009–16.

Gurr, T.R. 1993. *Minorities at Risk: A Global View of Ethnopolitical Conflicts.* Washington, D.C.: United States Institute of Peace.

Hare, A. P. 1982. *Creativity in Small Groups.* Beverly Hills, Calif.: Sage.

————. 1989. "Pre-negotiation as a Type of Consensus Building: Old Experience in a New Form." Paper presented at the Conference on Theory and Practice of Pre-negotiation. Hebrew Univ., Jerusalem. June.

Hare, A. P., F. Carney, and F. Ovsiew. 1977. "Youth Responds to Crisis: Curaçao." In *Liberation Without Violence.* Edited by A. P. Hare and H. H. Blumberg, 220–238. London: Rex Collings.

Harty, M., and J. Modell. 1991. "The First Conflict Resolution Movement, 1956–1971." *Journal of Conflict Resolution* 35: 720–58.

Heller, J. 1955. *Catch-22.* New York: Simon and Schuster.

Hicks, D., H. O'Doherty, P. P. Steiner et al. 1994. "Addressing Intergroup Conflict by Integrating and Realigning Identity: An Arab-Israeli Workshop." In *Group Development and Political Evolution.* Edited by M. Ettin, J. Fidler, and B. Cohen, 279–302. Madison, Conn.: International Univ. Press.

Hill, B. J. 1982. "An Analysis of Conflict Resolution Techniques: From Problem-Solving Workshops to Theory." *Journal of Conflict Resolution* 26: 109–38.

Holsti, K. J. 1992a. *International Politics: A Framework for Analysis* (6th edition). Englewood Cliffs, N.J.: Prentice-Hall.

———. 1992b. *Peace and War: Armed Conflicts and International Order, 1648–1989*. Cambridge, U.K.: Cambridge Univ. Press.

Hurwitz, R. 1991. "Up the Down Staircase? A Practical Theory of De-escalation." In *Timing the De-escalation of International Conflicts*. Edited by L. Kriesberg and S. J. Thorson, 123–51. Syracuse, N.Y.: Syracuse Univ. Press.

Independent Commission on Disarmament and Security Issues. 1982. *Common Security: A Blueprint for Survival*. New York: Simon and Schuster.

International Peace Academy. 1984. *The Peacekeeper's Handbook*. New York: Pergamon.

Institute for Multi-Track Diplomacy. 1995. "Consultation on Reconciliation II: Final Report." Washington, D.C.: Institute for Multi-Track Diplomacy.

Johnston, D. and C. Sampson, ed. 1994. *Religion: The Missing Dimension of Statecraft*. New York: Oxford Univ. Press.

Julius, D. A. 1991. "The Practice of Track Two Diplomacy in the Arab-Israeli Conferences." In *The Psychodynamics of International Relationships*. Volume 2, *Unofficial Diplomacy at Work*. Edited by V. D. Volkan, J. V. Montville, and D. A. Julius, 193–205. Lexington, Mass.: Lexington Books.

Kaplan, M. 1984. "The Pugwash Conferences on Science and World Affairs." In *The Arms Race at a Time of Decision: Annals of Pugwash 1983*. Edited by J. Rothblat and A. Pascolini, 281–83. London: Macmillan.

Keashly, L. 1988. "A Comparative Analysis of Third Party Interventions in Intergroup Conflict. " Unpublished doctoral dissertation. Univ. of Saskatchewan, Saskatoon, Sask.

Keashly, L., and R. J. Fisher. 1990. "Towards a Contingency Approach to Third Party Intervention in Regional Conflict: A Cyprus Illustration." *International Journal* 45(Spring): 424–53.

———. 1996. "A Contingency Perspective on Conflict Interventions: Theoretical and Practical Considerations." In *Resolving International Conflicts: The Theory and Practice of Mediation*. Edited by J. Bercovitch, 235–61. Boulder, Colo.: Lynne Rienner.

Keashly, L., R. J. Fisher, and P.R. Grant. 1993. "The Comparative Utility of Third Party Consultation and Mediation Within a Complex Simulation of Intergroup Conflict." *Human Relations* 46: 371–93.

Kelman, H. C. 1972. "The Problem-Solving Workshop in Conflict Resolution." In *Communication in International Politics*. Edited by R. L. Merritt, 168–204. Urbana: Univ. of Illinois Press.

———. 1978. "Israelis and Palestinians: Psychological Prerequisites for Mutual Acceptance." *International Security* 3(1): 162–86.

———. 1979. "An Interactional Approach to Conflict Resolution and Its Application to Israeli-Palestinian Relations." *International Interactions* 6(2): 99–122.

———. 1982. "Creating the Conditions for Israeli-Palestinian Negotiations." *Journal of Conflict Resolution* 26: 39–75.

———. 1983. "Conversations with Arafat: A Social-Psychological Assessment of the Prospects for Israeli-Palestinian Peace." *American Psychologist* 38: 203–16.

———. 1986. "Interactive Problem Solving: A Social-Psychological Approach to Conflict Resolution." In *Dialogue Toward Inter-faith Understanding*. Edited by W. Klassen, 293–314. Jerusalem: Ecumenical Institute for Theological Research.

———. 1987. "The Political Psychology of the Israeli-Palestinian Conflict: How Can We Overcome the Barriers to a Negotiated Solution?" *Political Psychology* 8: 347–63.

———. 1988. "The Palestinianization of the Arab-Israeli Conflict." *The Jerusalem Quarterly* 46(Spring): 3–15.

———. 1990. "Applying a Human Needs Perspective to the Practice of Conflict Resolution: The Israeli-Palestinian Case." In *Conflict: Human Needs Theory*. Edited by J. W. Burton, 283–97. New York: St. Martin's Press.

———. 1991a. The Costs and Benefits of Institutionalizing the Field of Interactive Conflict Resolution." Paper presented at the annual meeting of the International Society of Political Psychology. Helsinki. June.

———. 1991b. "Interactive Problem Solving: The Uses and Limits of a Therapeutic Model for the Resolution of International Conflicts." In *The Psychodynamics of International Relationships. Volume II: Unofficial Diplomacy at Work*. Edited by V. D. Volkan, J. V. Montville, and D. A. Julius, 145–60. Lexington, Mass.: Lexington Books.

———. 1992. "Informal Mediation by the Scholar-Practitioner." In *Mediation in International Relations: Multiple Approaches to Conflict Management*. Edited by J. Bercovitch and J. Rubin, 64–96. New York: St. Martin's Press.

———. 1993a. "Coalitions Across Conflict Lines: The Interplay of Conflicts Within and Between the Israeli and Palestinian Communities." *In Conflict Between People and Peoples*. Edited by J. Simpson and S. Worchel, 236–58. Chicago: Nelson-Hall.

———. 1993b. Social Psychological Approaches to Peacemaking in the Middle East." Invited address to the Third Symposium on the Contributions of Psychology to Peace. Randolph-Macon College. Ashland, Va. August.

———. 1995. "Contributions of an Unofficial Conflict Resolution Effort to the Israeli-Palestinian Breakthrough." *Negotiation Journal* 11: 19–27.

———, ed. 1965. *International Behavior: A Social-Psychological Analysis*. New York: Holt, Rinehart and Winston.

Kelman, H. C., and S. P. Cohen. 1976. "The Problem-Solving Workshop: A Social-Psychological Contribution to the Resolution of International Conflict." *Journal of Peace Research* 13: 79–90.

———. 1979. "Reduction of International Conflict: An Interactional Approach. In *The Social Psychology of Intergroup Relations*. Edited by W. G. Austin and S. Worchel, 288–303. Monterey, Calif.: Brooks/Cole.

———. 1986. "Resolution of International Conflict: An Interactional Approach." In *Psychology of Intergroup Relations* (2d edition). Edited by S. Worchel and W. G. Austin, 323–42. Chicago: Nelson-Hall.

Kende, I. 1978. "Wars of Ten Years (1967–1976)." *Journal of Peace Research* 15: 227–41.

Kimmel, P. R. 1985. Learning About Peace: Choices and the U.S. Institute of Peace as Seen from Two Different Perspectives." *American Psychologist* 40: 536–41.

Koocher, G. P. 1979. "Credentialing in Psychology: Close Encounters with Competence?" *American Psychologist* 34: 696–702.

Kriesberg, L. 1982. *Social Conflict* (2d. edition). Englewood Cliffs, N.J.: Prentice-Hall.

———. 1987. "Timing and the Initiation of De-escalation Moves." *Negotiation Journal* 3: 375–84.

———. 1991a. "Formal and Quasi-Mediators in International Disputes: An Exploratory Analysis." *Journal of Peace Research* 28: 19–27.

———. 1991b. "Introduction: Timing Conditions, Strategies, and Errors." In *Timing the De-escalation of International Conflicts.* Edited by L. Kriesberg and S. J. Thorson, 1–24. Syracuse, N.Y.: Syracuse Univ. Press.

———. 1992. *International Conflict Resolution: The U.S.-USSR and Middle East Cases.* New Haven, Conn.: Yale Univ. Press.

———. 1994. Personal communication.

Kriesberg, L., and D. Shomar. 1991. "Dialogues Aid Peace Process." *Syracuse Post Standard.* December 11.

Kriesberg, L., and S. J. Thorson, eds. 1991. *Timing the De-escalation of International Conflicts.* Syracuse, N.Y.: Syracuse Univ. Press.

Lafreniere, F., and R. Mitchell. 1990. "Cyprus: Visions for the Future." Working Paper No. 21. Ottawa: Canadian Institute for International Peace and Security.

Lakin, M., J. Lomranz, and M. A. Lieberman. 1969. *Arab and Jew in Israel: A Case Study in a Human Relations Approach to Conflict.* Washington, D.C.: NTL Institute.

Laue, J. H. 1989. "Getting to the Table: Creating the Forum for Negotiations in Deep-rooted Conflicts." Paper Presented at a Conference on Conflict Resolution in South Africa, Israel, Northern Ireland, and Sri Lanka. Stresemann Institute. Bonn, Germany. September.

———. 1991. "Contributions of the Emerging Field of Conflict Resolution." In *Approaches to Peace: An Intellectual Map.* Edited by W. S. Thompson and K. M. Jensen, 299–332. Washington, D.C.: United States Institute of Peace.

Lederach, J. P. 1995a. *Building Peace: Sustainable Reconciliation in Divided Societies.* Tokyo: The United Nations Univ.

———. 1995b. *Preparing for Peace: Conflict Transformation Across Cultures.* Syracuse, N.Y.: Syracuse Univ. Press.

Levi, A. M., and A. Benjamin. 1976. "Jews and Arabs Rehearse Geneva: A Model of Conflict Resolution." *Human Relations* 29: 1035–44.

———. 1977. "Focus and Flexibility in a Model of Conflict Resolution." *Journal of Conflict Resolution* 21: 405–25.

Lippitt, G., and R. Lippitt. 1986. *The Consulting Process in Action* (2d. edition). San Diego, Calif.: Univ. Associates.

Little, W., and C. Mitchell. 1989. The Maryland Workshops. In *In the Aftermath: Anglo-Argentine Relations since the War for the Falklands/Malvinas Is-*

lands. Edited by W. Little and C. Mitchell, 3–11. College Park, Md.: Center for International Development and Conflict Management, Univ. of Maryland.

Lund, B., C. Morris, and M. L. Duryea. 1994. "Conflict and Culture: Report of the Multiculturalism and Dispute Resolution Project." Victoria, B.C.: UVic Institute for Dispute Resolution.

Maclean's. 1991. "The People's Verdict: How Canadians Can Agree on Their Future." July 1, 10–76.

———. 1992. "An Action Plan for Canada." January 6, 8–45.

Mandell, B. 1993. "Evaluating the Process and Outcomes of Conflict Analysis Workshops." Symposium at the annual scientific meeting of the International Society of Political Psychology. Cambridge, Mass. July.

Maslow, A. H. 1970. *Motivation and Personality* (2d. edition). New York: Harper and Row.

McDonald, J. W. 1991. "Further Exploration of Track Two Diplomacy." In *Timing the De-escalation of International Conflict.* Edited by L. Kriesberg and S. J. Thorson. 201–20. Syracuse, N.Y.: Syracuse Univ. Press.

McDonald, J. W., and D. B. Bendahmane, eds. 1987. *Conflict Resolution: Track Two Diplomacy.* Washington, D.C.: Foreign Service Institute, Department of State.

Mitchell, C. R. 1966. "Cyprus Report." London: Centre for the Analysis of Conflict.

———. 1973. "Conflict Resolution and Controlled Communication: Some Further Comments." *Journal of Peace Research* 10(1): 123–32.

———. 1981. *Peacemaking and the Consultant's Role.* Westmead, U.K.: Gower.

———. 1993. "Problem-Solving Exercises and Theories of Conflict Resolution." In *Conflict Resolution Theory and Practice: Integration and Application.* Edited by D. J. D. Sandole and H. van der Merwe, 78–94. Manchester, UK.: Manchester Univ. Press.

Montville, J. V. 1987. "The Arrow and the Olive Branch: The Case for Track Two Diplomacy." In *Conflict Resolution: Track Two Diplomacy.* Edited by J. W. McDonald and D. B. Bendahmane, 5–20. Washington, D.C.: Foreign Service Institute, Department of State.

———. 1991. "Transnationalism and the Role of Track-Two Diplomacy." In *Approaches to Peace: An Intellectual Map.* Edited by W. S. Thompson and K. M. Jensen, 253–69. Washington, D.C.: United States Institute of Peace.

———, ed. 1990. *Conflict and Peacemaking in Multiethnic Societies.* Lexington, Mass.: Lexington Books.

Morris, C., and A. Pirie, eds. 1994. *Qualifications for Dispute Resolution: Perspectives on the Debate."* Victoria, B.C.: UVic Institute for Dispute Resolution.

Okumu, J. J. 1970. "Appraisal by a Kenyan." In *Resolving Conflict in Africa: The Fermeda Workshop.* Edited by L. W. Doob, 57–84. New Haven, Conn.: Yale Univ. Press.

Pettigrew, J. 1991. "Quaker Mediation." In *Peacemaking in a Troubled World.* Edited by T. Woodhouse, 226–46. Oxford, U.K.: Berg.

Prien, H. 1984. "A Contingency Approach for Conflict Intervention." *Group and Organization Studies* 9: 81–102.

PRIO. 1988. "Prospects for Peace: Sri Lankan Consultation." *PRIO Inform.* No. 2. August. Oslo, Norway: International Peace Research Institute.

———. 1989. "Political Violence in Sri Lanka: Report from a Consultation." *PRIO Inform.* No. 5. October. Oslo, Norway: International Peace Research Institute.

Pruitt, D. G. and P.V. Olzack. 1995. "Beyond Hope: Approaches to Resolving Seemingly Intractable Conflict." In *Conflict, Cooperation, and Justice: Essays Inspired by the Work of Morton Deutsch.* Edited by B. B. Bunker and J. Z. Rubin, 59–92. San Francisco: Jossey-Bass.

Pruitt, D. G., and J. Z. Rubin. 1986. *Social Conflict: Escalation, Stalemate, and Settlement.* New York: Random House.

Rosenau, J. N. ed. 1969. *International Politics and Foreign Policy: A Reader in Research and Theory.* New York: The Free Press.

Ross, M. H. 1993a. *The Culture of Conflict.* New Haven, Conn.: Yale Univ. Press.

———. 1993b. *The Management of Conflict.* New Haven, Conn.: Yale Univ. Press.

Rotblat, J. 1972. *Scientists in the Quest for Peace: A History of the Pugwash Conferences.* Cambridge, Mass.: MIT Press.

Rotblat, J., and J. P. Holdren, eds. 1989. *Building Global Security Through Cooperation: Annals of Pugwash 1989.* Berlin: Springer-Verlag.

Rothman, J. 1990. "A Pre-negotiation Model: Theory and Training." *Policy Studies.* No. 40. The Leonard Davis Institute, Hebrew Univ. of Jerusalem.

———. 1991. "Negotiation as Consolidation: Prenegotiation in the Israeli-Palestinian Conflict." *The Jerusalem Journal of International Relations* 13(1): 22–44.

———. 1992. *From Confrontation to Cooperation: Resolving Ethnic and Regional Conflict.* Newbury Park, Calif.: Sage.

———. 1993. "Unofficial Talks Yielded Mideast Peace." *Philadelphia Inquirer.* September 14.

Rouhana, N. N. 1993. "A Framework for Evaluating the Problem-Solving Workshop as a Method of Conflict Resolution." Paper presented at the annual scientific meeting of the International Society of Political Psychology. Cambridge, Mass. July.

Rouhana, N. N., and H. C. Kelman. 1994. "Promoting Joint Thinking in International Conflict: An Israeli-Palestinian Continuing Workshop." *Journal of Social Issues* 50(1): 157–78.

Rubenstein, R. E. 1992. "Dispute Resolution on the Eastern Frontier: Some Questions for Modern Missionaries." *Negotiation Journal* 8: 331–46.

Rubin, J. Z. 1991. "The Timing of Ripeness and the Ripeness of Timing." In *Timing the De-escalation of International Conflicts.* Edited by L. Kriesberg and S. J. Thorson, 237–46. Syracuse, N.Y.: Syracuse Univ. Press.

Rubin, J. Z., D. G. Pruitt, and S. H. Kim. 1994. *Social Conflict: Escalation, Stalemate and Settlement* (2d. edition). New York: McGraw-Hill.

Salem, N. ed. 1992. *Cyprus: A Regional Conflict and Its Resolution.* London: Macmillan.

Salem, P. E. 1993. "A Critique of Western Conflict Resolution from a Non-Western Perspective." *Negotiation Journal* 9: 361–69.

Sandole, D. J. D. 1991. "Institutionalizing Conflict Resolution: The First Decade." *ICAR Newsletter* 4(2): Fall, 1, 3–5.

Satir, V. 1967. *Conjoint Family Therapy* (revised edition). Palo Alto, Calif.: Science and Behavior Books.

Saunders, H. H. 1985. "We Need a Larger Theory of Negotiation: The Importance of Pre-negotiating Phases." *Negotiation Journal* 1: 249–62.

———. 1991a. "An Historic Challenge to Rethink How Nations Relate." In *The Psychodynamics of International Relationships. Volume I: Concepts and Theories.* Edited by V. D. Volkan, D. A. Julius, and J. V. Montville, 1–30. Lexington, Mass.: Lexington Books.

———. 1991b. "Officials and Citizens in International Relationships: The Dartmouth Conference." In *The Psychodynamics of International Relationships. Volume II: Unofficial Diplomacy at Work.* Edited by V. D. Volkan, J. V. Montville, and D. A. Julius, 41–69. Lexington, Mass.: Lexington Books.

———. 1992. "Thinking in Stages: A Framework for Public Intercommunal Problem-Solving from Experience in the Dartmouth Conference Regional Conflicts Task Force, 1982–92." Paper presented in a symposium on non-official interaction processes in the resolution of international conflict at the annual scientific meeting of the International Society of Political Psychology. San Francisco. July.

———. 1995. "Sustained Dialogue on Tajikistan." *Mind and Human Interaction* 6(3): 123–35.

Saunders, H. H., and R. Slim. 1994a. "Dialogue to Change Conflictual Relationships." *Higher Education Exchange,* 43–56.

———. 1994b. "Dialogue to Change Conflictual Relationships: The Tajikistani Dialogue." Paper presented at the annual scientific meeting of the International Society of Political Psychology. Santiago, Spain. July.

Schon, D. A. 1983. *The Reflective Practitioner: How Professionals Think in Action.* New York: Basic Books.

Schwartz, R. D. 1987. "Human Rights and Peace in the Middle East: A Conference Report." *Syracuse Journal of International Law and Commerce* 13: 391–548.

———. 1989. "Arab-Jewish Dialogue in the United States: Toward Track II Tractability." In *Intractable Conflicts and Their Transformation.* Edited by L. Kriesberg, T. A. Northrup, and S. J. Thorson, 180–209. Syracuse, N.Y.: Syracuse Univ. Press.

Shaffer, J. B. P., and M. D. Galinsky. 1974. *Models of Group Therapy and Sensitivity Training.* Englewood Cliffs, N.J.: Prentice-Hall.

Sheppard, B. H. 1984. "Third Party Conflict Intervention: A Procedural Framework." *Research in Organizational Behavior* 6: 141–90.

Sherman, F. 1987. "Partway to Peace: The United Nations and the Road to Nowhere." Unpublished doctoral dissertation. Pennsylvania State Univ. University Park, Pa.

Shipler, D. 1986. *Arab and Jew: Wounded Spirits in a Promised Land.* London: Bloomsbury.

Sites, P. 1973. *Control: The Basis of Social Order.* New York: Dunellen.

Sivard, R. L. 1991. *World Military and Social Expenditures 1991.* Washington, D.C.: World Priorities Institute.

————. 1993. World Military and Social Expenditures 1993. Washington, D.C.: World Priorities Institute.

Slim, R. M. 1991. "The Role of Supplemental Diplomacy in a Changing World." Symposium at the annual scientific meeting of the International Society of Political Psychology. Helsinki, Finland. July.

————. 1995. "A Framework for Managing Conflict in Divided Societies: The Tajikistan Case Study." Paper presented at the annual scientific meeting of the International Society of Political Psychology. Washington. D.C. July.

Smith, J. D. D. 1994. "Mediator Impartiality: Banishing the Chimera." *Journal of Peace Research* 31: 445–50.

Society of Professionals in Dispute Resolution. 1995. "Ensuring Competence and Quality in Dispute Resolution Practice." Washington, D.C.: Society of Professionals in Dispute Resolution.

Stein, J. G. ed. 1989a. *Getting to the Table: The Processes of International Prenegotiation.* Baltimore: John Hopkins Univ. Press.

————. 1989b. "Getting to the Table: The Triggers, Stages, Functions, and Consequences of Prenegotiation." In *Getting to the Table: The Processes of International Prenegotiation.* Edited by J. G. Stein, 239–68. Baltimore: John Hopkins Univ. Press.

Stephenson, C. W. ed.. 1982. *Alternative Methods for International Security.* Lanham, Md.: Univ. Press of America.

Stewart, P. 1987. "The Dartmouth Conference: U.S.-U.S.S.R. Relations." In *Conflict Resolution: Track Two Diplomacy.* Edited by J. W. McDonald and D. B. Bendahmane, 21–26. Washington, D.C.: Foreign Service Institute, Department of State.

Stockholm Initiative on Global Security and Governance. 1991. *Common Responsibility in the 1990's.* Stockholm: Prime Minister's Office.

Talbot, P. 1977. "The Cyprus Seminar." In *Unofficial Diplomats.* Edited by M. R. Berman and J. E. Johnson, 159–67. New York: Columbia Univ. Press.

Thompson, S. W., and K. M. Jensen, eds. 1991. *Approaches to Peace: An Intellectual Map.* Washington, D.C.: United States Institute of Peace.

United Nations. 1992. *An Agenda for Peace.* Secretary-general's report. New York: United Nations.

United Nations Educational, Scientific, and Cultural Organization. 1995. *UNESCO and a Culture of Peace.* Paris: UNESCO.

United States Institute of Peace. 1993. *Conflict and Conflict Resolution in Mozambique.* Conference report. July 13–15, 1992. Washington, D.C.: United States Institute of Peace.

Van der Westhuizen, J. E. 1993a. "Beyond Pre-theory? Third Party Consultation as Pre-negotiating Problem-Solving Workshops and the Resolution of South African Community Conflict." Paper presented at the biannual congress of the South African Political Studies Association. Bloemfontein. October.

————. 1993b. "Towards a Contingency Model of Third Party Intervention in South African Community Conflict: A Case Study Analysis." Unpublished master's thesis. Univ. of Stellenbosch. Stellenbosch, South Africa.

Volkan, V. D. 1985. "The Need to Have Enemies and Allies: A Developmental Approach." *Political Psychology* 6: 219–47.

————. 1988. *The Need to Have Enemies and Allies: From Clinical Practice to International Relationships.* Northvale, N.J.: Jason Aronson.

————. 1990. "Psychoanalytic Aspects of Ethnic Conflicts." In *Conflict and Peacemaking in Multiethnic Societies.* Edited by J. V. Montville, 81–92. Lexington, Mass.: Lexington Books.

————. 1991a. "Official and Unofficial Diplomacy: An Overview." In *The Psychodynamics of International Relationships. Volume II: Unofficial Diplomacy at Work.* Edited by V. D. Volkan, J. V. Montville, and D. A. Julius, 1–16. Lexington, Mass.: Lexington Books.

————. 1991b. Psychological processes in unofficial diplomacy meetings. In *The Psychodynamics of International Relationships. Volume II: Unofficial Diplomacy at Work.* Edited by V. D. Volkan, J. V. Montville, and D. A. Julius, 207–22. Lexington, Mass.: Lexington Books.

————. 1992. "Ethnonationalistic Rituals: An Introduction." *Mind and Human Interaction* 4: 3–19.

————. 1995. "Developing Institutions to Reconcile Groups in Conflict in Estonia." Paper presented at the annual scientific meeting of the International Society of Political Psychology. Washington, D.C. July.

Volkan, V. D., and M. Harris. 1992. "Negotiating a Peaceful Separation: A Psychopolitical Analysis of Current Relationships Between Russia and the Baltic Republics." *Mind and Human Interaction* 4(1): 20–39.

————. 1993. "Vaccinating the Political Process: A Second Psychopolitical Analysis of Relationships Between Russia and the Baltic States." *Mind and Human Interaction* 4(4): 169–90.

Volkan, V. D., D. A. Julius, and J. V. Montville, eds. 1991. *The Psychodynamics of International Relationships. Volume I: Concepts and Theories.* Lexington, Mass.: Lexington Books.

Wallensteen, P. 1991. Report from the workshop chairman. *Cambodian Workshop on Reconstruction and Development. Penang, Malaysia. August 18–25, 1991.* Penang, Malaysia: Unit for Peace Research and Education, School of Social Sciences, Univ. Science Malaysia.

Wallensteen, P., and K. Axell. 1994. "Conflict Resolution and the End of the Cold War, 1989–93." *Journal of Peace Research* 31: 333–49.

Walton, R. E. 1969. *Interpersonal Peacemaking: Confrontations and Third Party Consultation.* Reading, Mass.: Addison-Wesley.

————. 1970a. "A Problem-Solving Workshop on Border Conflicts in Eastern Africa." *Journal of Applied Behavioral Science* 6: 453–89.

————. 1970b. "Strategic Issues in Designing Workshops." In *Resolving Conflict in Africa: The Fermeda Workshop.* Edited by L. W. Doob, 136–61. New Haven, Conn.: Yale Univ. Press.

————. 1987. *Managing Conflict: Interpersonal Dialogue and Third-Party Roles* (2d edition). Reading, Mass.: Addison-Wesley.

Warfield, J. N. 1988. "Do as I Say: A Review Essay of John W. Burton, Resolving Deep-rooted Conflict: A Handbook." *International Journal of Group Tensions* 18: 228–36.

Wedge, B. 1967. "Psychiatry and International Affairs." *Science* 157: 281–85.

———. "A Psychiatric Model for Intercession in Intergroup Conflict." *Journal of Applied Behavioral Science* 6: 733–61.

———. 1979. "Reflections on 'A Psychiatric Model for Intercession in Intergroup Conflict.'" In *Organizational Change Sourcebook II: Cases in Conflict Management.* Edited by L. D. Goodstein, B. Lubin, and A. W. Lubin, 101–4. La Jolla, Calif.: Univ. Associates.

———. 1983. "Peacemaking." *Psychiatric Annals* 13(2), 135–37, 140–41, 144.

———. 1987. Mediating Intergroup Conflict in the Dominican Republic." In *Conflict Resolution: Track Two Diplomacy.* Edited by J. W. McDonald and D. B. Bendahmane, 35–52. Washington, D.C.: Foreign Service Institute, Department of State.

Wedge, B., and D. J. Sandole. 1982. "Conflict Management: A New Venture into Professionalization." *Peace and Change* 8: 129–38.

Wickes, T. A. 1970. "The African Context and the Schedule." In *Resolving Conflict in Africa: The Fermeda Workshop.* Edited by L. W. Doob, 26–37. New Haven, Conn.: Yale Univ. Press.

Willard, A. R., and C. H. Norchi. 1993. "The Decision Seminar as an Instrument of Power and Enlightenment." *Political Psychology* 14: 575–606.

Wright, Q. 1965. "Escalation of International Conflicts." *Journal of Conflict Resolution* 9: 434–49.

Yalem, R. J. 1971. "Controlled Communication and Conflict Resolution." *Journal of Peace Research* 8(3): 263–72.

Yarrow, C. H. M. 1978. *Quaker Experiences in International Conciliation.* New Haven, Conn.: Yale Univ. Press.

———. 1982. Unofficial Third-Party Conciliation in International Conflicts. In *Alternative Methods for International Security.* Edited by C. M. Stephenson, 121–26. Lanham, Md.: Univ. Press of America.

Zartman, I. W. 1985. *Ripe for Resolution: Conflict and Intervention in Africa.* New York: Oxford Univ. Press.

Zartman, I. W., and J. Aurik. 1991. Power Strategies in De-escalation. In *Timing the De-escalation of International Conflicts.* Edited by L. Kriesberg and S. J. Thorson, 152–81. Syracuse, N.Y.: Syracuse Univ. Press.

Index